D0414681

Underwood and Underwood

Jane F. Hoops: F.P.G.

F.P.C

From Rome to Ringling

CI

Marian Murray

RCUS!

GREENWOOD PRESS, PUBLISHERS
WESTPORT, CONNECTICUT

Library of Congress Cataloging in Publication Data

Murray, Marian.
   Circus! From Rome to Ringling.

   Bibliography: p.
   1. Circus--History.   I. Title.
[GV1801.M8 1973]   791.3'09   74-171420
ISBN 0-8371-6259-9

Designer: Ernst Reichl

The rare heralds and rare circus drawings which are not otherwise credited come from the private collection of Roland C. Butler and from The Museum of the Circus, Sarasota, Florida. They are reproduced with the kind permission of the owners.

The circus terms in "Lingo" are reprinted from "Circus Glossary—Lot Lingo," *White Tops*, August–September, 1939, with the kind permission of the Circus Fans Association of America.

Originally published in 1956 by Appleton-Century-Crofts, Inc., New York

Reprinted with the permission of Marian Murray.

Reprinted in 1973 by Greenwood Press
A division of Congressional Information Service
88 Post Road West, Westport, Connecticut 06881

Library of Congress catalog card number 74-171420
ISBN 0-8371-6259-9

Printed in the United States of America

10 9 8 7 6 5 4 3

To the men and women, now and yesterday,

who have created that timeless delight, that imperishable fantasy,

the circus

FOREWORD

THE HISTORY of the circus is almost as long as that of civilization itself, and to attempt to confine it within the covers of one book is both complicated and hazardous. Even if the historian were able to read hieroglyphics and cuneiform tablets, and to go directly to written source material in many tongues, he would still find it no easy task to trace the intricate pattern of those disparate threads that make up the fabric of today's great extravaganzas.

It is probably impossible to learn the whole truth, for many of the early records have disappeared. He must depend largely on reports and interpretations, and the problem is inevitably made more complex by distortions, deliberate or unintentional. Exaggeration is the very spirit of the circus, and certain circus men seem to have tried to outdo each other in mendacity. Later writers have often perpetuated those distortions, and added others, so that it is possible now only to weigh one conflicting report against another.

To trace the development of Ringling Brothers and Barnum & Bailey is comparatively simple; but when one attempts, for example, to follow the hundreds of small circuses that crisscrossed America at the end of the nineteenth century, the task becomes inordinately complex. Nevertheless, although no one can accurately define every curve in the pattern, the picture that emerges still confirms the historian in his conviction that the circus is indeed the greatest show on earth.

For assistance in the preparation of this book, my gratitude to innumerable individuals is beyond expression. Thanks go especially to:

Those men and women who have written books and articles touching on the circus and its forerunners—above all to Henry Thétard, for the rich results of his years of research, and to those American circus fans who have delved into records and written down the results of their observations;

15

To Dr. Edith W. Ware, Dr. Charles C. Mierow and Dr. Henry Field, for checking classical material; Julie Allen Field, for guidance in the understanding of jungle animal training and exhibition; Otto Koegel, for data concerning the Zoological Institute; Jack White and Harry Nutkins, for material on contemporary British and Continental circuses, and for checking my manuscript; to Henry Ringling North, John L. Sullivan and the Rev. Dr. H. Chester Hoyt for help concerning the American circus of today and yesterday, and Roland C. Butler for permission to reproduce rare heralds from his collection;

To the Circus Fans Association of America for permission to reproduce in part their "Circus Glossary—Lot Lingo" from the August–September, 1939, issue of *White Tops;*

To the gifted performers who furnished information and explained techniques—especially to Antoinette Concello, William Heyer, Con Colleano, Massimiliano Truzzi, Fannie McClosky, Teobaldo Zacchini, Mogador Cristiani, Genoveffa Canastrelli and Ermide Loyal;

To Marjory Stoneman Douglas, Janet Ormond, Eric Hodgins and others who have acted as sounding boards;

To the Florida State Board of Control and officials of the Ringling Museums, for permitting me to have time to work on this book;

To Ella Russell, for typing a complex manuscript; to Barbara Watt, for all manner of practical assistance, and for standing by from beginning to end. Without her support and encouragement, this book might never have been completed.

Sarasota, Florida   MARIAN MURRAY
March, 1956

Contents

17

18

Errata

Page 65, line 14: *For* a Barbary ape
   read an orangutan
Page 100, line 17: *For* Maheu *read* Mahyeu
         lines 19, 26, 30: *For* Mayheu's
            read Mahyeu's
Page 139, line 12: *For* Crowenshield
   read Crowninshield
Page 169, line 27: *For* forerunner of
   read first cousin to
Page 195, line 9: *For* 1845 *read* 1856
Page 198, line 3: *For* Neville *read* Melville
Page 239, line 1: *For* Must *read* Just
Page 285, line 5 from bottom: *For* first trip
   out in 1875 *read* one of the early trips
Page 287, line 23: *For* Jane *read* June
Page 296, line 23: *For* Alfred Stonehouse
   read Alpheus Stonehouse
         line 2 from bottom: *For* 1906
            read 1907

CIRCUS!

1

Bettmann Archive

The Imperishable Fantasy

THE circus is a creature of fact and fantasy, of experienced age and perpetual youth. Its father was a charioteer; its mother, a juggler. It took its first steps in an open ring, spent its youth on a galloping horse, and grew to maturity in a tent. In its prime, Barnum named it the Greatest Show on Earth.

The swift and dramatic spectacle we call circus is so suited to the American temperament that it seems to us typically our own. Nevertheless, it is ours only by adoption, for it first acquired form and vitality in London. Philip Astley, an eighteenth-century British trick rider, is called Father of the Circus; but even Astley did not invent the complex form. He merely put together into cohesive and orderly arrangement numerous pieces that had been taking shape during thousands of years. In its essence, the circus is the most ancient and persistently popular form of entertainment devised by man.

The form in which the circus appears has differed with time and place, and continues to do so. In other countries, it has been traditionally a welcoming host with a permanent home. For us in the United States, it is, and almost always has been, a transitory guest, coming to us from afar, bringing its house on its back, to stay a little while and then move on.

Not so long ago, innumerable small or isolated communities saw almost no entertainment except that provided by the periodic visits of the circus. It was like a visitor from another world, carrying unimaginable delights in its tents. And even today, when it competes with countless easily available and insistent attractions, the circus still produces an incomparable thrill, and maintains its unique ability to evoke delight, amazement, and incredulity. Since the time of Philip Astley, in the hands of daring entrepreneurs, this spectacle has reached fantastic heights.

Watching a three-ring circus, it is not easy to pick out the essential elements. So many things are going on at once that the design is confused. The precise synchronization of the pieces making up the pattern is obscured in a mélange of form and movement, color and sound. Terrifying suspense is interrupted by uproarious farce. Beauty of form, line and color, blended into swift and intricate movement, is contrasted with bizarre grotesqueries. Brilliance runs side by side with dinginess; comedy with horror; the meretricious with the genuine; the mediocre with the sublime.

When we divorce ourselves from the immediate miracle, three basic elements emerge, essential and timeless: the acts that can be presented

in a ring (riding, tumbling, juggling, equilibrism), a clown of some type, and the ring itself. Without those three, there can be no true circus. When the ring, the ring acts, and the clown are combined, whatever else there may or may not be, the circus lives.

Alongside these elements, three others have developed, not truly essential, not constant, but adding color and vitality whenever they do appear. They are the menagerie, the side show, and the parade.

Men and women began to balance on tightropes so long ago that the time when the art emerged is only a matter of conjecture. Thousands of years before the Christian era, horses obeyed the will of clever trainers; jugglers, acrobats and various types of balancing artists had already begun to appear. One people taught another; and, despite wars, pestilences, and the inroads of barbarians, the chain by which those skills have been transmitted from one generation to another has never been broken. The clown appeared, developed, and changed slowly through the centuries. A setting was devised, and then fell into ruin, to be built up again when the time was ripe.

When primitive man, first controlling his lust to kill, took home a wild animal and made a pet of it, the menagerie began. The person who first exploited the abnormality of some other human being anticipated the side show. The first pagan priest who arranged a procession in honor of his god was the true originator of the circus parade.

Onlookers responded with amazement. Here was something new, something strange, something that looked impossible. They applauded. Those who created the entertainment practiced their skills, developed them, added new ones. In time, performers grouped together, and moved from place to place, adding or substituting as they went, on the lookout always for feats that would amaze the audience and loosen its purse strings.

As the strange became familiar and the difficult commonplace, new wonders were added. When men and women ceased to marvel at a man juggling three balls, he threw lighted torches. When it was no longer astonishing to see a rider standing on his galloping horse, he must needs throw a somersault above it. Once an elephant had become a familiar object, someone taught it ballet. Above all else, and at all times, the performer, the trainer, the entrepreneur must stimulate excitement and suspense in those who watch.

How the arena, the ring acts, the clown, the parade, the side show, and the menagerie acquired substance and evolved, how each became more or less important as time went by, and how the entire concoction was modified by the time, the place and the individual genius—that is the history of the circus. It is the story of an imperishable fantasy that began to take recognizable shape far away and long ago.

2

Egyptian Pomp and

Grecian Circumstance

ON THE banks of the Nile, at least as early as 2500 B.C., rich and poor were entertained by all kinds of equilibrists. Wall paintings in tombs at Beni Hasan on the eastern edge of the Nile Valley show young men standing erect and swinging girls in great arcs, maidens juggling balls, and athletes doing some of the very stunts performed today by "carpet" acrobats. There were prestidigitators too. Archeologists have found records in Egypt of conjurers baffling their onlookers with thimblerig, usually known to Americans as the shell game—the rigged sleight-of-hand that used to fleece the unsuspecting a generation ago (and sometimes still fleeces them) around circuses, fairs, and carnivals.

The early Egyptians were a gay people, fond of music and dancing. Bands of dancers often dressed themselves in ribbons, tassels, fools' caps, and cavorted through the streets to the accompaniment of drums. Groups made up of dancers, musicians, jesters, and other entertainers roamed from village to village, putting on their stunts, and passing the hat for whatever they could collect. Such itinerant entertainers must have been very like the mountebanks who were to travel across Europe in the Middle ages.

Of course this kind of entertainment in Egypt was not circus. Nevertheless it represented the emergence of some of the vital components of the circus.

Sacred Crocodiles

The menagerie also goes back to Egypt, where, long before the Christian era, the training of wild beasts was already an astonishingly developed art. Animals were always a part of Egyptian life, and death. Profuse records have been unearthed proving that animals were worshiped as sacred, were used for hunting, and were kept in parks that much resembled our zoos.

All sorts of beasts, domesticated and savage, were worshiped in Egypt, and some of the most predatory were tamed. When visitors to the temple at Arsinoë called across Lake Moeris, the sacred crocodiles used to swim over and take tidbits from their hands. The crocodiles wore collars, and rings around their ankles, and (as with other sacred animals) when one died it was embalmed and buried in the necropolis reserved for its kind of mummy.

Dogs, hyenas, leopards, cheetahs, lions, and even cats were trained for hunting. Domestic cats have seldom been taught to perform, but in Egypt they were persuaded to retrieve birds, stunned or killed by boomerangs, which had fallen in the reeds. Cats, by the way, were almost unknown in Europe until they were imported from Egypt in the fifth century A.D. to cope with a devastating scourge of huge Asiatic rats that came in the wake of the Huns.

Lions of the Pharaohs

Lions are shown in many monuments as pets of the Pharaohs, and even the name of the lion owned by Rameses is known. He was called Anta-m-nepht, and he accompanied his master to battle. Ordinarily Anta-m-nepht was chained outside Rameses' tent, but when the fighting began he ran in advance of the war chariot, beside the horses, mixing in the fight, and knocking aside anyone who approached the Pharaoh. Pet lions became so popular that, at least during the time the Romans dominated Egypt, virtually every rich man possessed one. In the first century A.D., Apollonius of Tyana recorded that he saw a lion walking on an ordinary leash, following its master. The creature appeared to be very gentle.

No one now knows how the ancients trained the great jungle cats, and present-day trainers are inclined to be skeptical concerning the extent to which they could have been tamed, but it seems probable that quiet "gentling" methods were used, which were later to be almost forgotten for centuries, except as they may have been revived by an occasional genius. Furthermore, in all likelihood the Egyptian who wanted to keep a lion as a pet took certain precautions. He would choose an animal from stock he knew to be comparatively gentle and amiable, have its canine teeth removed, and keep its claws cut. A male animal undoubtedly would be castrated. And even then, once the lion was full-grown, its liberty might have to be drastically curtailed. Unless the great carnivora have changed their natures, which seems doubtful, it would have been dangerous to allow them any real freedom, unless they were accompanied by trainers whom they respected and feared. Still, despite the understandable skepticism of those who handle animals today, it is difficult to deny or ignore completely the numerous apparently authentic records of achievements during the early Mediterranean civilization, many of which seem much more remarkable than anything known in modern times.

In ancient days at Memphis, there were parks and other great tracts of land where domestic and savage beasts were kept. In the VIIIth Dynasty (fifteenth century B.C.) Queen Hatshepsut sent five vessels through the Red Sea to Punt, to bring back frankincense, myrrh, gold, ebony, and

30

ivory. They also returned with many animals Egypt had not known before, such as monkeys, greyhounds, oxen, a giraffe, and various kinds of birds, as well as numerous plants, including thirty-three myrrh trees wrapped in balls of earth. Hatshepsut had the trees planted on the terraces in front of the temple at Thebes, and the animals were kept in special preserves.

The Egyptians were very clever indeed at catching animals, and hordes of specimens of different varieties were often driven into single-doored corrals, and there kept alive. It was the style to procure lion whelps, bear cubs, and tiny ruminants, and bring them up. A tomb at Karnak shows one of the officers of Thothmes III supervising the arrival in Egypt of a baby elephant and a little blond bear.

In the fourth century B.C., Alexander the Great and Ptolemy introduced into Egypt the Asiatic cults of Serapis and Dionysus. Temple menageries were enlarged, and the use of animals in ceremonials became much more elaborate. A permanent menagerie was attached to the museum in Alexandria, and great collections of animals were made for it by the Ptolemies. At its largest it covered 100 acres. The beasts became features of the triumphs of the rulers, and of great religious festivals, which also included chariot races, combats, and tremendous processions.

Ptolemy's Magnificent Parade

Atheneus, an Egyptian Greek, tells of a magnificent parade presented by Ptolemy II (309–247 B.C.). Various sections were devoted to the popular deities, among them Dionysus, who, according to legend, caught and trained even the most ferocious beasts. Because it was natural that any procession in his honor should utilize the menagerie, in paying homage to their god, the priests of Dionysus also unwittingly fostered the ancestor of that incomparable spectacle, the circus parade. The procession of Ptolemy II began at dawn and took all day to pass through the stadium. The animals came toward the end, after satyrs, winged victories, and such features as a chariot pulled by twenty-four men, bearing a statue of Bacchus surrounded by priests, priestesses, and girls wearing crowns, which must have resembled an elaborate nineteenth-century float.

Barnum and Bailey themselves would have envied the turnout of animals. First came an elephant caparisoned in gold and crowned with ivy leaves, bearing a satyr astride his neck. Then followed 24 cars drawn by elephants, 60 by he-goats, 12 by lions, 6 by she-goats, 15 by buffaloes, 4 by wild asses, 8 by ostriches, and 7 by stags. Behind camels hitched to

chariots came mules, drawing other cars, each carrying a woman dressed as a slave, and a tent constructed "in the manner of the barbarians." Camels loaded high with spices and perfumes were followed by Ethiopians bowed down under elephant tusks, ebony, gold and silver goblets, and powdered gold; hunters leading thousands of dogs; men holding branches to which numerous kinds of animals were attached; exotic birds in cages made of reeds; hundreds of sheep; and an Ethiopian rhinoceros. Next in line came statues of the gods, and of Alexander and Ptolemy, followed by richly clad women displaying the names of Greek cities. As the line of parade moved on, there were horses; more wild beasts, including 24 enormous lions; statues of still other kings and gods; a choir of 600 men, 300 of whom played on gilded citharas and wore gold crowns; 2,000 bulls, all of matching color high-lighted with gold; censers, palms, and statues of Jupiter and Alexander (in undoubtedly noncoincidental juxtaposition). The last feature was a chariot filled with incense.

This sort of procession was presented periodically as long as menageries lasted. Toward the end of the fourth century A.D., however, Egyptian temples began to be destroyed, and the animal preserves were abolished, making such magnificent displays impossible.

Animal collecting and training of a similar character went on among the Assyrians, Chaldeans, and Persians, and in the Far East. It is

32

not really certain whether the custom of maintaining animal preserves started in Egypt and spread thence to the rest of the world, or whether it began in the East, perhaps in China. In Mesopotamia there were sacred menageries, and it is known that the Babylonian kings had captive elephants, rhinoceroses, leopards, and numerous smaller or less dangerous beasts. Gala expeditions went out to capture them, and they were transported in strong wooden cages (of which pictures still remain), from which they could be released into big hunting preserves. Many rulers seem to have kept lions in their palaces, as the Pharaohs did in Egypt.

Apollonius of Tyana, who was something of a globe-trotter, wrote that he saw leopards and cheetahs in India, wandering around entirely free in the gardens and inside the palaces, and was so astonished at their docility that he asked how they had been trained. The answer was that the animals were never beaten, flattered or coaxed too much, but were approached with amiable calmness, and led on to do as was desired, by caresses backed up by warnings of retribution if they misbehaved.

From China, sparse records indicate that as early as the twelfth century B.C. a great animal park existed on the road between Peking and Nanking. In the domain of the Great Khan, at the end of the twelfth century A.D., Marco Polo saw lions and tigers wandering around at liberty in the most intimate apartments of the palace; leopards and lynxes trained to hunt bears; and a mammoth park at Xanadu where there were lodgings for lions, tigers, hunting leopards, elephants, rhinoceroses and myriad other beasts.

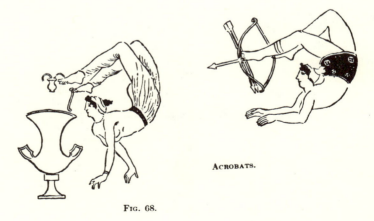

ACROBATS.

FIG. 68.

Jugglers in Xanadu—Acrobats in Crete

Just how early juggling and acrobatic stunts were developed in the Far East is not known, though tightrope walking is said to have originated in China; but such skills were certainly familiar there when, to the Mediterranean world, "Cathay" was still an incalculably distant and mysterious country. Writing about the court of Kublai Khan, Marco Polo reports that, "when the repast is finished, and the tables have been removed, persons of various descriptions enter the hall, and amongst them a troop of comedians and performers on different musical instruments. Also tumblers and jugglers, who exhibit their skill in the presence of the Great Khan, to the amusement and gratification of all the spectators."

Acrobatics on the backs of moving domestic animals (to become the basic attraction of the early modern circus, and remain so for almost a century) was carried on in the Mediterranean island of Crete. In the palace at Knossos, which was built in 2000 B.C., and stood for almost six hundred years, wall paintings showed the life of the times. One of them, which has been carefully reconstructed, portrays what scholars call bull-leaping. In a beautiful and astonishingly naturalistic design, the artist depicted a young man facing a charging bull, catching hold of the horns. The attitude of a second figure shows that the trick was to let oneself be tossed over the animal's head, turn a somersault on his back, and land in the hands of a person standing behind the bull. Because of the custom of painting masculine figures in chocolate brown and feminine ones

The acrobatic tradition has endured through the centuries. These are medieval tumblers

34

in yellow ochre, the catcher in this picture appears to be a young woman. Although Cretan bull-leaping originated as a religious ceremony, it is very much like the sort of feat on horseback with which Philip Astley was to astound the London world at the end of the eighteenth century, and so can be said to anticipate the modern circus.

On the northern shore of the Mediterranean, gangs of jugglers and tumblers, fortune tellers, dancers, and musicians were moving through the towns and cities of Greece. These itinerant bands must have been very similar to those of Egypt—a motley crowd, taking over from the folk festivals anything acceptable to a street-corner audience, and developing each trick and spectacle as the occasion demanded and their skill permitted. Athletes experimented with new forms of acrobatics. There are records of ropedancers (called *schoenobates*), who had not been seen in Egypt, and stories of women jumping through hoops of fire.

Along with these acrobatic entertainers, comes a jester who has now grown important in his own right. That is the Greek mime, ancestor of the modern circus clown. Some version of the mime certainly appeared as early as 800 B.C., when one Susarion presented his comic actors in Icaria, but the form is said to have originated in Dorian Hellas, and to have developed somewhat in Megara. The phallus was an accepted and indispensable part of the costume, and the entertainment presented by the mime was very broad farce indeed, accompanied by gestures that would undoubtedly shock even the far from squeamish audiences of today. The comic character, by the way, has always borne a close relationship to the acrobat and the juggler, and the ability to perform difficult acrobatic feats with deceptive ease is traditionally part of the clown's stock in trade. Only in the past few decades has the public been willing to accept a clown who was not also a tumbler, vaulter, and equilibrist.

In the early days there were at least seven roles assumed by mimes: an old man with a peaked beard, a fool, a doctor, an old, haglike woman, a bald, ruddy glutton who was either a cook or a sailor, two slaves who occasionally were thieves, and a leading slave who had reddish hair, bushy eyebrows, big feet, and a potbelly, and wore his hair in a formalized coiffure known as a *speira*. The majority concealed their features and expressions behind masks. Others put soot on their faces, foreshadowing, of course, the "blackface" clowns who have been so popular with American audiences.

35

It is traditional to give the Romans credit for creating the background for the circus arena in which the ring acts and the clown are presented. We usually think of the development of the ring in terms of the catch line *From Rome to Ringling,* but with a good deal of justification it is possible to say that the circus owes its characteristic setting equally to the Greeks. Neither Greeks nor Romans developed what we think of as true circus; but between them, at approximately the same period, they did devise forerunners of the modern arena.

Chariot Races and Dancing Bears

During the great days of the city states, the Greeks worshiped the perfection of the human body, and played innumerable games calculated to make and keep themselves fit. Among the athletic contests in which they indulged were running, jumping, boxing, throwing the weight, the discus and the javelin, and racing horses. As some sort of marked-off area was essential for such pursuits, the stadium and the hippodrome came into being. The *pentathlon,* a combination of five events—running, wrestling, jumping, throwing the discus, and throwing the javelin—was given in the stadium. Horse and chariot races were the spectacles in the hippodrome.

From earliest times, games of all kinds had centered around religious festivals, and it was natural that both a stadium and a hippodrome should be built at Olympia, where stood the greatest of all temples to Zeus and Hera. This Olympian Stadium was a parallelogram, with markers for starting, and posts to indicate the turning point for the racers. There were no seats, except for officials, and the spectators stood for hours. All around ran a stone runnel, with basins here and there from which they could quench their thirst.

No trace remains today of the Hippodrome (literally a horse course), built somewhat south of the Stadium. It was merely a larger rectangle surrounded by rising ground, and the course was marked by a pillar at either end, where chariots and horses turned. At the western end there was a colonnade, the Portico of Agnaptos, and in front of it an elaborate starting gate shaped like the prow of a ship. The sides of the prow were divided into parallel pairs of stalls, where the chariots were kept when not in use. A temple stood in the center of the portico, holding on its altar an eagle with outstretched wings, and a bronze dolphin. The eagle was the bird of Zeus, the dolphin a symbol of Poseidon, one of the gods who presided over horses. At a signal for the race to begin, the starter

touched a piece of mechanism; the eagle rose and the dolphin dropped, and the horses leaped away from the gate.

At the beginning of the fifth century B.C., the only hippodrome events were the four-horse chariot race and the horse race. The charioteer, in his long white robe, holding his whip or goad, had barely room to stand in the two-wheeled chariot with the rail at front and sides. Two horses were attached to the poles; two others were on traces. In the horse race, the jockey wore no shoes, and had no stirrups. After either event, the prize, a leafy crown, went to the man who owned the horses, as the purse does today. In Greece too, the owner seldom rode, and the racing was done by professionals.

As time went on, other races were added, and the true sporting instinct was supplanted by an exaggerated enthusiasm for competition. Before long, professionals were going from city to city looking for prizes. Even at worst, however, the Greeks never had a taste for the Roman entertainment of watching wild animals being killed in great numbers. They did enjoy quail and cockfighting, and presented Thessalian bull-fights, in which the men were mounted, and the skill shown was closely related to that of the modern rodeo, but by and large their interest in animals seems to have been benign.

In the days of the independent city states, Greece did not have the immense wealth of some of its Mediterranean neighbors, who sent all over the known world to satisfy their acquisitive instincts. In Hellas there were no great collections of savage beasts. In later days, however, the Greeks provided halfway stations for wild beasts on their way to Rome. In fact, such numbers of purveyors went through the country, stopping between Asia and Italy, that eventually the Greek language developed three words for the different kinds of cages in which wild animals were transported.

The great achievement of the Greeks, as far as animals were concerned, was in training them to do tricks; and in that field they achieved astonishing results. As with the Egyptians, the original impetus came from religious ceremonials. Sacred menageries were set up in Greek temples, where lions and leopards were associated with Cybele, dogs with Hecate, eagles with Zeus, and snakes with Aesculapius. All these and other creatures were trained to be exhibited in the festivals of the various cults. In processions, though the ferocious beasts sometimes were confined in cages, they often walked quietly, drawing vehicles.

The first traveling menageries of which there are records were created by wandering Greek priests, called *agyrtes,* who went from village to village as early as the fourth century B.C., showing captured animals and putting them through all manner of tricks. By exhibiting dancing bears, those priestly showmen initiated a taste that has not died down in our own time. Lions, which were to be found in the mountains of Greece up to perhaps the third century B.C. (but were hunted relentlessly after they attacked the camels in Xerxes' army), were taken alive and trained by the *agyrtes* to pull chariots and other vehicles, or even to become house and temple pets. A famous Greek cup showed a bacchante playing a tambourine while a lion danced. In training wild beasts, the specialists of Hellas always used music.

Although Europeans of the sixteenth century usually receive credit for first training horses to go through the routine now known as *haute école* or "high school" (in which the animals dance, bow, kneel and perform various other graceful gyrations to musical accompaniment), Greek literature tells us of horses dancing to music almost 2,000 years before the development of so-called Spanish riding in Vienna. One especially delightful story concerns the Sybarites, who were unusually clever trainers, and taught their horses to respond enthusiastically to lively rhythms. In a battle between Sybarites and Crotonites, the latter took advantage of that fact, and began to play dance rhythms loudly and clearly, whereupon, according to the legend, the Sybarites' steeds danced off the field, carrying their helpless riders into the arms of the enemy. Pleasant as it is, this legend must be discounted, for a horse trained to *haute école* is controlled entirely by his own rider, and responds only to that rider's firm though imperceptible direction.

As the glorious days of Greece drew to a close, and the Christian era approached, the center of civilization swung westward, to Rome, where, for the next several hundred years, circus received a strong and invigorating impulse.

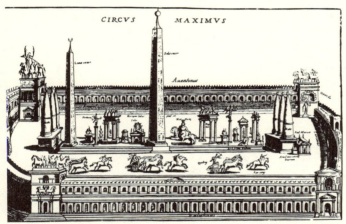

3

CIRCVS   MAXIMVS

Bettmann Archive

Emperors and
Amphitheatres

ALTHOUGH the Greeks drew up preliminary plans for the arena, it was the Romans who really constructed it, developed its potentialities, and gave it a name.

Two kinds of arenas grew out of Roman enthusiasm for spectacles—the circus and the amphitheatre—both of which exerted a profound effect on the ring entertainment that was to be christened in the eighteenth century. Of the two, the circus was used primarily to satisfy the desire to watch horses—an urge that was to spur development of the modern circus. The amphitheatre became the special setting for diversions that were almost always considerably less innocent.

In its circuses, Rome developed horse racing to a degree that would have made Saratoga of the great days look amateurish. In its amphitheatres, Rome watched carefully prepared programs that somewhat resembled those of a modern circus—except for one basic difference. No entertainment in a Roman amphitheatre could be repeated exactly, because the cast seldom survived the sport. The entertainments, ironically called *ludi* (games), came to be almost always such brutal affairs that even the twentieth century, accustomed to its own peculiarly sinister horrors, is revolted.

"Bread and Circuses"

As was true everywhere in the ancient world, religious festivals furnished the original impetus for games of some sort. Before long, any excuse was sufficient. Even during the Republic, popular leaders began to give shows, ostensibly for the people's enjoyment, actually for their own aggrandizement. In Imperial times no emperor could hope to control the populace without giving it *panem et circenses,* an expression usually translated "bread and circuses," which actually meant "bread and races," and was used to indicate all sorts of *ludi.* Officials who wanted to impress their contemporaries presented games on special occasions—more and more games, more and more extravagant and, except for the races, more and more bloody. In the mid-fourth century, 175 days in the year were holidays, all celebrated by public spectacles.

Two hippodromes, the Circus Maximus and the Circus Flaminius, were built in Rome itself, and innumerable others sprang up in the provinces. The earlier and more important of the two in the city was the Maximus. According to tradition, Lucius Tarquinius Priscus, Etruscan king of Rome, put up the original building, a wooden structure, in the sixth century B.C., when the first games were held. Thereafter, up through the time of Trajan (emperor from 98 to 117 A.D.) changes in the building were made every now and then.

The Circus Maximus stood between the Aventine and Palatine hills, similar in form to the Greek hippodrome, but differing in many respects. It was a long rectangle with a curved end at the south, surrounded by risi g banks of seats—an obvious ancestor of our race tracks, football stadiums, and circus tents. Incidentally, in the circus tent, the runway between the seats and the ring or rings is still known as the hippodrome track. At its greatest capacity, the Circus probably held between 180,000 and 190,000 spectators, though some estimates are lower.

At the north end, on either side of a central gate, were six *carceres* or stalls, each big enough to hold a chariot and its horses. Above were boxes for officials. The line of *carceres* was at an angle, carefully designed to give everyone a fair start.

Out in the center, approximately along the longitudinal axis of the arena, ran a long wall called a *spina,* on which were various ornamental structures, including pillars, altars, statues, shrines, and two obelisks. Just beyond each end stood three *metae*—cone-shaped pillars to mark the turnings. On the *spina,* a small structure held seven dolphins and seven egg-shaped balls, emblems of Neptune, and of Castor and Pollux, which served to mark the score. Each race was run in seven laps and, as a lap was finished, one egg and one dolphin were taken down.

The Latin word *circus,* meaning "round," was applied to the hippodrome not because of its shape but because the drivers sent their horses around and around. A charioteer, dressed in a short tunic, and wearing a helmet to protect him in case he was dragged, stood in the two-wheeled cart, a whip in one hand and the reins in the other, urging his horses on to try to get closest to the *spina* at the end of the stretch. In his belt was a knife, with which he hoped to be able to cut himself free if chariots, men, and horses collided or tangled, as they often did. From dawn to dusk, with only a short intermission at noon, the chariot races roared around the *spina,* as many as twenty-four in a day, while the crowds cheered or booed.

Trick riders in the modern circus would have felt at home in the Roman arena, for in addition to the chariot races the Romans promoted competitions on horseback, in which *desultores* leaped from horse to horse, lay down on their running steeds, jumped over obstacles, and picked things up off the ground.

The races were preceded by a procession, which started at the Capitol, wove through the city, and entered the Circus through the main entrance, passing around the goal posts. The magistrate who presented the spectacle led off. Then came the musicians. Next, in a high chariot, was a praetor or proconsul dressed as a conquering general. Statues of the gods on ornately decorated chariots were followed by members of the priesthood. The procession moved to the accompaniment of flutes and trumpets. This kind of parade, beginning in comparative simplicity, in time grew to the great size and magnificence of the triumphal processions with which Julius Caesar and later conquerors celebrated their military achievements.

The arena of the Circus was occasionally used for gladiatorial combats and the beast baitings known as *venationes,* but after the Republic most of those were held in the amphitheatres. The first true Roman amphitheatre, which was not unlike a circus, but was a short ellipse rather than a rectangle, was built by Julius Caesar for his triumph in 46 B.C. It was a wooden structure, however, and was soon pulled down. The best known and most completely developed amphitheatre was the Colosseum, which was equipped to produce the most elaborate and expensive spectacles the world has ever seen.

The trained animals, which delighted audiences then as now, form the closest link between the Roman amphitheatre and the modern circus. Trainers of today can do little that was not done at least as well by those in Rome. According to writers of the time, almost incredible results were produced by the Roman *mansuetarii,* who had learned from the Alexandrian experts.

Lions Drew Chariots

If we can believe these writers, Mark Antony, with the actress Cytheris beside him, drove from Brindisi to Rome in a chariot drawn by lions. The notorious Heliogabalus was fond of driving on the Vatican Hill, with lions, tigers, or stags pulling his chariot. He also loved practical jokes. He would put lions and tigers, whose teeth and claws had been extracted, into the bedrooms of his drunken guests—several of whom, on awakening, died of fright.

In the third century B.C., after the consul Metellus showed in his triumph 142 elephants he had captured in Carthage, the strange animals were killed because no one knew what to do with them. But the Romans quickly grew accustomed to the elephant, and developed into skillful and ingenious trainers. During Caesar's triumph in 46 B.C. he was escorted

A Roman stone engraving of elephants drawing a chariot

to and from the Capitol by forty elephants carrying blazing torches. In the arenas, the mighty beasts fought like gladiators, danced to cymbals clashed by other elephants, and threw weapons into the air. It is also recorded that with their trunks they wrote Greek and Latin words on tablets. Four carried a fifth one in a litter. They could walk through crowded rooms and sit neatly at table. In the time of Tiberius, an elephant walked across the Circus Maximus on a tightrope.

Other animals were trained with equal skill. Bears fought or danced at command. So did cranes. Wild bulls walked on their hind feet. An eagle flew, carrying a baby in its talons. Dog-faced baboons pointed out letters in the alphabet, and plucked the cithara. Lions, leopards, tigers, even boars and wolves went through the same kind of turns we see in the ring today. When the Romans felt good-natured it amused them to watch a lion chase a hare, catch it, play with it as a cat does with a mouse, and then carry it back unharmed to the trainer.

As in Egypt and Assyria, lions were used as house pets. The style was to clip them much as we do our poodles, and sometimes they were powdered with gold. Caracalla owned a lion named Acinaces, which sat with him at table and slept in his bedroom. Valentinian had two bears, Innocentia and Mica, which always spent the night at his chamber door.

44

The wealthy made pets of large and small dogs, monkeys, Barbary apes, baboons, and grass snakes. Even the poor had their trained pets. During the reign of Tiberius, a shoemaker picked up a raven that had fallen from its nest and taught it to perch on the edge of the rostrum in the Forum, calling out the names of Tiberius, Germanicus, and Drusus. One day a rival shoemaker killed the raven in a fit of envy. The mob gave it a solemn funeral—and killed the envious shoemaker. Another raven was trained to call out, "Ave Caesar, victor, imperator!" which so delighted Augustus that he bought it for 20,000 sesterces (about $2,000).

The Romans continued the tradition of persuading many creatures to do stunts in contradiction to their inherent natures. Wild bulls let boys dance on their backs. Gentle antelopes butted each other to death.

In training savage animals, the Roman *mansuetarii,* like the Greek, had recourse to music, which they played on the cithara, syrinx, flute, and drum. Snake charmers added incantations and magic chants. One trainer put his head into a lion's mouth. Another kissed a tiger.

And then there was the legendary incident of Androclus, recorded by several supposedly responsible writers, which forms the basis of Shaw's play *Androcles and the Lion.* Androclus was a slave who ran away from his master in Africa, and was condemned to be torn to pieces by wild beasts. In the arena, so the story goes, he was recognized by a lion from whose paw he had extracted a thorn, years before in the desert. The lion now refused to touch him and, at the people's demand, Androclus was pardoned. Thereafter he went in and out of the taverns of the city, leading his lion on a slender leash.

Just as had happened in Greece, interest in looking at unfamiliar animals or watching them perform was aroused by traveling priests—in this instance those of Cybele and Isis, who came from Asia Minor or Egypt to wander through Italy. Showmen called *circulatores* also went about showing lions, bears and snakes, and monkeys and other small animals.

By the time the republic turned into an empire, all rulers were gathering tremendous collections, and many rich citizens had their own private zoos, though elephants could be owned only by the emperor. In or near the imperial city, three kinds of zoological gardens were maintained—one where the animals received ordinary care; one where the sick were treated; and one where they were prepared for the games. Eventually, schools for trainers were established.

45

The ruins of the Colosseum in Rome

During a fifteen-year reign, Augustus collected 3,500 animals, including 420 trained tigers, 260 lions, 600 African leopards, cheetahs and other spotted carnivora, one rhinoceros that he sometimes showed to the public, one hippopotamus (the first to be seen in Rome), and 36 crocodiles, plus seals, eagles, elephants and bears. Travelers had orders to keep an eye out for animals, and to bring back any natural curiosities they came across. Marcus Aurelius also had a large and varied zoological collection, and Heliogabalus, in addition to the usual species, owned several hippopotami, one rhinoceros, and a crocodile.

After Roman times, it was to be many years before some of these animals were seen on the European continent. No hippopotamus was known in Europe again until 1850, when a specimen was sent from Egypt to the London Zoological Gardens.

Beast Baitings

However, from the first, the Romans' interest in wild animals had its sinister side. Few of the *ludi* were harmless exhibitions of skill. Apparently the people were deliberately conditioned to be cruel. A hundred years after the killing of the war elephants from Carthage, soldiers who had deserted from the army of Paullus were crushed under the feet of elephants. After the destruction of Carthage, in 146 B.C., the deserters were given to the wild beasts in the arena, to make games for the people. Thereafter, combats involving wild animals were common throughout Italy, and the patrons were sometimes hard-pressed to think up new cruelties.

The first *venationes* in the arenas of Rome were merely developments of the kind of hunting that had always been done in the country. In the beginning, the arena hunters chased elephants, lions, and leopards, as well as stags, boars, and other familiar European game. By the opening of the Christian era, many new types had been brought in, and most of them were hunted. The first giraffe, called a *camelopardalis,* was seen in Europe at the time of Caesar's most famous triumph. As time went on, even the strangest beasts became commonplace in the arena, and were hunted by the hundreds and thousands. The numbers necessary for a satisfying *venatio* increased constantly. Pompey offered a mere 500 lions, 410 leopards, and 17 elephants; but when the Colosseum was dedicated, 9,000 wild and tame animals were killed in a hundred-day show. At Trajan's triumph, 11,000 were destroyed. In one great festival, enough animals were killed to stock all the zoos of modern Europe.

Occasionally the emperor himself got into the act. In the Colosseum, with his own hand, Commodus killed elephants, hippopotami, rhinoceroses, tigers, bears and lions. It is said that in one day he killed 100 bears, and on another, using different weapons, finished off 100 lions turned loose at once.

Obviously, for putting on such exhibitions, a very special kind of building was desirable, and the Colosseum was built by Vespasian and his son Titus on the site of an artificial lake near Nero's Golden House. The building has been hit by lightning, knocked about by earthquakes, and defaced by men, but in its heyday it was an architectural masterpiece, perfectly adapted to the uses to which it was put. In the floor of the arena were various trap doors to subterranean regions where scenery, accessories, and machines for operating them were stored, and where corridors led out to the dens of the wild beasts. Processions entered through monumental doors at either end of the long axis of the amphitheatre. Under the loges occupied by the elite stood the Doors of the Dead, through which the dead or wounded were removed.

Around the arena was the *podium,* a wall on which dignitaries could sit or stroll about, and behind the *podium* rose grandstands, with a capacity of 40,000 to 50,000. Spectators were seated according to importance. Except for the Vestal Virgins, women were relegated to the very top. Here a roof protected them from sun and rain, but their view was impeded by huge awnings over the seats below. These *velaria* were made of silk, and their color depended on the whim of the patron. Nero chose dark blue with stars.

The Colosseum was divided into three stories with a fourth added later, but the most elaborate part of the structure was below ground. Great high-arched cellars were hidden under the arena, and under the grandstands there was an intricate system of corridors, ramps, and rooms. Animals were sometimes released through doors in the *podium* called *cavae,* and sometimes came up through the arena floor. The *podium* was supposed to be high enough to protect the spectators; but for additional safety, nets were run along it, with grilles at the top, and revolving ivory wheels were attached to the gates where there were no nets. Eventually a low barricade was built between the *podium* and the central part of the arena, at some distance from the seats, which in addition to shielding the spectators offered some protection to the slaves who had to move cages and traps while ferocious beasts were at large.

Despite all precautions, animals did sometimes get out of bounds, and at one time a canal was built at the foot of the *podium,* especially to restrain the elephants. The most ingenious safety device, however, was the *cochlea*, which the Romans invented to give a trainer or roustabout a moment of respite when he was being pursued. Four panels, affixed at right angles to a movable axis, turned as one was pushed. The contrivance was nothing more nor less than a revolving door.

A *venatio* was announced far in advance by criers and posters. The night before the games, the final preparations were made below ground and the arena was sprinkled with sand, sawdust, or, for the effete Nero, with cinnabar and gold powder. At dawn a parade of animals was held in the arena, for which the beasts wore bells and were covered by variegated scarves, plaques of metal, or gold leaves. To look especially smart, oxen were painted blue, sheep purple or scarlet, and ostriches cinnabar red. Occasionally a touch of unkind humor was introduced by covering the bears with glue, so that when they rolled in the arena they picked up sand, leaves, feathers, and straw.

On the night before the show, the wild animals were taken to the Colosseum from the big menagerie outside the Praenestine Gate. Recent arrivals were carried across the city in their heavy traveling dens, two on a wagon, with the heaviest and sturdiest boxes holding the bears, which are among the strongest and most dangerous of all animals.

When the creatures arrived from the stockyard, they were put into cages under the arena itself, or placed in a two-story area under the *podium*. For the show, they could be pulled up to ground level by windlasses, or driven into underground corridors and forced into the arena. Wild animals are easily frightened, and their instinct is to hide and cower. To drive them out of the cages, the Romans used to put burning straw behind them, or prod them with hot irons.

With the advent of Christianity, and increasing concern for human life, the *venationes* gradually lost much of their cruelty. As animals became increasingly difficult to obtain from Africa, they were treated with greater consideration. In 326 A.D. Constantine was to issue a law against the spectacle, and abolish the profession of gladiator. Antiquity's last spectacle was a hunt given in 519 by Entaricus.

As time went on, with each person who presented games trying to outdo his predecessors, the artificial setting and accessories developed until they became very important in themselves. Daylight games were not enough. Bonfires and innumerable flaring torches illuminated the arenas for sumptuous pageants after dark. Virtually every type of spectacle that has been seen in the circus had its origin in the blood-soaked arenas of Rome.

4

Colossal
Spectacles

I NGENIOUS presentations in Rome's Colosseum were lineal ancestors of the comparatively simple mystery and miracle productions of the Middle Ages, the sumptuous pageants of the Renaissance, and the elaborately devised performances at seventeenth- and eighteenth-century courts. Through them the line runs directly to the modern circus spectacle.

Shipwreck in the Colosseum

Using trap doors in the floor of the Colosseum and elevators worked by windlasses, the Romans produced fantastic mechanical effects. In the time of Septimius Severus, a ship was drawn up from the Colosseum underground, and "wrecked" in view of the populace, spewing forth lions, leopards, bison, wild asses, and ostriches. During the same reign, after a dead whale had been picked up on a beach, a model whale was constructed for the amphitheatre, and became a dramatic container for fifty bears, from which they rushed out to meet swords and javelins.

Imagination, backed by immense wealth, produced an extraordinary variety of conceits; but the most original of all spectacles invented by the Romans was the *naumachia,* the sham sea battle. The original *naumachia* was given by Julius Caesar for his quadruple triumph, during which he showed the first giraffe and was escorted to the Capitol by the torch-bearing elephants. On a lake dug for the occasion in the Campus Martius, he offered a facsimile of a fight between Tyrian and Egyptian fleets, with 1,000 marines and 2,000 oarsmen manning biremes, triremes, and quadriremes, and killing each other in sufficient numbers to satisfy even the most jaded spectators. When Augustus wanted to present a water show, he dug another lake out of the bank of the Tiber, and showed a battle between the beaked biremes and triremes of the Athenians and Persians, carrying 6,000 soldiers and innumerable rowers. And in a first-century *naumachia* in the amphitheatre built by Nero on the Campus Martius, novelty was added by having fish and large marine animals swimming around the ships, and by draining off the water afterward to make a place for a land fight.

In one of the biggest of all the *naumachiae,* presented by Claudius on Lake Fucinus to celebrate the completion of an aqueduct, the fighters represented Sicilians and Rhodians, and the signal to begin was blown by a silver Triton, rising out of the water like a true demigod. The contestants, who were criminals, fought so bravely that the survivors were

51

reprieved. Finally Domitian outdid all his predecessors by presenting in the Colosseum itself a mock battle so stupendous that it looked as if real fleets were fighting.

Strolling Tumblers and Ropedancers

Just as the Roman *venationes* and *naumachiae* were the ancestors of spectacular sham fights in the circus amphitheatres of the early nineteenth century, so modern acrobatic ring acts are descended from entertainments in the streets of Rome. Rome was a crowded, cosmopolitan city, and along its streets wandered jugglers, acrobats, fortune tellers and snake charmers. Trained animals appeared on corners and in squares, where crowds gathered openmouthed to watch. It was not uncommon to see tightrope walkers, whom the Romans called *funambuli,* balancing high above the crowd.

Ordinarily, such exhibitions were spontaneous affairs, put on wherever a strolling entertainer could catch an audience. The emperor Galba is credited with being the first person to sponsor a performance in a formal setting, and in the third century the emperor Carinus offered a performance (probably on a theatre stage) with sword swallowers, fire-eaters, prestidigitators, stilt walkers, jugglers, boys doing tricks on the top of ladders (in what today we call the perch act), ropedancers and fixed trapeze artists. Along with these attractions there were performing bears and great numbers of flute players and trumpeters. When the consul Flavius Mallus Theodorus gave a festival, in addition to chariot races, athletic contests, music, theatricals and animal baitings, the entertainment included all kinds of circus acrobatics. Ropedancers balanced on threads; men formed pyramids; jugglers threw colored balls; acrobats jumped from scaffolds and hurled themselves through flames.

After Christianity had somewhat moderated the brutal and bloodthirsty desire to watch human and animal agony, the Romans saw entertainments in their arenas that aroused more interest in skill than in danger for its own sake. The *cochleae* (those revolving doors) became a feature of a lively game. Several of them were set up in the floor of the Colosseum, and the crowds roared with delight to see an athlete adroitly evade a pursuing beast, leaping into the angle between the panels, and whirling to safety just as the animal thought he had cornered his prey.

As emphasis on the comic developed, new stunts were added. Two men hung in baskets on either end of a pole, balanced like a seesaw. When a wild beast approached one of the baskets, it went into the air. Naturally,

the animal ran toward the basket on the ground, which in turn rose out of his reach. The Romans found it excruciatingly funny. There was another trick, worked by a contortionist inside a *canistrum,* an iron sphere pierced with holes just big enough for him to get his arm through. The contortionist thrust a hand out to prick and prod the beast, and then pulled it back as quickly as possible. Sometimes he lost an arm, but he was not likely to be killed.

Monstrous Miracula

Interest in wild animals seems to be a universal psychological trait. A more complex drive, undoubtedly, lies behind the impulse to gawk at human abnormalities; and, when civilization was younger, all such deviations from the norm were objects of unabashed curiosity. The Romans collected freaks whenever and wherever they could, occasionally contrived the abnormalities, and exhibited all such oddities under the general head of *miracula.*

The people were familiar with dwarfs, which were kept in all the houses of the powerful, as they were to be later, especially, at the court of Spain. Hermaphrodites were discovered from time to time. Giants and giantesses, cretins, men without calves, men with short arms, men with three eyes, and men with pointed heads were all sold in a Roman monstrosity market. In the time of Claudius, a giant was sent from Arabia who was nine and three-quarters Roman feet tall (about 8 feet 4 inches). The emperor also received from Phrygia an androgynous creature, first girl, then boy. One Artabenus sent to Tiberius a Jew named Eleazar, recalled as a fairy-tale giant 7 ells high. Augustus exhibited to the public a boy named Lucius Icius, who was not quite two feet tall but had a voice like a man's. A giant and giantess, Posio and Secundilla, were kept in a vault in the gardens of Sallust.

According to a record of the year 354, there lived in Alexandria a glutton, Arpocras by name, who must have been the ancestor of all side-show fat men. At one meal he ate a boiled wild pig, a live hen (with feathers), 100 eggs, 100 stone-pine kernels, a suckling pig, a bundle of hay, some broken glass, a few hobnails, a batch of palm broom twigs, and four tablecloths. He said he was still hungry.

The fakes had also begun. Fabulous monsters were carried into Rome—creatures with animal bodies and human limbs, such as a "hippocentaur" supposedly caught in the mountains of Arabia, which had died and been preserved in honey. Nereids, Tritons, and other fabled sea creatures came along, and Pausanias says he saw in Rome a Triton with green hair, large teeth, scales, hands covered with shells like mussels, and a fish's tail. Barnum's "Fejee" mermaid was a simple thing compared to that.

It was bruited abroad that there were *skiapodes* in Libya, the soles of whose feet were so large that they could be turned up and used as umbrellas. St. Augustine remarked that he thought that story might be pure invention, though he did know that in Hippo Diarrytus there was a man whose hands and feet were almost crescent-shaped, ending in only two digits on each, and that in the East there was a man of remarkable length, with two heads, two breasts, and four hands, but only two legs.

Ancestor of the Clown

Although the Roman theatre at first imitated Greek comedy, and the form only gradually became truly Latin, the ancestors of our clowns made their appearance at this time. The pseudo-Greek comedies exerted no great influence on the development of the clown, except through such characters as the boastful soldier, butt of the jokes. who was to develop into one of the most popular figures of the Italian Comedy.

The type of Roman theatrical performance most important for its effect on the circus was one for which there was little or no written text, for the clown grew out of the improvisational spirit. One such vehicle, the *fabula Atellana* (developed in Atella in Campania) was a burlesque rather like a Punch and Judy show, woven around a thin plot, with much of the

54

dialogue improvised, and innumerable riddles, known as *tricae,* introduced. Included among its stereotyped characters were Maccus, awkward, stupid, and gluttonous; Bucco, another glutton who babbled foolishness and lies; Pappus, a gullible greybeard; Cicirrus, a strutting braggart; and Dossenus, a sardonic hunchback, clever and boastful, recognized by a hooked nose, a large mouth, and a wart on his brow. Their descendants still tread both boards and tanbark.

In the *versus Fescennini* (so named after a town in Etruria), actors broke forth into jokes and sarcastic jibes such as originally had been sung at rustic festivals and weddings, and here one can discern the origin of comic repartee, which was to hit a high spot shortly after the middle of the nineteenth century, with the creation of a type of circus comic known as the august.

Slapstick and buffoonery, an inevitable aspect of all these vehicles, were a part too of the Roman *fabulae togatae,* which eventually took the place of the Greece-inspired comedies.

In discussions of Latin comedy, constant references are made to the *mimus,* or mime. The word originally meant a type of burlesque performance rather like a harlequinade, and only later came to indicate the actor who took part in it. According to our standards, the plots of the mimes were indecent, the humor coarse, the jokes unsavory. Often an undercurrent of political satire ran through the continuity, worked out by stock characters. Among those characters there was always he who got slapped; and it was a mime who first wore the *centunculus,* a patchwork costume that was to develop into the diamonds and lozenges of Harlequin.

The Italians have always been a people who gesticulated freely, and gestures came to play such a part in the comedy that eventually all dialogue was omitted. The resulting pantomime attained an immense popularity in Rome, partly because it could be understood as easily by a Roman citizen from Macedonia or Carthage as by one born within the ring of the Seven Hills. But finally the increasing use of pantomime put an end to the true comedy of the Romans.

Though much of the early comedy was performed in theatres, in the great days of Rome, ambulant groups of players still went from town to town, giving their farcical shows in the streets, and perhaps selling nostrums as a side line. In the Middle Ages, wandering groups were to play a much more important role.

5

Mountebanks,
Monsters, and Fairs

WHEN Rome fell, in the fifth century, the type of entertainment that had developed through a thousand years in its circuses and amphitheatres fell with it. However, during the Middle Ages, the itinerant mountebanks, carrying their acrobatic turns from city to city and country to country, kept alive the tradition out of which eventually the circus developed.

The Middle Ages were a time when long-range communication of any kind was slow and extremely difficult. Roads were narrow, pitted, and dangerous. Those who could afford to do so traveled on horseback, but even they were beset by great perils and inconveniences. The poor went on foot, whatever the weather and whatever the distance. Carts were simple and primitive.

The pitifully inadequate roads were alive with messengers, men looking for work, pedlars hawking their wares, serfs who had broken away from their masters, mendicant friars and pilgrims, drug sellers, thieves of every stripe, and the minstrels, gleemen and perambulating mountebanks who offered entertainment. The greater part of the world, however, led passive lives, seldom venturing forth from home, and avid for word of what was going on beyond its bounds. All those who came from a distance, bearing news or bringing variety, were hailed with enthusiasm, no matter what their purpose.

Medieval Medicine Show

Most popular among them were the bands of mountebanks, each of which would inevitably include a seller of nostrums. The brightly clad troupe would stop in some market place or on some village green, spread a carpet on the ground, and break into its routine. One of the number would jump up and begin a harangue full of tall tales and big words, promising health, long life, and happiness from a concoction that might be made largely of ground-up crickets, glowworms, beetles, and bats. That seller of nostrums was, of course, the direct ancestor of the snake-oil merchant of our grandfathers' time.

After the spiel, the acrobats would produce their fantastic entertainment. They juggled, turned somersaults, walked on their hands, danced on ropes, swallowed swords, jumped through hoops, did conjuring tricks, and tied themselves into knots.

Among them there might be several who could sing. Certainly there would be a number who could play on some of the light, small, string, wind and percussion instruments of the time. More and more, the true minstrel became associated with the bands of tumblers, jugglers, conjurers, and ribalds, who were as welcome at castle gates as in the town square.

These folk were not gypsies. The Romanies, who abounded early on the Continent, though there were none in England until the fifteenth century, were the tinkers, the basket weavers and, unfortunately often, the chicken and horse thieves. It was usually a lone gypsy who wandered the country with a performing bear, thus keeping alive the tradition of the traveling menagerie. As time went on, however, animal trainers often became a part of mountebank troupes, as the menagerie was later to attach itself to the circus.

In the troupes, the performers came from far and wide, speaking many tongues, and their encampments must have sounded very like a modern circus lot. We call all these gentry mountebanks, but strictly speaking the mountebank is the one who climbed onto some slightly elevated structure and harangued the crowd. The name derives from the Italian *montambanco,* contraction of *monta in banco,* that is to say, "hop onto a bench." It is possible that the bench also served as a kind of springboard from which an acrobat catapulted himself into a somersault. And while the man on the bench was distracting the crowd with his spiel—and from his vantage point keeping a sharp lookout for possible trouble— some of his companions would undoubtedly be investigating the contents of the onlookers' pockets, before they themselves went into their tumbling, juggling, or ropewalking acts. Speed, variety, and confusion were essential stocks-in-trade of the ambulant troupes of entertainers.

Eventually the bench became a little stage, usually of a semicollapsible variety, which could be drawn through the countryside on wheels and set up at will. Side curtains were dropped to make skirts, behind which machinery could be concealed; and the whole thing could be folded up very quickly, ready to move on again.

An eighteenth-century etching of acrobats

Miracles at St. Bartholomew's

It was not only the medieval laity who greeted traveling mountebanks with enthusiasm. They were encouraged by the Church itself, through the specific instrument of the fair.

Some persons say the word "fair" comes from the French *foire,* a place where merchandise is sold. Others derive it from the Latin *feria,* meaning a festival. In German, the word is *Messe,* which is also the word for the Church Mass. A medieval fair partook of all three ideas. It was not unlike a modern carnival. It was also a market. And in addition, it had the support of organized religion, in a period when the Church wielded tremendous power.

The first fairs were formed by the gatherings of worshipers and pilgrims around sacred places, and especially within the walls of abbeys and cathedrals on the feast days of their saints. Often such buildings were in open country, and accommodations were insufficient for the pilgrims. Consequently, tents were pitched, and merchants set up stalls roundabout.

There were scores of such fairs, but most famous of all those established in medieval times was St. Bartholomew's, in England. In 1123, a priory was built in Smithfield, in a marsh just outside the north wall of London, where a market was set up. That area became the site of the fair.

The prior was one Rayer, who had been a jester or minstrel to King Henry I. No sooner had Rayer set himself up at St. Bartholomew's Priory than a spate of miracles broke out there. The blind regained their sight; the crooked were straightened; cripples walked; a woman's tongue, which had protruded, went back into her mouth. And, it was recorded by Rayer's successor, there was a young man named Osberne, whose right hand stuck to his left shoulder, while his head stuck to his left hand. He came unstuck when he was taken to the church.

There were those unkind enough to say that Rayer was trying to draw crowds to Smithfield by working false miracles. Be that as it may, in 1133 he persuaded Henry to grant him a charter with special privileges for a fair. The charter provided, for everyone, freedom from taxation for three days—the first, arriving; the second, on the spot (the Feast of St. Bartholomew); and the third, returning. That system came to be the customary schedule.

In the early days, fairs were held in the churchyard, or even in the church itself. Later they were forced to move outside; then Edward II forbade anyone to hold a fair in a churchyard; and Henry VIII dissociated the church and fair entirely.

The fair that Rayer set up in the twelfth century endured for 700 years. Originally, a fairgoer could transact business, take care of the needs of his soul, and have an uproarious holiday, all at the same time. After 400 years, the religious aspect disappeared. Trade gradually became less important, and eventually nothing was left but increasingly degraded amusement. In the great days, however, St. Bartholomew's and other fairs like it in England and on the Continent were patronized by both commoners and kings.

The fairs dedicated to the chief saints became especially popular, and prospered accordingly. Merchants gathered their wares from the ends of the earth. Owners and governors were enjoined to make sure that weight and measure were accurate, and a court of prompt justice was set up on the spot. This bore the name of Piepowder Court, perhaps coming from *pied poudré,* indicating that it dealt with travelers, whose feet were powdered with dust. There were stringent rules against extortion. Fairs could not be held within seven miles of each other, and all independent shops in the neighborhood were closed for the three days.

Though worship and trade provided sufficient reasons for attendance, the amusements must often have furnished the real reason that Johnny lingered so long. Inevitably the fair attracted traveling mountebanks, and it is said that the entertainment was the best offered anywhere at the time, delighting even royal visitors. The aristocracy made up pleasure parties and traveled long distances to attend.

In the thirteenth century a friar of the priory of St. Bartholomew's recorded several feats of skill: a woman balanced herself head downward on two sword points; and a woman with a water jug on her head held a baby and walked on stilts.

As time went on, the three-day limit of the fair was ignored. In the

Hogarth's engraving of South-wark Fair, made in 1733

Restoration period, it was extended to a fortnight, and then to six weeks, during which there was a riot of amusement. The lines of booths became streets, which were paved and railed early in the seventeenth century. Entertainment features increased in number and excitement. In one of his comedies, published in 1614, Ben Jonson told what Bartholomew Fair was like, with booths and stalls, rattles, drums, halberts, pipes, horses, puppet shows, gingerbread men, ballads, fruit, mousetraps, hobbyhorses, and innumerable other attractions great and small. He wrote also of "monsters"—living wonders. There were a trained dog named Toby, dogs that danced the morris, an eagle, black wolves, a bull with five legs, a hare that played the tabor.

During the Great Plague of 1665, the fair was suppressed, but reopened the next year. In 1667 Samuel Pepys (who went often to Smithfield) wrote of Jacob Hall's "dancing on the ropes, a thing worth seeing and mightily followed." Jacob Hall, who established a ropedancing booth at Charing Cross, was, it seems, a "very pretty man," said by gossip to share Charles II's mistress, Lady Castlemaine.

Pepys wrote also of a mare that told money and did "many other things to admiration." Trick horses had been known in England from the time of the Saxons. Among the most famous was a bay, Morocco, owned by one Banks, a Scot who had served with the Earl of Essex, instructor of horse to Queen Elizabeth. Morocco, who was shod in silver, could stand and leap about on his hind legs, and even dance the "Canaries" (probably the can-can). When he was exhibited in London, by rapping he told the

61

number of coins in a purse or how many spots there were on dice. When told to "fetch me the veriest fool in the company," he chose Dick Tarlton, a favorite low comedian of the London public. While Banks was exhibiting the horse in Orleans in 1608, these tricks looked so uncanny that Morocco was accused of harboring a devil. Banks saved the day by having the horse bow to the Cross on the bonnet of one of the bystanders.

Two years after Pepys' report, William Blaythwaite saw Jacob Hall at St. Bartholomew's, along with an elephant, and a Dutch ropedancer who did wonderful tricks. A bill of 1702 tells of the wonders in the "great Booth over against the Hospital Gate," where a famous company was dancing on the low rope, walking on the "Slack and Sloaping Ropes." It was stylish to have the entertainers come from abroad, and tumblers and ropedancers from France were advertised.

Horses on Tightropes

Through the Middle Ages and the Renaissance, almost incredible stunts were performed on the ropes. Men went from the top of one tall building to another, or up and down ropes that slanted from high points to the ground, sometimes dancing and posturing as they went. In the thirteenth century, a Frenchman rode a horse on a horizontal tightrope. In 1385, an intrepid soul went from the top of a bridge to a church tower in Paris, carrying two lighted candles. In 1685, an Englishman rode a horse up and down a slanting rope.

In his famous engraving of Southwark Fair, Hogarth showed Cadman, the Wingless Bird-Man, performing in the background above the heads of the crowd. He could go down a 150-foot rope in six or seven seconds, so fast he left a trail of smoke. He was killed while performing in Shrewsbury in 1740, and his gravestone recorded that the rope was drawn too tight. Violante, who appears in the foreground of the engraving, once went headfirst down a slack rope from the arches of St. Martins-in-the-Fields to the Royal Mews. He married another cord dancer, whose special feats were to dance a minuet on a board placed on the rope, and to perform on the rope with two boys fastened to her feet. For more than two hundred years their descendants have followed in their path.

Medieval and Renaissance Italian *funambuli* were as adept as their Roman ancestors had been. One Italian danced on a rope, holding a duck on his head, pushing a wheelbarrow containing two children and a dog, and singing as he went. A print from the second half of the sixteenth century shows a scene in St. Mark's Square, Venice. A man in loose clothes, with a black or blackened face, holding a balancing pole, has nearly reached the upper end of a rope that is moored to a platform in the water and runs at a 45-degree angle to the top of the Campanile. Below him the crowd in the square and gondoliers in the boats stare in amazement.

Throughout the Renaissance, and up to the eighteenth century, England and much of the rest of Europe made up one vast and increasingly avid side-show audience. It was a period when explorers were bringing back from distant lands all sorts of astounding objects, animals, and human beings. The time was, of course, a credulous one, and it is small wonder that exhibitors were tempted to show anything the public would accept, and on occasion to manufacture wonders more startling than nature provided. The public would accept almost anything, as P. T. Barnum was to prove several hundred years later.

Contortionists and Freaks

Each fair developed its own peculiarities. In some of them there were areas given over to what we should call side shows, where the curious could pay a fee at the door to see dwarfs, midgets, monsters, trained fleas, fat women, contortionists, and all manner of other human and animal oddities. Certain fairs emphasized theatrical entertainment.

Puppet shows are said to have been developed at the fairs by "legitimate" local players who wanted to keep the popular foreign mountebanks from offering too much competition. To attract the public, they devised puppets that acted like acrobats, jugglers, trained animals, and comics. Out of this came the nineteenth-century Punch and Judy show and many

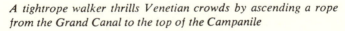

A tightrope walker thrills Venetian crowds by ascending a rope from the Grand Canal to the top of the Campanile

aspects of the pantomimes that developed in England alongside the circus.

Bartholomew Fair became a kind of headquarters for the entrepreneurs who exhibited over the rest of the country during the remainder of the year. At fairtime, they took up their lodgings in Smithfield, and had their addresses printed on paper. At other times of year, many of the monsters were prepared to give private appearances "at any gentleman's house, if desired."

The greatest number of handbills extant comes from the times of Charles II, Queen Anne, and William and Mary. In those prints, the attraction is usually said to be presented by His or Her Majesty's authority —a notation indicating that the license fee had been paid. By the seventeenth century, the thirst for monsters had become an obsession alike in England and on the Continent. A handbill from the time of Charles II shows a man with a twin depending from his chest, and the potential spectator is informed that both halves of the creature received names at baptism, the larger one being called Lazare, and the smaller one, Jean Baptiste.

The British Museum contains another bill of approximately the same time, showing a "Miracula Natura: or a Miracle of Nature." This is a "Gyant-like man aged 23 last June." We are informed that both his "late and present Majesty" went to see him, and "his late Majesty [Charles II] was pleased to walk under his arm." The young gyant "now reaches with his hand three yards and a half, and spans 15 inches." He is to be seen "at Cow-Lane End, in Bartholomew Fair, where his Picture hangs out." This may well be "O'Brien the Irish Giant the Tallest Man in the Known World Being Near Nine Feet High," as there is a record that Charles II walked under the arm of the "Irish Giant" at St. Bartholomew's.

Mr. Edward Bright weighed 621 and a quarter pounds, though he was only 5 feet 9 inches tall, and was so enormous in girth that, in December, 1750, someone bet that five men could be buttoned up inside his coat— and easily won the wager.

Crowds flocked to St. Bartholomew's to see a man with one head and two bodies, a hermaphrodite, a "Mail child with a Bear growing on his back alive," a monster from the Coast of Brazil, with a "Head like a child, Legs and Arms very wonderful, with a Long Tail like a serpent, wherewith he Feeds himself, as an Elephant does with his Trunk." There was also a woman with three breasts ("an Admirable Work of Nature"), a child with three "Leggs," and a man without hands, feet or thighs, who played the oboe and drew pictures.

The dividing line between the normal and the abnormal, between the possible and the impossible, was still not clear. In such prescientific days, the mental world of even the most sophisticated adult was very like the world of a small child, where everything is wonderful and nothing is unthinkable.

In 420 B.C., the Carthaginian Hanno had taken a long sea voyage out beyond the Pillars of Hercules and along the coast of West Africa. There he and his men stopped on an island, where they found very hairy wild men and women, whom the Carthaginians had to kill in order to capture. They were probably gorillas. As late as 1784, two thousand years later, a handbill was circulated in London, showing a picture of "The Ethiopian Savage," otherwise known as the "Oriental Satyr or Real wild-Man of the Woods," offered as "the Link between the rational and brute Creation." Obviously it was a Barbary ape.

The medieval fair also did its part in maintaining the tradition of animal training and exhibition. Rich and poor shared an enthusiasm for watching exotic animals at close range. Records from the Middle Ages are scanty, and it has been customary to assume that little expert animal training was practiced anywhere, that few animals except bears and monkeys were carried from place to place, and that almost no important collections were made from the great days of Rome until modern times. Actually, this is not the case.

This "most astonishing creature, called the Oriental Satyr, or Real Wild-Man of the Woods," was an orangutan. An example of ingenious eighteenth-century English showmanship

Fabulous Royal Menageries

Like the Roman emperors, Charlemagne collected exotic beasts, and was especially fond of an elephant, called Abul-Abbass, given to him in 797 by Harun-al-Rashid. As the Crusaders entered Constantinople in 1101, lions and leopards were sent out to intercept them. Soldiers of the conquering army killed the lions and pursued the leopards into the palace, where they caused great grief and consternation by destroying a favorite pet lion. Though Constantinople's theatre was torn down and the menagerie was dispersed when the city was sacked in the Fourth Crusade a century later, the emperors continued to keep strange animals, as rulers in eastern Europe had always done.

The first known menagerie of western Europe after classical times, set up at the Sicilian court of Frederick II in the thirteenth century, included a giraffe Frederick had received from the Sultan of Egypt in exchange for a bear. The emperor sent a group of animals traveling all over Italy, and paraded them when he went to Worms to marry the sister of Henry III of England.

Like the ancient Romans, all wealthy Italians had their own zoological collections. In 1245 a beggar looked into a garden in Pisa and ran quickly to tell that he had seen wild beasts lying there placidly while boys and girls strolled about playing on vielles and citherns. In the next century, at the court of the Visconti in Milan, two leopards were led about by silken leashes attached to their velvet collars. On the other hand, in 1332 at the house of one of the Frangipani family, a woman was killed by a leopard. In Rome, lions were kept until the fourteenth century in a pit at the foot of the Capitol. Florence, in the mid-thirteenth century, set up a place for wild beasts near the Bargello, and a few decades later built a lions' house behind the Palazzo Vecchio.

Many of the little *seigneuries* in the Low Countries had their own menageries, some of which were of impressive size. During three months in the year 1384, the Dukes of Guelder killed 200 wolves to feed their animals, and two years later, within six months, fed 260 sheep to their lions. As a rule, the lords of Holland and Belgium kept bears, and in 1399 the Bishop of Tournai's bears got loose and ran through the streets, scaring the inhabitants into fits.

In France the Popes kept lions in Avignon, and the menageries were still maintained after 1377, when the headquarters of the Church went back to Rome. Louis IX, Philippe III, Philippe IV, and Louis X were all so fond of animals that they took collections with them on their travels, thus establishing what were really private ambulant exhibits. Philippe IV built the first menagerie of the Louvre in 1333, calling it l'Hôtel des Lions du Roi. When Charles V was Dauphin, he took the animals to l'Hôtel St. Pol (whither Good King Wenceslas once went to see the lions), and built a garden with gates, fountains, trees, and flowers. Thereafter for a century and a half the gardens were periodically enlarged and made more elegant, while the collection of animals increased. After a while, the wealthy *bourgeoisie* of France began to ape the *grands seigneurs* but, unable to afford the great jungle beasts, contented themselves with smaller animals. Thus enthusiasm for the menagerie spread throughout Europe.

Though there had always been animals in English preserves, William the Conqueror set up in England the first real collection of wild and strange beasts. Subsequent rulers added to it. Henry I sequestered lions, leopards, a lynx, and several camels in a walled park at Woodstock. In 1251, Henry III acquired a white bear, which was kept in the Tower of London and was accustomed to going on a leash down to the Thames, with a keeper who waited while it fished for its food. Three years later, Henry's brother-in-law, Louis IX, gave him an elephant—the first ever to be seen in London. Everybody went to look at the extraordinary creature, and the city built a house for it. For another century and a half, the city was obligated to house and feed the royal animals, and provided a quarter of a sheep daily for Edward II's lion, which was lodged in what was now called the Lion Tower. Edward III acquired more lions, but they were not properly cared for, and they all died. By that time, arched dens had been constructed for the Royal Menagerie, and the royal family could watch the feeding from a special gallery. Bear gardens were built on the banks of the Thames, in Southwark. Scaffolds were constructed around the pit for the safety of the onlookers, and bears and bulls were baited there frequently until at least the end of the sixteenth century.

At Bartholomew Fair, animal exhibits were amplified gradually until at last they constituted a small menagerie, which was on view in 1708, the year in which the first traveling menagerie set forth in England.

Long before that, however, the Renaissance had already revivified the more spectacular antecedents of the circus, and had provided material from which the comic was to shape the colorful motley he wears today.

6

The Zany and
the Parade

IN ITALY, under the influence of the Renaissance, the tradition of the parade was revived and the clown gained new color and prominence. Italian courts were centers of artistic production in every possible field, including the pantomime and pageant. From the beginning, more festivals, and more splendid ones, had been presented in Italy than anywhere else in Europe. The Italian courts had always enthusiastically sponsored such displays. Often they were adaptations of the original mystery play, which had been devised in the tenth century by the Church, to teach its illiterate flock the Bible narrative from Creation to the Day of Judgment.

Trap Doors and Flying Angels

In the thirteenth and fourteenth centuries, mysteries were occasionally presented in settings the Romans themselves had built, such as the ancient amphitheatres in Nîmes, Orange, and Arles, in a type of presentation that recalled the spectacles seen in the time of the mighty emperors, and foreshadowed the circus. The audience, of course, sat on the sloping grandstands, and the actors appeared in the center on a platform containing trap doors and machinery. Christ rose through a trap door. Yawning jaws opened to spout fire and sulphurous smoke from hell, or to give a glimpse of the fiery furnace of Nebuchadnezzar—which must have constantly imperiled the papier-mâché scenery. Saved souls ascended to heaven on a platform, while the damned fell into the pit. There were machines to make angels fly, to bring animals on stage, and to create the illusion of thunder, lightning, and wind.

Though the Devil, with a host of lesser attendant spirits, was included in the medieval cast ostensibly to build up fear of hell, in him lurked the rudiments of a comic type, and his diabolical intrigues evoked much merriment from the onlookers. The standard costume for the Devil was leather, hair, or black cloth, and he and his ilk inevitably wore masks. The mask might have a ram's horn, but often it was human, with a crooked nose, projecting jaw, and wart on the side of the face. Dossenus of the *Atellanae* had had a wart on his face, and a later and more familiar figure was to wear the same blemish in the Italian Comedy.

As the Renaissance progressed, profligate amounts were often poured into such productions. The ecclesiastical significance of the early festivals gradually disappeared, in favor of the secular. Characters and symbols from allegory and comedy usurped the place of the religious ones. If some local achievement warranted a real triumphal procession, so much the bet-

69

ter. If not, a Roman triumph could be copied, complete with conquering hero and triumphal chariots. In 1500, Cesare Borgia copied Julius Caesar's triumphal procession, showing eleven magnificent chariots. A few years later, the Florentine Guild of Merchants built ten parade chariots, some of which were painted by Andrea del Sarto.

Most elaborate illusions, sometimes created by the greatest artists, were evolved for important occasions. For the Feast of the Annunciation in the Piazza San Felice, Florence, Brunelleschi invented a celestial globe surrounded by circles of angels, from which Gabriel flew down in an almond-shaped machine. Leonardo da Vinci himself devised numerous intricate machines for the Duke of Milan. On one occasion, the great artist created a device by means of which heavenly bodies, developed in colossal scale, moved in intricate orbits, permitting the planets to open and reveal divinities who stepped out and sang. When Duke Borso d'Este went to Reggio, in 1453, to receive the homage of the city, he was met by a machine out of which St. Prospero seemed to float under a baldachin held by angels. Two of eight singing cherubs on a revolving disc below gave to the duke the key and scepter of the city. Among other floats in the parade was one in the form of a ship, moved by concealed men. As the procession passed the Church of San Pietro, the saint, accompanied by two angels, floated down in an aureole, put a laurel wreath on the brow of the distinguished visitor, and floated back up again.

Mechanical animals reminiscent of the whale in the Roman arena, and sometimes of gigantic size, were very popular. When Charles VIII visited Milan, Leonardo created a mechanical lion that advanced a few steps and opened its breast, which was full of lilies. For a public reception in Siena, a ballet of twelve persons stepped out of a golden wolf.

Florentine Floats

Here, in Renaissance Italy, was the completely developed forerunner of the modern circus parade. The ancient games had probably never entirely ceased in Rome, and sham fights of cavalry were now held in the Piazza Navona in carnival time, presaging the early equestrian spectacle of the circus. In one of the Florentine pageants, which re-enacted a triumphal procession, Julius Caesar stood on a revolving globe, such as was to be a feature of elaborate parade wagons in the nineteenth century. And in that same procession in Florence one of the high lights was a float with a tall tower, on which an angel with drawn sword guarded a door. Such a chariot would be modified centuries later into the "telescope" wagon—a fantastic feature of the great days of the circus parade. In the mid-nineteenth century, an English showman even put Britannia and a great black-maned lion onto the top of a telescope wagon.

Lions may have been carried on Renaissance floats. It is certain that they sometimes walked in the processions. As in medieval times, many of the great princes and popes collected jungle beasts, and almost all of them kept lions.

Both spiritual and temporal rulers hunted with cheetahs, and staged bullfights and other bloody contests. One day Cesare Borgia followed the example of Commodus and himself killed six bulls in the arena. Savage beasts fought dogs, horses or bulls, and men were pitted against all kinds of dangerous beasts. The most extensive game preserves of Italy were in Florence, where Cosimo de' Medici showed twenty-six lions in a pageant in honor of Pope Pius II, and tried to stage a Roman hunt. Into one enclosure his keepers turned loose lions, bears, wolves, untamed bulls, wild horses, and Corsican dogs. But after promenading in a prefight parade, the lions lay down in a corner and refused to budge.

Though French rulers were not so anxious to imitate the Roman emperors as were Italian princes during the Renaissance, a similar enthusiasm for owning wild beasts continued in France. Probably the most extensive collection in that country, before Louis XIV established the menagerie at Versailles, was that of René d'Anjou, who in Angers and Provence built pits for lions and bears, most of which died from lack of elementary sanitation. Louis XI, who was extremely fond of animals, owned a pet lioness that slept in his bedroom, tied by a cord attached to a window. Louis was much distressed when the lioness jumped out the open window one night, and strangled. François I usually slept with a lion or bear at the foot of his bed, hunted with a leopard, and drove to church followed by equipages drawn by lions and two kinds of leopards. Charles IX, on the other hand, felt no such pleasure in animal company. One of his pastimes was staging combats with beasts from his menagerie, and on the night of October 14, 1572, after such a combat, he dreamed that the animals turned on him. The next morning he went out to his zoo and killed them all.

These royal collections of animals continued to grow throughout Europe, providing a pattern for the public menagerie, that later was to attract all people, and eventually became a feature of the circus. The sudden swift development of comic types, along with the parade, took place almost exclusively in Italy.

Harlequin, Punch, Pierrot

It was in Italy during the sixteenth century that, in *il Commedia dell' Arte all' Improviso,* the comic really began to turn into a clown. This dramatic form had its roots in the Roman theatre and *mimi,* and more immediately in the comic novels of the fourteenth and fifteenth centuries, written in North Italian vernacular. And yet, its development was so spectacular that it seemed almost to burst on the scene full-grown.

In 1558, one Angelo Beolco, called *Il Ruzzante,* wrote a play in dialect, using Paduan peasants as characters. The Italians found it hilarious, and each wanted to see and hear his own fellow townsmen parodied. Gradually the whole family of types appeared, with each representing the supposed characteristics of the inhabitants of a given city. The most popular and long-lived among those masks were Arlecchino and Brighella, out of Bergamo; Pulcinella, Scaramuzzo and Il Capitano, from Naples; Pantalone, from Venice; and Il Dottore, from Bologna.

As its full name implies, the most important characteristic of the Italian Comedy was its basis in improvisation. It used no true plays, only scenarios giving a bare outline of plot and action. The scenario was tacked up off stage and, though an actor knew from it what direction the action must take, how he worked it out was his own responsibility. The only coaching was done by the chief actor, who was also producer, director, and stage manager. The comedian memorized certain stock phrases, formal exit lines (*uscite*), which often were rhymed couplets, and other lines, known as *chiusette,* to terminate the discourse. In general, however, he made up his speeches as he went along. Altogether some 700 scenarios have been unearthed, with the earliest known one of 1568, and all the remainder dating from the seventeenth and early eighteenth centuries. From these and from other records, it seems certain that the basic structure remained the same for centuries.

The bones of the scenario were covered by the muscles of dialogue, witty, allusive, and often very obscene. An actor needed a rich imagination, fluency and grace of expression and gesture, ready wit, colorful ingenuity, and a quick response to others. In addition, he had to be able to spice the action with all sorts of interpolated gags, known as *lazzi,* which were usually rough-and-tumble slaps, trippings up, and crude practical jokes. He had to be a dancer, musician, and poet, as well as a mime, comic, and acrobat. He had to possess a repertory of songs and stories to fit every conceivable occasion, to develop a scenario based on impersona-

Emmett Kelly, the saddest of all modern clowns

tions, kidnapings, caricatures, and misunderstandings. Speed, confusion, and noise were an essential aspect of the Italian Comedy, as they had been part of the bag of tricks of the medieval mountebank.

The *Commedia dell' Arte* took all Europe by storm. Troupes wandered from country to country, playing their improvised farces on the corners and in the squares. Usually they performed only two or three times in any city. A scaffolding would be quickly erected in the open air and, before the buzz of curiosity and expectation had died down, the actors would mount the stage, delighting the spectators with their vivacious and uninhibited shenanigans. The scenic backgrounds were rudimentary, easy to transport and easily replaced, showing sketchily painted suggestions of a corner or square.

As time went on, the witty qualities of the comedies came to predominate over the coarse; and by the eighteenth century, in the last days of the *Commedia dell' Arte,* the robust improvisations were almost forgotten, and the form approached more closely that of the legitimate stage.

Very early in the life of the Italian Comedy, the companies of actors often accompanied troupes of mountebanks. Rain or shine, they traveled in oxcarts, staying overnight at cheap inns, finding shelter in stables, or even lying in open fields. Back and forth across Europe they wandered, setting up their scaffolds in each town, for fairs and feast days especially, trying their luck with the eager public.

Almost always their plays were given out of doors; but occasionally some member of the aristocracy would offer the use of rooms in his palace or villa. The first indoor performances by the Italian Comedians were given at the Italian courts. The dukes of Mantua and Ferrara became celebrated patrons, and eventually presented the comedians in sumptuous productions. Meantime, France had heard about those delightful entertainers who were performing at the Mantuan and Ferrarese courts, and a company of them was invited to go to Paris in 1571 to become a part of the festivities surrounding the marriage of Charles IX. For the next century and a half, the Italian Comedy was in demand at all the courts of Europe, and became sought after as no acting group had been before or has been since.

As the troupes of actors and mountebanks traveled up and down the European continent in the late sixteenth and early seventeenth centuries, inevitably the comedians assimilated more and more of the acrobatic tricks and fancies of their companions, and gradually the types of characters they portrayed changed.

The great number of stock characters that evolved may be divided

74

more or less arbitrarily into two classes, the serious and the comic. Only the latter are related to the circus, and not all of them. The most important are the *zanni,* those two comic servants who are recalled in modern speech by the English "zany." The first of these two servants is witty and adroit, a wily trickster and cheat. His companion is oftenest a stupid, dull-witted peasant, who does everything upside down, and is always on the wrong end of the joke—and the stick. Although they have changed outwardly, they are both still with us, perpetrating their slapstick buffooneries on the vaudeville stage and in the circus ring.

At the outset, each of them wore a full white shirt, long, loose pantaloons, and a peaked hat. Each carried a wooden sword and wore a leather mask with a full face-beard. The mask of the first zany had an enormous wart on the forehead, in the tradition of the Atellan Dossenus and of the medieval Devil. Both of the Italian Comedy servants were bald-headed, like the mimes of Greece and Rome.

Though he may have many names, the first zany is most popularly called Arlecchino. He is, of course, the figure we know as Harlequin, in his costume of varicolored lozenges or triangles. Arlecchino's nature did not stay in one mold, but he is best known as a lively, quick-witted, not too ill-natured creature, full of tricks and capers. Like the acrobats of the mountebank troupes, who certainly influenced him, he danced, tumbled, and leaped about with abandon. Especially he delighted in perpetrating jokes on his companions, and the one who played opposite him always was slapped, buffeted, and boxed on the ears.

Pulcinella, the Neapolitan, is the longest-lived of all the comedy characters, having started as Cicirrus, strutting braggart of the Atellan mimes, and appearing today as Punch of the English pantomime. In the Italian Comedy, normally he was a greedy and villainous servant, possessed of a certain amount of sly wit. He wore a loose-fitting costume and a hat with two enormous points, and had a peaked beard and a pair of pointed mustachios.

In the sixteenth century, Pedrolino, the forefather of today's white-faced clown, was a vague figure; but in the seventeenth he was developed by one Giuseppe Giaratone (or Geratone) into a sort of second Pulcinella who was a stupid fool instead of a clever rogue. In Paris, in the nineteenth century, Gaspard Debureau was to create out of Pedrolino the character of Pierrot—he of the loose white garments, the wide frill at the throat, the tall pointed hat, the dead-white face. Gentle and sad, in much the same costume, he often beguiles us in the contemporary circus ring.

While the clown and parade were developing on the Continent, Eng-

75

land was steadily approaching the time when all the elements of the circus were to be gathered together to make one coherent whole. As the sixteenth century passed into the seventeenth, and the seventeenth into the eighteenth, the fair continued to be the most easily accessible center of entertainment for the masses. At the fair, the ropedancers, jugglers, contortionists, prestidigitators still offered the incredible. Peep shows, puppet booths, and freaks still drew their crowds. Individual comics danced, sang, and cracked bawdy jokes. Companies of players presented the near-clown in diverse vehicles. The public gaped before collections of unfamiliar beasts. Royal collections of animals grew in size. The traveling menagerie was beginning to carry its wonders out into the countryside. But England was fondest not of the more exotic beasts, but of the horse.

After Roman days, when *desultores* delighted huge audiences by leaping skillfully from one horse to another, there seems to have been little exhibition riding in Europe until the thirteenth century. At that time, a troupe of ropedancers and horsemen came into Italy from Constantinople, and made a triumphal progress through Europe to Spain, thrilling the populace by walking on ropes from one ship's mast to another, and turning somersaults on horses running at full speed.

Thereafter there is another hiatus until 1532, when Henry VIII paid the equivalent of 23 pounds to "one Dompne peter Tremesin that dud Ryde ij horses at ones." Probably "dompne" is the equivalent of the French *dompteur*—animal trainer. Slightly more than a century later, Joseph Zinzan acted as riding master in a cavalry "manage" in the yard of Winchester House. According to the *Gentlemen's Dictionary* of 1705, the word "manage" comes from *manège*, "the ground proper for managing horses, being sometimes a covered place, as in your great academies, for continuing the exercise in bad weather; while sometimes 'tis open in order to give more liberty and pleasure, both to the horse and horseman." Even today, around the circus lot the equestrian acts are known as the "manage," though it is doubtful if many of those who use the term have any idea of its derivation.

During the seventeenth century, several other English and French centers began to specialize in the teaching of horsemanship, and numerous expert riders came into the public eye. In 1652, William Stokes, first "vaulting master," published the *Art of Vaulting*, giving pictures to show how he leapt onto a horse, sometimes landing erect in the saddle, and sometimes astride, in a fashion not to be accomplished again for two hundred years. A *New Method of Training Horses,* by Cavendish, Duke of Newcastle, appeared two decades later. A military academy was established at the rear of Leicester House, and John Evelyn wrote in 1684 of seeing the railed-in manage there, where young gallants were taught. They ran at the ring, flung javelins, fired pistols at the mark, and took up gauntlets on the points of swords—all at full speed.

Several extraordinary riders set England agog in the years during and just after the middle of the eighteenth century. In 1750 Mr. Price gave demonstrations in the yard of a pub, "The Three Hats," in Islington. In a print depicting "Surprising Performances," vignettes show him in a half-dozen demonstrations, always "on full speed." He appears "between 2 Horses resting only on his Arms; Leaping a Bar standing upon 2 Horses with one foot on each Saddle . . . ; Takes his Whip from the Ground . . . ; Laying across 3 Horses . . . ; Standing upon His Head and Fireing a Pistol . . . ; Riding backwards standing on the Saddle." Price was ousted in 1767 by Mr. Sampson, who created a sensation by riding with one foot on the saddle and the other on the horse's head. With him was Mrs. Sampson, the first "female equestrian." As early as 1758, Thomas Johnson, the "Irish Tartar," rode in Bristol on three horses simultaneously, and performed a number of other daring tricks. During the next decade Jacob Bates, who could ride four horses at one time, became famous throughout Europe, appearing before the rulers of Germany, France, Sweden, Denmark, and Poland, as well as England. Before our Revolution, he came to America and repeated his triumphs here.

All these equestrian demonstrations were given in the open, in fields, gardens, and the yards of taverns and inns. But the time was at hand when they were to go into an especially created setting, when all the spectacular feats that had been developing through many centuries would be put together to make one breath-taking and improbable spectacle.

The centuries-long preliminaries were ended; the performers were ready and waiting; the scenario had been tacked up off stage. The hour had struck for the appearance of the genius who would set the stage and coordinate players and play, to make the circus.

Philip Astley entered.

Astley and the Modern Circus

IN LONDON, toward the end of the eighteenth century, the ring, the ring acts, and the clown, those basic elements of the circus, were brought together for the first time in history, to make an entertainment that could be repeated day after day. At that time, Philip Astley combined them to make a brew so powerful and so agreeable that its components have not been radically changed to this day.

Astley, the Father of the Circus, was born in 1742 in the little English village of Newcastle-under-Lyme. His father, a cabinetmaker, tried to bring up his son in his own respectable footsteps, but Philip lived for nothing but horses from the time he was big enough to pat one. At seventeen he ran away and enlisted in the 5th regiment of Dragoons as a horsebreaker and rough rider. After the regiment went to the Continent, the young man won his stripes as a noncommissioned officer and, in 1760, in a battle at Emsdorf in Hesse, became the envy of his fellows by capturing the French standard. Six years later, Astley was discharged, something of a celebrity among military men, but with very little money and no prospects.

He was strong and lusty, more than six feet tall, with a voice that could be heard for blocks, and manners that left a good deal to be desired. There was one thing he could do. He could ride. Moreover, he had a horse of his own, given to him by his colonel—Gibraltar, the white horse he had ridden when he captured the French standard. At Smithfield Market he bought two more horses, for five pounds apiece, one of average size, the other more nearly a pony, named Billy. With them he decided to open a "riding school."

In 1768, after taking to himself a wife who also loved to ride, Philip Astley bought a field called Halfpenny Hatch, in Lambeth near Westminster Bridge, and advertised that he would teach vaulting on two or three horses, and saber attacks and defenses such as were in use among the Hussars. Naturally, he also gave exhibitions of his own superlative skill. Performances were in an open ring enclosed by a rough fence of palings. To attract the crowds, one or two fifers stood on a small platform in the middle, and produced shrill tootings while Mrs. Astley beat on a bass drum. At the end of the performance she passed the hat.

The venture was a success and, after a year or so at Halfpenny Hatch, Astley acquired a piece of ground some 200 yards away, facing Westminster Bridge, and put up a permanent building. It was a simple wooden structure, with a great circular ring open to the sky and enclosed by railings, overlooked by covered grandstands 120 feet long. On the side facing the bridge, the audience was admitted through a two-story entrance, with galleries overhead for the gentry, and stables stretching out at either side. The building front was decorated with five large showbills, and with a dozen small equestrian figures that seemed to be galloping along the edge of the roof. Above the ridgepole, a somewhat larger figure on a horse raised his whip. This was the first home of the modern circus.

It seems to have been 1770 by the time Astley opened the building, which he called the New British Riding School or the Amphitheatre Riding House. In the morning he gave lessons in horsemanship. In the afternoon, there was a program of entertainment, which included other features besides equestrian play but deliberately emphasized the military angle. When time came for the performance to begin, the ex-cavalry officer sat at the end of the building on his white charger, and with outstretched sword indicated the way to the entrance. From all accounts, he presented an impressive appearance, in dragoon's uniform of skin-tight trousers, red spencer, boots with spurs, and a bicorne hat with a plume perched gaily on his powdered hair. "That there," he would shout, "is the riding school! I will hold on by one arm and leg, with my toe in my mouth."

Admission was a shilling, and posters out in front indicated that those who paid the shilling would witness feats of horsemanship, acrobats forming a human pyramid, performers on the tightrope, and slack-wire artists whose headliner was "Sieur Jones." Among the cord dancers and tumblers was Garmon, who had just been exhibiting at Sadler's Wells. A trainer showed dancing dogs.

"Billy Button," The Tailor's Ride

In addition to obvious skillful riding, Astley's company very soon offered *Billy Button, or the Tailor's Ride to Brentford,* a skit on horseback satirizing the military tailor, which for many years was to delight audiences all over the world. Army tailors were notoriously awkward with horses, and England was still laughing at a play, *Tailors: A Tragedy for Warm Weather,* which had been produced a few years before at the Haymarket Theatre. Inevitably, when Astley's presented Billy Button, the clumsy little fellow who apparently couldn't stay on, or even get onto, a horse, thousands rushed to see him. *The Tailor's Ride* was a headliner in the Amphitheatre for three-quarters of a century, and was seen in this country at least as early as 1793, before the true American circus had been established.

In presenting the comic rider, Astley demonstrated that he was as

80

The first home of the modern circus—Astley's "New British Riding School," opened in 1770

astute a psychologist as he was a showman, for with all the tense excitement of swift and perilous spectacle, it was essential to give relief and release to the audience in laughter. The inventors of the Billy Button skit were a pair of clever riders, Saunders and Fortunelli, who thus became the first comics on horseback. A little later, an acrobatic comedian named Porter performed often without benefit of horse—and in so doing achieved the metamorphosis from the comic rider to what we think of as the circus clown. By that time, Astley was already famous and making a fortune, and the modern circus had become a thriving institution.

The French circus, like the English, owes its existence directly to Philip Astley. At least as early as 1774, and probably in 1772, the Briton took his troupe to Paris to give performances in the Razade manège in the rue des Vieilles-Tuileries. It was probably on that same trip to the Continent that Astley visited the principal manèges of France and Germany, and published a series of maps for travelers, apparently to guide horse lovers to centers where they could find exciting exhibitions.

The Magic Combination

By then he had set up a program containing almost all the types of acts that were to be represented in the circus for the next half century. It included equestrian stunts, cord dancers, acrobats, trained animals, equilibrists, tumblers and vaulters of all kinds, plus ballet and pantomime performances. Astley himself was showing how to control four horses going

81

at full speed in the manner of Mr. Sampson, with one foot on the saddle and the other on the horse's neck, possibly brandishing a broadsword as he went. A favorite trick was to ride with his feet in the air, and his head on a "common pint pot." He was assisted not only by Mrs. Astley but by Mr. Taylor, Signor Markutchy, Costmethopila, Mrs. Griffiths, Miss Vangable, and other "transcendent performers." In France as in England, this exciting new type of entertainment was an immediate success.

Another landmark in the history of the circus was established in 1779, when the London ring acquired a roof. The whole Amphitheatre Riding House was covered over and the establishment was rechristened "Astley's Royal Amphitheatre." Lighting was installed so that performances could be given after dark. Doors opened at five o'clock, and the show began at six.

Three years later Charles Hughes, one of Astley's riders, a colossus of magnificent presence and enormous strength, set up his own Royal Circus nearby in Blackfriar's Road. The resulting feud between the competitors was much like those conducted in the most flamboyant period of

The interior of Astley's amphitheatre as it was rebuilt after the 1794 fire, a design which influenced early circuses everywhere

the circus. Astley rode around town proclaiming that Hughes was an impostor. Hughes retorted by writing ads in which he sneered at Astley. When the latter went to Paris, Hughes informed the nobility that his "Antagonist has catched a bad cold so near the Westminster Bridge, and for his recovery is gone to a warmer climate which is Bath in Somersetshire. He boasts, poor Fellow, no more of activity, and is now turned Conjuror, in the character of 'Sieur the Great.' Therefore Hughes is unrivalled." Hughes also wanted the public to know that he himself "has no intention of setting out every day to France for three following Seasons, his ambition being fully satisfied by the applause he has received from Foreign Gentlemen who came over the sea to see him." Already one smells the "rat bill," which in the nineteenth century was to become an accepted circus weapon for attacking a competitor.

The Royal Circus of Hughes, which had not only a roof but a stage for "burlettas," did very well for a time. Among the feats the owner advertised as early as 1783 were: leaping over a horse forty times without stopping between springs; leaps over a bar, standing on the saddle with back to the horse's tail, and vice versa; riding full speed on the saddle with his left toe in his mouth ("two surprising Feet"); Mrs. Hughes standing on pint pots, mounting higher, pot by pot; recitation by a young gentleman of verses of his own making, and acting out Marc Antony between the leaps. There was also a Little Lady only eight years old, who "rides Two Horses," and "is enough to put anyone in fits to see her."

A decade later, at the Royal Circus, young Crossman, a rider who had been at Astley's, challenged all Europe. Mr. Porter, also from Astley's, jumped over a garter 15 feet above the ground. Mr. Ingham from Dublin turned innumerable flip-flaps and the famous Saxoni from Rome walked the tightrope.

It was already the fashion to present, or pretend to present, artists from France, Italy, and "other genteel parts of the globe." A half century later, the English mulatto, William Darby, was to call himself Pablo Fanque, and throughout circus history many a Bill Jones or Mary Smith has appeared as Signor Machiavelli or Mlle Fifi. The foreign pseudonyms were assumed usually by performers of such feats as dancing on the high wire or tumbling and juggling—skills that with some justification were felt to be the peculiar inheritance of the Latins. Riding was an English sport, and nobody expected an equestrian virtuoso to bear a name more exotic that Astley, Johnson, Hughes, or Price.

Hughes' career as a producer was a difficult one. He antagonized the public, and got into debt. In 1793, he went to Russia where, scandal said, he was a favorite of Catherine the Great, then more than seventy to his forty-five. Four years later, when he was still only forty-nine, Hughes returned to London to die. In 1805 the debt-ridden Royal Circus burned to the ground.

After that, Astley had no circus rival, though there were numerous theatres where circus acts were given—Sadler's Wells, Covent Garden, Coburg, Vauxhall Gardens, Drury Lane, and others. Already, performers had begun to move from one company to another, as they have done ever since. The exchange was constant, and to try to follow the adventures of an individual is like tracing the erratic pattern of a firefly.

Marie Antoinette's "English Rose"

In 1783, Philip Astley, who loved Paris, had gone back at the invitation of Marie Antoinette. He bought land in the Faubourg du Temple, and erected the first Parisian circus—a circular building 64 feet in diameter, with two tiers of boxes, lighted by 2,000 lamps. With him was his son John, a very handsome young man who, according to Horace Walpole, was as graceful as the Apollo Belvedere. Father and son were billed in the "rue et Fauxbourg du Temple" as *les Sieurs Astley*." After an appearance at Fontainebleau, the Queen, who called John her "English rose," gave him a gold medal studded with diamonds. Thereafter, at the end of each London season Astley took his company to Paris. He and his son had become two of the most famous figures of their day.

With understandable arrogance, he ignored both letter and spirit of his French permit, which gave him the right to present equestrian performances in the faubourg arena. In addition to his riders, he showed tumblers, cord dancers and other entertainers. Rival entrepreneurs, outraged, protested. Astley was instructed to remember that his permit from the King and the Lieutenant-General of Police entitled him to give nothing except exhibitions "on horseback." A French print, distributed for performances in Paris in 1786, indicates the ingenuity with which he met the challenge. In that print, sixteen horses with as many grooms are standing in the arena. Onto the back of each horse is strapped a sort of inverted wicket, and those wickets support a good-sized platform. On the platform, and therefore literally on horseback, acrobats turn somersaults in the air, and two equilibrists balance on the back-bent torso of a third.

As a showman, Philip Astley has seldom been excelled. He was will-

84

The ruse by which in Paris Astley circumvented the King's permit allowing him to give only exhibitions "on horseback"

ing to try anything to draw a crowd. In 1784, on March 12, in order to bring people to the Surrey side of the Thames, he sent up a balloon from St. George's Fields. The occasion was probably the first time a balloon ascension had ever been tried in England, though Montgolfier had promoted one at Lyons two months previously. A writer in the *Gentleman's Magazine* reported somewhat naïvely that at St. George's Fields there had gathered "a greater number of spectators than were, perhaps, ever assembled together on any occasion," and somewhat cynically that "a more ample harvest for pickpockets never was presented."

One of Astley's prize attractions through the years was Billy, the pony he had bought at Smithfield Market. Billy was known as the Little Military Learned Horse, and seems to have been a truly extraordinary animal. He could dance, jump through hoops, take off his own girth, wash his feet in a pail of water, pretend he was dead, play hide and seek, "calculate," set a tea table, and lift a pot of boiling water and make tea. With his master he rode around in a hackney coach. He lived to be forty-two years old.

When Astley, who was a little uncertain about his H's, introduced Billy, he told his audience that "this 'ere hanimal has bright eyes, lively, resolute and himpudent that will look at an hobject with a kind of disdain." He also had a rhyme he spoke when he put the little horse through his paces:

> *My horse lies dead apparent in your sight,*
> *But I'm the man to set the thing aright;*
> *Speak when you please, I'm ready to obey—*
> *My faithful horse knows what I want to say;*
> *But first just give me leave to move his foot*
> (moves the horse's foot)
> *That he is dead is quite beyond dispute.*
> *This shows how brutes by Heaven were designed*
> *To be in full subjection to mankind.*
> *Rise young Bill and be a little handy*
> *To serve that warlike hero Granby*
> (horse rises of its own accord)
> *When you have seen all by Bill's exprest,*
> *My wife, to conclude, performs the rest.*

Obviously this jingle was devised in the early days, and the last line was a cue for Mrs. Astley to pass the hat.

When war broke out between England and France in 1793, Astley went off to fight. He left the great London enterprise in the hands of his

Ducrow at Astley's Royal Amphitheatre, London

86

son John, while the Paris circus was taken over by the Franconis, a family who had worked with him there. In 1794, fire (then and always the greatest threat to the circus) burned the London amphitheatre to the ground. It was rebuilt on the plan of Hughes' Royal Circus, a plan that offered actually a combination of amphitheatre and theatre, and influenced early circuses everywhere. Seats rose in tiers around the ring, surrounding it except where they touched the stage. Riders and tumblers performed in the ring. Ropedancers appeared on the stage, which also became a theatre for the pantomime—a type of entertainment already popular in London, especially at Christmas and New Year's, that was rapidly becoming more so. James Lawrence, a member of the company, created a furor in the first season by turning the hazardous front somersault from a trampoline, over twelve horses. For the benefit of a public still obsessed by an interest in monsters, all sorts of freaks were put on exhibition.

The Ring's the Thing

There seems to be no record of exactly when Philip Astley established the size of the circus ring. Undoubtedly he went through a process of trial and error; but certainly he had set the size by the time he built the ring-and-stage amphitheatre. The ring there was 42 feet in diameter. And 42 feet in diameter the standard circus ring remains to this day. Astley is said to have made his decision because, when he stood on his head, he discovered that centrifugal force would best assist him if he set the horse loping in a circle of just that dimension. Trick riders since that time have agreed that 42 feet is an admirable diameter, although occasionally the ring may be as small as 38 feet or as large as 45.

When hostilities ceased, Astley went back to Paris, but in 1799 war broke out again, and he was kept prisoner in France. By holding a pistol to a driver's head, he managed to escape across the border and eventually got back to London by way of Holland. There he found that his wife had died while he was gone. In September, 1803, fireworks set his London amphitheatre ablaze, and it burned to the ground, destroying fifty valuable horses. The loss was estimated at 30,000 pounds and there was only 5,000 pounds' insurance. In the conflagration, Mrs. Woodhams, Astley's mother-in-law, was burned to death.

While he was waiting for the structure to be rebuilt, this time in stone, he leased a plot of ground and put up a temporary building where the famous Olympic Theatre was to rise later. With his usual resourcefulness, Astley made the frame of parts of an old man-of-war that had been captured from the French, and roofed it with sheet iron covered by canvas. This circus, which he called the Olympic Pavilion, had a single tier of boxes, with a pit and a gallery. There was no orchestra, but a few musicians sat in the stage boxes on each side. Astley sold the Pavilion in 1812 and moved his clever equestrians, ropedancers, and tumblers to the new and more luxurious version of the Royal Amphitheatre.

Philip Astley died in Paris in 1814 at the age of seventy-two, leaving direction of his still-growing enterprise to John Astley and William Davis. During the next few years, the Astley company of vaulting horsemen invented the feature known as the equestrian or hippodramatic spectacle— a pantomime episode on some dramatic theme, performed on horseback. Such a pantomime became so popular that, for almost a century, no circus could pretend to exist without one.

While Astley's was leading the world, the equestrian spectacle assumed innumerable forms. It could be based on some glorious military incident, on some vivid theme from poetry, or on some historical, Biblical, exotic, fantastic, mythological, or allegorical story. To bring the theme to life, men and animals rushed in and out of the arena, engaged in mock battles, carried on rescues, fled before the victorious enemy. Music blared. Guns thundered. Lightning flashed. The amphitheatre was ablaze with color and sound. Certain of the spectacles were received with such enthusiasm that they were in demand in every circus on both sides of the Atlantic.

When John Astley, too, died in Paris, seven years to the day after his father's death, management of Astley's passed into the hands of Andrew Ducrow, a member of the company. It was Ducrow, one of the most spectacular and glamorous figures in all circus history, who actually raised Astley's to its highest renown.

The Swaggering, Talented Mr. Ducrow

Andrew Ducrow danced on horseback, created riding feats he christened *poses plastiques,* and devised and popularized innumerable equestrian spectacles in which he played all sorts of characters. He could go through a series of quick costume changes on horseback, maintaining his equilibrium on a swiftly moving steed without the slightest apparent difficulty, while he danced ballet steps, and performed acrobatics that kept the public openmouthed.

Ducrow was born in Southwark in 1793, the son of an extraordinary

athlete, the Bruges-born Peter Ducrow, who was known as the Flemish Hercules. One of the elder Ducrow's specialties was to jump over the backs of seven horses and through a hoop of fire.

Andrew's career began when he was scarcely more than an infant. At four, he was billed as an "Infant Hercules." At five, he walked a rope. He made his debut at Astley's at the age of seven, and the story goes that he broke a leg at that time. If he did, it was well set. He continued his acrobatic training, and also attended the best actors' school in London, which helped to develop his innate capacities as a mime. At fifteen he was earning ten pounds a week, not only as a rider but as a cord dancer.

In 1814, the year Philip Astley died, Ducrow made a first appearance in Paris, as Eloi the Dumb Boy, in *The Forest of Bondy*. The perfection of the young man's body was such that, when he was with Astley's in Edinburgh in 1816, the great surgeon Barker advised his students to go to see him if they wanted to know what the human body could be like at its best.

Five years after the death of Philip Astley, and while John Astley was still in charge of the circus, Andrew Ducrow went to Paris, to appear in, and share the profits of, the Franconi Cirque Olympique, which had been established in 1807. With him went three Astley clowns, whom he took along to fill in spots when the actors and horses, winded, needed a breather. The engagement was highly successful.

Soon after 1821, when he became director of the Royal Amphitheatre, Ducrow married Adelaide Hinne, equestrienne daughter of a German circus director, bought a group of horses, and traveled the continent, where he quickly became noted for his quick changes on horseback.

During the twenty years of his control of Astley's, Ducrow carried that institution to its greatest days, in a period that is considered the peak of the indigenous English circus. At the high point there were some 150 persons on his payroll, which amounted to 2,000 pounds a month. The personnel included the three clowns who had gone to Paris; William Wallett, who was to be famous for years as the "Shakespearian Jester"; Andrew Ducrow's brother John, who was "Mr. Merryman," a clown; the riders Powell, Clarke, and Polaski (who vaulted over obstacles); the mulatto Pablo Fanque, who was later to have a circus of his own; and an extraordinary American named Robert Stickney, probably the best vaulter who ever appeared in the ring and one of the few able to do a double somersault on horseback. The first elephant ever seen in a modern circus arena was shown at Astley's in 1828.

At this time, according to a British periodical, *The New Monthly*

Ducrow as "The Courier of St. Petersburg"

Magazine, Astley's in London was a "circular riding house" some 50 feet in diameter, boarded up to a height of about three feet, with "seats rising amphitheatrically all round," balconies above, and "the whole spectacle illumined with a blaze of gas till it rivals noonday sunlight." This, we read, was "the arena of Ducrow's triumphs, the scene of all his glory."

His contemporaries have left records that Andrew Ducrow was a vain and swaggering man, difficult to get along with, and much given to cursing and foul language. Apparently the company, or at any rate the equestrians, traveled the provinces in the summer. One year, when the company arrived in Sheffield, the master cutler and members of the town council appeared at the head of scores of carriages filled with potential circus audience, asking to see Mr. Ducrow. The latter sent out word that he waited only on crowned heads. His circus was boycotted in Sheffield.

Ordinarily, in whatever amphitheatre he might be appearing, immense audiences gathered to watch Ducrow perform his colorful equestrian miracles. In *The Indian Hunter* he rode bareback with one foot on the neck of the horse. As "The God of Fame" he wore a tunic, was decked out with plumes and wings, and carried a shield and trumpet. "The Yorkshire Fox Hunter" wore top hat and tails for his two-horse jumps. As a "Chinese Enchanter" Ducrow bestrode three horses. The sailor in *The*

91

Vicissitudes of a Tar pretended to be in a boat with an ape that threatened to throw him out and after a series of difficulties concluded the number by dancing a hornpipe and appearing in a succession of national costumes, waving the flag of each country.

A clipping from *The New Monthly Magazine* recalls something of the awe Ducrow evoked. The writer, describing a solo performance, was much impressed by the fact that the great horseman, whose face was long and thin, looked like a horse—the ideal Phidian horse from the pediment of the Parthenon. The pantomime described was a series of metamorphoses in which Ducrow changed his costume four times without coming to earth, and progressed from grotesque acrobatics to the most subtle and graceful ballet. He was at first a sort of pilgrim version of Billy Button; then a Pulcinella "floundering and flinging about his limbs as if they were so many fly-flappers"; then a young peasant of the Campagna, going through a pantomime with an imaginary loved one; and thereafter a Harlequin, dancing "every pas and attitude" on a stage a few inches square, moving under his feet at twenty miles an hour. Finally, Ducrow, "still moving around in his endless path, like the wind around the 'earth globose,' " transformed himself "into a symbol of that wind itself . . . like a winged Zephyr pursuing, with the speed of light, the invisible Flora," of whom he was enamored.

The critic grew poetic about "the miraculous skill with which the rider took advantage of the centrifugal and centripetal forces that were counteracting each other . . . merely touching the horse with the tip of his foot—his whole frame literally pendent in the supporting air." In Paris, another writer proclaimed that the laws of equilibrium seemed not to exist for the English rider, who looked as if he were effortlessly suspended in space.

Such a furor of excitement greeted Ducrow when he appeared in these solos that riders in other arenas immediately began to copy them. At the Haymarket in 1831, Cooke's Equestrian Circus presented "Mr. J. Cooke, a first-rate horseman of the present day," in the *Fox Hunter,* and the true *British Sailor*. Mr. Taplin made his first appearance as "The Inebriated Soldier"—on horseback, of course. With a certain disregard for mythology, the bill announces that "Miss Emeline Margurete, the INFANT PRODIGY . . . will appear for the first time in an entire new Equestrian Scene, as the LILIPUTIAN BACCHUS! With the Metamorphosis to Felicitas, the Goddess of Happiness and Peace." The program concludes with *Sir Billy Button's Vote*.

Despite his success in other roles, the pantomime on horseback for which Ducrow is deathlessly remembered is *The Courier of St. Petersburg,* which he invented in 1829 and showed in Paris in the same year. Behold, he is a Russian courier, with one foot on each of two wildly galloping horses. Four other horses, riderless, go between his legs, one after the other. As they pass, he snatches the reins, planting on each a flag bearing the name of a city through which he supposedly has passed. Thereafter, he drives all four horses tandem, still balancing on the original two. (A rare old print inaccurately shows three horses all rushing side by side between his legs. Even Ducrow would have experienced some difficulty in achieving that posture.)

Misfortune cut short his career. In 1841, the Royal Amphitheatre burned for the third time, in a fire set off by the guns used in a spectacle, *The Wars of Cromwell,* destroying all the circus property, including the horses. A contemporary artist's impression of the fire depicts the interior of the amphitheatre blazing, with walls falling and balconies crashing as human figures try to control the panic-stricken horses, which dash frantically around the ring, back and forth across the stage, and up and down the connecting ramps. The scene is caught in a moment of unmitigated terror.

During more than a century since that time, numerous amphitheatres and countless tents have become similar death traps. In many instances, circus owners have taken inventory, gathered themselves together and started all over again. Sometimes ruin has been so complete that they have given up. Andrew Ducrow lost his mind. On January 27, 1842, he died at the age of fifty-one.

In twenty years, Ducrow had made of Astley's an institution that will be remembered as long as men love the circus. Artists who had been trained in his ring went out all over the world, and an increasing number of circuses began to roam the British Isles.

In London, approximately a year after the death of Astley's great successor, the New Royal Amphitheatre was rebuilt on plans drawn up by Dickie Usher, a clown, and William Batty, a rider. Batty sent his circus out tenting through England in the summer, and presented it in the amphitheatre during the winter. It prospered, and the enthusiasm for circus spread even more widely. But the supremacy of Astley's was ended.

The true center of circus had shifted to France, where the Franconis had usurped the place once held by Astley, and set up the first of the great circus dynasties.

8

Francis C. Fuerst: Black Star

Dynamic

Dynasties

THE GREATEST period of the French circus, which was to encompass forty years, developed around the Franconis. The last member of that family did not bow out until 1907, and the career of its four generations is without peer in the annals of the circus, toward which, as artists, organizers, and builders, they made an inordinately important contribution.

The Fabulous Franconis

The Franconis were Venetians, and it was Antonio, born in Venice in 1737, a notoriously hot-tempered, vital, and courageous man, who transferred the family allegiance to France. When he was twenty-three, Antonio killed a young fellow citizen in a duel, and fled to Lyons, where he arrived without money or friends. A traveling circus was in town, and the owner offered him a job training a lion. Though he knew nothing whatever about controlling wild animals, the young man accepted without hesitation, and persevered even after his arm was badly mauled. He might have become a wild animal trainer and nothing more, if one of the other employees had not been jealous of his success. Antonio hit the fellow on the jaw, and departed.

In his pocket he had only six crowns. With these he bought a few canaries, trained them to stand on their heads, to pull tiny cars, and to fire little guns, and exhibited through France and Spain. In Spain he saw several bullfights, and decided that he would like to promote such contests in France. Backed by a wealthy patron, he put on a bullfight in Rouen in 1773 and made a little money, but gave up the enterprise immediately afterward. Two years later he married a girl named Elizabeth Massacuti and with her and his canaries went on to Paris, where Philip Astley had just opened his amphitheatre in the Faubourg du Temple. The birds made an engaging act and Franconi rapidly became such an important associate of Astley's that he took over management of the amphitheatre whenever the owner went to England. The Franconis had two sons, Laurent Antoine and Jean Gérard Henri, born in 1776 and 1779, respectively.

Very soon Antonio thought he might branch out for himself. So in 1786 he bought some horses, trained them, and in Lyons erected a circus (first a wooden building, and later, one of stone). Then in 1792 England declared war on France, and Astley left Paris. Franconi offered to take over l'Amphithéâtre Astley, and on March 21, 1793, it became l'Amphithéâtre Franconi. The Franconi dynasty had been established.

Though Antonio Franconi was one of the greatest of circus men, he often fell into financial and other difficulties. For instance, a bombardment destroyed his Lyons circus, and in 1794 the Convention awarded him 83,866 francs compensation—in those days, a goodly sum. But this was during the Reign of Terror. Political complications ensued and it turned out that Franconi never got a sou. Then he himself became politically suspect when he gave refuge to one of his Lyons partners who was running from possible arrest. As soon as authorities got wind of what Franconi was up to, delegates arrived to arrest him. They reckoned, however, without Antonio's courage and popularity.

Barricading himself in the foyer of the circus, he shouted defiance at them. The crowd growled and crowded nearer in sympathy. The delegates retired, announcing that they would come back with enough men to control the situation. They did not return. However, a few days later he discreetly left Paris and was not seen there again until several months after the fall of Robespierre.

Laurent was nineteen, Henri seventeen, and their father himself fifty-eight when he reopened l'Amphithéâtre Franconi. As a boy in Italy, he had learned the art of riding, and now taught his sons. They became members of a company that also included Antonio's brother-in-law, a nephew, and a number of other good riders. The program was based, as Astley's had been, on acrobatic riding, but the Franconis also introduced *haute école*. "High school" horses, those that dance to music, are the most expertly trained of any that appear in the ring. The lowliest are the "rosinbacks," whose role is merely to jog along at a rhythmic trot without shying or breaking pace, while their riders pose, do acrobatic turns, or dance. The backs of the plodding mounts are sprinkled with rosin so that the riders' shoes will not slip. The third category is the "liberty" horses, who go through their paces without riders. The "educated," like Astley's Billy, are of course individuals that have evidenced peculiar adaptabilities. All types of ring horses were shown in the Paris arena.

In 1801, the Franconis left the old faubourg amphitheatre and built nearby in l'Enclos des Capucines of the rue Neuve-Saint-Augustin, where a French version of *The Tailor's Ride* was one of the numbers on the program. Great excitement was created for years by Coco, a trained stag that went through various features of the manège, jumped ribbons, soared over eight soldiers and four horses, played dead, lying motionless even when his master fired a pistol in his ear. Later, Coco was exhibited in many of the pantomimes with an equally famous little elephant, Baba, who

96

A typical nineteenth-century circus herald

played with balls, turned the handle of an organ, drank out of a bottle, danced a gavotte, and fired a pistol. Almost all the kinds of attractions that were to characterize the circus through the nineteenth century were presented by the Franconis in their early days. In addition to equestrian spectacles and trained animals, they offered cord dancers, tumblers, dancers, and pantomime actors. They even presented acts on the rigging, though not on the flying trapeze, which did not appear until 1859.

Antonio and Laurent, father and son, were especially remarkable riders, showing great delicacy and finesse. Laurent, who was exceedingly strong, often produced *Les Forces d'Hercule,* with his wife, his sister-in-law, and three other riders. Two horses were led out with Laurent between them. He grasped the bridles, and put a foot in a stirrup of each. The two girls stood on the saddles, and three men were supported on the

97

shoulders of Laurent, who urged the horses into a gallop. Henri, who was never so good at vaulting as the others, began to specialize in pantomimes and equestrian scenes, to supplement the simpler numbers. The Franconis and their young equestrienne wives were the toast of Paris.

The amphitheatre that Astley had built in 1783 in the Faubourg du Temple, which Antonio had inherited, contained a simple ring surrounded by seats. In 1806, when the rue Napoléon was cut through the Enclos site, he and his sons built the Cirque Olympique in the rue St. Honoré. There they followed the style that Hughes had established in his Royal Circus and Astley had copied in the London Royal Amphitheatre. Here, by means of ramps, movable platforms and curtains, an equestrian spectacle in the ring could give way gracefully to an entr'acte on the stage, and vice versa. An important feature was two openings at the sides of the stage, through which horses and riders could enter the ring. The building became really a theatre-circus, where pantomimes could be given as great spectacles.

Four years after Antonio and his sons had moved into the Olympique, he had a terrific row with them, and the sons betook themselves back to the faubourg. When a public building was put up in the rue St. Honoré, and Antonio had to give up the Olympique there, he rejoined them, and they transferred the Cirque Olympique title to the faubourg establishment.

More hard luck came along. While a conflagration spectacle was

Lions sometimes make unruly pupils.

being featured on the night of May 15, 1826, the old faubourg building went up like a torch, carrying with it a house that Laurent had built nearby when he held three winning tickets in the national lottery. The Franconis were ruined, but they would not stop. They gathered together all their resources, amplified by subscriptions, with the name of Charles X first on the list, and put up a new building on the site.

This new Cirque Olympique was a stone structure. Bronze riders dominated the pediment above its rectangular façade, and it had a glass peristyle hung with multicolored lanterns. High over the roof, above the name FRANCONI, an immense tricolor floated in the breeze. One of the sights of Paris during the Restoration was to see old Antonio sitting on the sidelines of the Olympique, watching his sons and grandsons. Even at ninety, when he had lost his sight, he still haunted the circus.

All seemed to augur so well at the new amphitheatre that the showmen began to present unusually elaborate pantomimes. Those productions were so expensive, however, that in 1835 the Franconis went bankrupt and the business passed into the hands of the owner of the land, Louis Dejean. Dejean put Henri's son Adolphe in as manager, and the enterprise again prospered, especially after Dejean and Adolphe opened still another amphitheatre, the Cirque des Champs-Élysées. Antonio did not live to see the revival, for he died in 1836 at the age of ninety-nine. All Paris followed his funeral cortege, in which his sons, grandsons, and great-grandsons led the way, and his riderless horse, in black and silver, proclaimed the passing of a great public figure.

After the fiasco of 1835, Henri retired to the country, and Laurent, who was an excellent mime, traveled the foreign circuit, even playing in London. In 1845, he built the first modern hippodrome in Paris, at the entrance to l'Étoile. Four years later he and his brothers died of cholera. Other Franconis were to continue the family tradition during the ensuing half century, but their achievements were far less spectacular.

In the German-speaking countries, the spark that Astley had lighted caught almost as quickly as it did in France, and pioneering beacons began to burn here and there even while the original Franconis were tending the flame in Paris.

The military style, in the Astley tradition, predominated beyond the Rhine, fostered especially by Juan Porté, a Spaniard who flourished in Austria in the time of Astley. Porté went from city to city with his company of acrobatic horsemen, giving exhibitions in the military manèges, and became so popular with the soldiers that when he and his troupe entered a village the drums began to beat, the fifes to play, and a military band escorted them to the manège.

Before his death in 1810, Porté had founded a successful circus on the Mehlmarkt in Vienna, directing the enterprise and exhibiting not only as a horseman but as a "Hercules." His son, also named Juan, inherited his father's strength, and one of his most spectacular stunts was to lie on his back and on hands and feet hold up a platform loaded down by a carriage, horse, and coachman. In a circus that Juan the Younger helped found in Vienna's Lerchenfeld, one of the spectacles, *Captain Cook or the Savages of Tahiti,* ended with Porté and an associate holding up a pyramid of forty persons, though Porté was then more than seventy years old. Despite his great popularity, fortune eluded him and, to keep the wolf from their door, his wife Anna, a remarkable ropedancer, still danced on the cord at country fairs when she was eighty.

During the first three or four decades of the nineteenth century, circuses were set up across the Rhine by three men, all pupils of one teacher, Pierre Maheu, who at the end of the eighteenth century gave exhibitions of horsemanship in Vienna. The first of those pupils, Christoph de Bach, joined Maheu's Vienna company in 1805, and three years later broke away to build his own Circus Gymnasticus in the Prater. It was an elegantly decorated amphitheatre that would seat 3,000, covered by a glass cupola that permitted daytime performances without artificial light. For six months of the year, the de Bach company performed there; the rest of the time it traveled in Germany, Italy, and, later, Russia, carrying the first ring entertainment to the people of the Czar, who have always been especially avid for any spectacular production. The second of Maheu's pupils, Brilloff, himself had a number of pupils, among whom were two great early directors of German circuses, Edward Wollschläger and Ernst Renz—the latter a fabulous character who was to be for many years the king of the German circus world. Maheu's third important pupil, Johann Hinne, founded a circus dynasty of his own, and it was his daughter, Adelaide, who married Andrew Ducrow. When Johann Hinne's son founded his own circus in Berlin, a decade after Ducrow's death, he called it the Hinne-Ducrow.

The Ingenious Cookes

Meanwhile, in Great Britain another family was setting up a comparable dynasty, which was to assume an enviable position in its homeland and carry its wares far and wide.

100

From the late eighteenth century to the mid-twentieth, there have been in the circus literally hundreds of men and women named Cooke, all more or less related, and almost all descended from Thomas Cooke. Even more significantly than the Sangers (who were to start with a peep show) and certainly more directly than Astley (whose training was military), the Cooke family presents a link in the unbroken tradition of the traveling mountebank, straight from the Middle Ages to our own time. At least as early as 1750, Thomas Cooke was following the fairs in Scotland, setting up his little show wherever opportunity offered.

Just what that show was like is not known; but certainly in 1784 it was something like a small circus. Possibly, if more were known about his early activities, Thomas Cooke, instead of Astley, might have won the title "Father of the Circus." There is no record of how Cooke himself contributed to the performance he offered; but without doubt he was an accomplished rider and acrobat, and probably he was a ropewalker. At one time or another, his descendants up to the present generation have been experts in all those fields.

A fuller record is available on Thomas Taplin Cooke, son of the original Thomas. He rode, walked a rope, and was so strong that on his

chest he could hold ten men balanced on a board. Thomas Taplin had at least a dozen children, whom he brought up to follow his pattern as far as each was able. Wives, husbands, children, brothers and sisters, nieces and nephews and all sorts of in-laws have often helped out in circus projects. Cooke's was probably the first real family circus. Without calling in any outsiders, the family could easily put on a whole program.

Cooke's was also the first true traveling circus. While Ducrow was confining his activities largely to London and Paris, in buildings designed especially for such performances, Cooke was already roaming the Continent. Although others very shortly began to copy him, it was a long time before most of them offered shows that could compare with his.

Such a thirst was developing for this kind of entertainment that very little was required to satisfy it. An early traveling circus might have only three or four horses, a couple of acrobats who did flip-flaps, a clown who pulled a few wheezes and perhaps rode as the Tailor, a tightrope walker, and little else. The performance would be short, and repeated from noon until nearly midnight, and a proprietor would just set up shop in an open field, as Price and Sampson had done. Everyone doubled in everything, and at the end the proprietor passed the hat. Of course the company traveled by wagon. In the earliest days, some of the troupes owned no canvas at all, but as soon as they could manage it most of them put up either sidewalls or little canvas umbrellas. After the full round tent was invented, everyone who could afford to do so adopted that.

In traveling about England, mud was the most dire and omnipresent enemy, and the lot itself could become a quagmire. When a circus went abroad, there was an additional hazard on the open seas, and many a vessel was lost. In 1816, when Thomas Taplin Cooke was only twenty-four, he traveled as far as Lisbon, where he and his company were received with wild enthusiasm, and he filled his pockets with gold. On the way home, the ship was so nearly wrecked in the Bay of Biscay that he lost forty ring horses. Despite that catastrophe, the young manager saved from the Portuguese venture enough to replace the horses and to set up a circuit, building wooden amphitheatres in several cities in the north of England.

The Cookes were an ingenious tribe, not content to follow paths too frequently trodden. In their amphitheatres they invented new pantomimes and spectacles, and in their programs presented an immense variety of acts, for which they attracted superlative performers. Thomas Taplin Cooke acquired such a reputation that in 1830 he was commanded to give a performance in the Brighton Pavilion before King William IV and

Queen Adelaide. Thereafter Cooke bills inevitably bore the British coat of arms, and eventually the "Equestrian" became the "Royal" Circus.

By the mid-nineteenth century, there were Cookes all over the globe, with almost every one of them distinguishing himself. William, one of Thomas Taplin's sons, a clown, ropewalker, and strong man, was to lease Astley's in 1853. James Cooke would be in Seville in 1860, and win a contest with a troupe of Arab vaulters, by going above the heads of eleven horses from a springboard, and above nine when he took off from a stone. John Henry, born in America, made his circus debut at four, at fifteen was in his Uncle William's circus in Birmingham, and at eighteen was billed as the Champion Equestrian of the Universe. He traveled a great deal in Portugal and America, and was shipwrecked and attacked by bandits. Before John Henry, too, set up his own company, he was chief rider and ringmaster of the Cirque d'Hiver and the Cirque d'Été in Paris. Another Cooke, Hubert, was to establish a circus in France.

One of the most dramatic contributions the Cookes made to the circus was a modern version of the Roman *naumachia,* which became a specialty in the family's amphitheatres. Like the equestrian spectacle, this production was essentially a pantomime, deriving directly from a form of entertainment that had been developing for some time on the stages of London theatres.

By way of theatre pantomime, and especially through the wit, antics, and buffoonery of Joseph Grimaldi, theatre pantomime's most popular exponent, another metamorphosis had taken place in the arena. The circus clown had come of age.

Harlequinade

T O CIRCUS FOLK, any clown is, and long has been, a Joey. In labeling him so, they are honoring the first great modern clown. His name was Joseph Grimaldi, and he was a pantomime clown in English theatres a century and a half ago.

Clown Prince Grimaldi

In an institution that abounds in anomalies, none is stranger than that the circus comic should really have got his start in life from a man who never entered a circus, except perhaps as a spectator. Grimaldi did not of course invent the genus he represented. It was he, however, who injected lifeblood into a tottering figure already named Clown, and set him up as a personage embodying comedy in so vital a fashion that all subsequent manifestations of the comic figure have been his descendants, direct or collateral.

Although Joseph Grimaldi developed his art in pantomime, for him dumb show—gesture, motion to replace words—was just one tool out of many, as it had been for the Italian comedians, from whom, no doubt, he was literally descended.

In 1717, pantomime was the name John Rich gave to the programs he began to offer at Lincoln's Inn Fields Theatre. London flocked to see the dumb show, in which Harlequin always played the lead. That Harlequin was a comic character, wearing the half mask and carrying the wooden sword that had characterized him among the Italian comedians. Without saying a word he could send audiences into paroxysms of laughter. John Rich's pantomime became the rage, and other theatres copied him.

Little by little, Harlequin began to perform transformation tricks with his magic sword. Machinery like that of the ancient spectacles was used. Anything could turn into anything, and the audience loved those transformations. Before many years had passed, a pantomime consisted of two parts—a short opening, like a fairy tale or Mother Goose story, followed by a lengthy harlequinade, for which a character called Clown took the limelight. After the first part, at the wave of a wand, the original characters were transformed into Harlequin, Pantaloon, Columbine, Clown, and other stock figures, and a cow might become a pump, or a goldbeater's shop turn into the Mint. Audiences young and old waited eagerly for that second part, which was packed full of practical jokes and horseplay in the *Commedia* tradition. The fairy-tale introduction became shorter and less important.

It was into a pantomime of that nature that Joe Grimaldi's father

105

stepped, and that Joe himself was born in 1778. In their hands, Harlequin was sent back into the wings for keeps, Clown was established on center stage, squarely in the limelight, and words and music were brought on to assist wordless gesture.

Giuseppe Grimaldi was an Italian ballet master who had come to England after a career as dancer at Italian and French fairs. His first appearance in London was in 1759 as Pantaloon in one of the pantomimes at Covent Garden, and he stayed on there to appear in subsequent plays, for which he invented a great deal of business that his audiences thought very funny indeed.

Clown had been a clumsy oaf, who never did much except stand around and look stupid, get into people's way, and fall over his own feet. Giuseppe gave him more to do, and made him into a character who was later to be bequeathed to his son for even more expert development.

Joe made his first public appearance when he was a mere baby, wearing a tiny clown suit exactly like that of his father. The child was so small and so agile that he was dressed up on occasion as one or another of the animals that were already a part of pantomime. One day, when Joe was representing a monkey, his father, who had hitched him to a chain, swung the chain so lustily that the youngster sailed out over the audience, straight into the arms of a spectator. That time the child was not hurt. However, somewhat later, at Christmas in *Hurly Burly,* when he was taking the parts of both a monkey and a cat, his cat costume was so awkward that he had difficulty seeing where he was going. He fell through a trap door, broke his five-year-old collar bone, and could not go back until Easter.

When Giuseppe died, leaving his wife and two children without a penny, Joe was ten years old. He was working then at two theatres—Drury Lane and Sadler's Wells—on one stage or the other from ten in the morning until nearly midnight, except for the time it took to get out of one costume, dash through the streets, and climb into another. Richard Brinsley Sheridan, at that time proprietor of Drury Lane, raised Joe's pay to a pound a week during pantomime season. At Sadler's Wells, they reduced him from 15 shillings to three. For that stipend, in addition to taking the part of any kind of grotesque human being or animal, he helped the stage carpenters and painters. Occasionally he went on in a straight role, and through the years often played Bob Acres in *The Rivals*. Obviously Grimaldi could have made an excellent straight comic.

By the time he was sixteen, Drury Lane had advanced his wages to four pounds, and he had already made a reputation. Like many great clowns, Joe Grimaldi seems to have been essentially a somewhat morose person, and he appeared almost to attract misfortune. When he was twenty, he married a daughter of the Sadler's Wells manager, but at the end of the year she died in childbirth. Before he was thirty, his health began to fail and he was increasingly crippled by a disease that manifested itself in cramps and spasms.

An accident in 1802 brought him first bad luck, then good. On the stage, as he was drawing a pistol from his belt, he inadvertently fired it into the broad-topped boot he was wearing. His stocking caught fire, and he writhed in agony as he finished the scene, while the audience laughed uproariously, thinking that this was some new stage business. Mary Bristow, an actress at Drury Lane, helped nurse him while he was laid up for a month, and soon afterward they were married. Joe had become such a popular favorite that four years later Sadler's Wells was paying him 12 pounds a week, plus two clear benefits during the season.

That system of giving a benefit for a performer was to persist for nearly a century. Apparently the benefit started as a kind of bonus, as with Grimaldi. It came to be expected every so often, and even occasionally was part of the bond. In the early days, average clowns were poorly paid; but almost any one of them could depend on a substantial benefit. A clown was permitted and, in fact, expected to insert into his routine any kind of advertising gags he could think up, and the support for his benefit came chiefly from tradesmen whose goods he had touted.

As time went on, writers lauded Joe Grimaldi as the "Michael Angelo of buffoonery . . . the Jupiter of Joke . . . the Garrick of Clowns." According to one reporter, "He tickles the fancy and excites the risibility of an audience by devices as varied as they are ingenious. He uses his folly as a stalking-horse under cover of which he shoots his wit."

All Grimaldi had to do to send his audience into paroxysms was to appear on the stage and say, "Well, how are you?" He could simply drop his chin to look at his waistcoat, and everybody would roar. In order to hold an audience in the hollow of his expressive hand, Joe Grimaldi would caricature an Indian sword swallower with a blade as big as an oar, or take off a ballerina, or merely pretend that he was making love, or was committing larceny, or was afraid of someone or something. The best-known anecdote about him is one that had been told also about Giuseppe Domenico Biancholelli, a seventeenth-century Bolognese Harlequin. Grimaldi felt very melancholy, and in search of a remedy consulted a doctor who did not recognize him. The doctor's prescription for melancholy was to go to see Joe Grimaldi in the pantomime.

Grimaldi was a master of make-up, and evolved for himself a strange mask of paint. Large, bright spots shone here and there on his mobile face, which, he explained, he painted to look like that of a "greedy boy who had smeared himself with jam after robbing a cupboard." He never adopted the motley we associate with Harlequin, but decked himself out in all sorts of outrageous gear. A comic costume could be extemporized in a moment. In one pantomime, during which a wicker basket turned into a fashionable carriage, as the driver Joe wore a coat made of a blanket with tin plates for buttons. He topped it off with a pie-plate hat, and carried a bouquet of carrots and greens.

Clowns making up before the show

Phot. Hutton, London: Black Star

"A Oyster Crossed in Love"

The public especially liked his comic songs. The most popular of them was "Hot Codlins" (toffee apples), which he introduced in *The Talking Bird,* a harlequinade at Sadler's Wells. "Hot Codlins" was such an instantaneous hit that many years were to go by before the public would accept any clown who did not sing as part of his act. "Me and My Neddy," in *Harlequin and the 40 Virgins,* the Easter pantomime of 1806, was another special favorite. It was in a song about the love life of an oyster, however, that Grimaldi showed most clearly his skill in playing on the emotions—an artistry that lifted him far above the ordinary comic of any period. He sat in the glow of the footlights, on one side of him a big cod's head, on the other a large oyster that opened and shut its mouth in time to the music, and he sang "A Oyster Crossed in Love." It was hilarious, but, as one writer said, "Such touches of real pathos trickled through his grotesqueness—that all the children were in tears."

At Christmas in 1806, the pantomime was *Mother Goose,* a farce by Thomas Dibdin. Grimaldi was Squire Bugle afterwards Clown; his friend Jack Bologna was Avaro afterwards Harlequin. The audience saw no expensive costumes, no elaborate scenery, no spangles except on Harlequin's jacket, but the entertainment was such an overwhelming success that it was repeated the following season. After Covent Garden burned in 1808, the farce was revived at the Haymarket, and later even came to the Bowery Theatre in New York. As a matter of fact, *Mother Goose* established a tradition which endured so strongly in the circus that it was given as a spectacle in approximately 1840, and P. T. Barnum procured Mother Goose floats for his parades in the late 1880's.

One role after another was made famous by Joe Grimaldi. His contemporaries wrote glowingly of his incomparable foolishness as Clown in *Harlequin and the Red Dwarf,* and Dr. Tumble Tuzzy in *Harlequin and the Swan,* and grew eloquent about his burlesque of the dagger scene from *Macbeth.*

In 1816, Joe Grimaldi left Sadler's Wells after a dispute with the management, but returned the following season, having acquired a share in the theatre. Before another five years had passed, he was so ill with the crippling spasms and cramps that sometimes he could scarcely get through the show, though he kept on faithfully. In *Harlequin and Poor Robin, or The House that Jack Built,* his son, in whom he had put great hopes, replaced him and was well received. But soon afterward the young

Grimaldi and Mr. Norman in the popular pantomine of **The Red Dwarf**

man, who was to die of insanity at thirty, left home. Joe became so ill that he could appear very seldom. His second wife had died. As before, when he most needed money, Sadler's Wells reduced his salary—first to four pounds a week, and then to two pounds. In 1828, farewell benefit performances were given for him by both the Wells and the Garden. For the benefit at Covent Garden, Grimaldi, game to the end, tried to go through with one of his famous old roles in *Harlequin as Hoax*. He was so weak that he was forced to play one scene sitting down.

On the proceeds from the benefits, plus a pension of 100 pounds a year from the Theatre Fund, Joe Grimaldi, increasingly ill and unable to work, managed to exist for nearly a decade. He died in 1837. Every evening, to the very end, he was carried to the Marquis of Cornwallis Tavern in Pentonville, where there was fun and laughter.

Though Grimaldi was never of the circus, he was the sculptor who took the clay marked "clown" and formed it into a shape the circus could use as its own. For at least forty years after the first Joey had cracked his last joke, the clown was formed very much in his image, though each newcomer might have his own specialty—singing, dancing, acrobatics, or buffoonery. The true circus clown, who had his origin in Astley's early days when Saunders and Fortunelli produced *The Tailor's Ride to Brentford,* merely assimilated certain of Grimaldi's manners and methods, and progressed by a somewhat different road. By the time the circus had become firmly established as a popular entertainment, the clown in the ring had acquired the personality that characterizes him to this day.

The spectacles in the arena grew even more directly out of the stage pantomime that had been delighting London for a hundred years. The type of entertainment the Grimaldis offered at Sadler's Wells and Covent Garden was in such demand that Hughes had built a stage in his Royal Circus, to take advantage of that popularity, and from the beginning pantomimes very much like those produced by John Rich were shown in all circus arenas.

These productions, complete with scenery and machinery, noise and colored fire, had brought the spectacle to the stages of London theatres. Characters emerged from trap doors. Mythological or fairy-tale creatures flew on or off by means of elaborate contrivances. Grotesque papier-mâché heads were worn. With accompanying sound and fury, evil spirits rose or descended, sometimes in nontraditional directions. Don Giovanni flew *up* to the infernal regions, surrounded by fire and demons. Where streets had been, beds of flowers or serpents appeared. Dry land sank, and there was the sea, beating on dangerous rocks. Harlequin touched someone with his bat, and that person vanished in a puff of smoke or was instantly transformed.

A great deal of that fantastic character and spirit, copied and absorbed by the circus stage, was put forth also in its early pantomimes on horseback. With the use of both stage and ring, often with the hippodrome track, plus various platforms, ramps and additional temporary structures, incredibly elaborate combinations of riding, acrobatics, and pantomime could be presented.

In advertisements for 1788, Astley offered *The Humours of Gil Blas,* and *The Magic World,* in which action took place on the four quarters of the globe, behind a transparent curtain painted to show the enchanted world. The great man himself sat on his charger, Gibraltar, surrounded by a sea of fire. Incidentally, in that year's program he may also have initiated the minstrel show, for notes about the *Ethiopian Festival* point out that "whimsical actions and attitudes are made use of by the Negroes."

The earliest true equestrian spectacle, naturally in the military tradition, was *The Battle of Waterloo,* invented by Andrew Ducrow after he had visited the battlefield. He revived it in 1828, and it was continued for many years. Other glorious military episodes were immortalized in such productions as *The Battle of Salamanca,* and *Napoleon before Moscow.* For the lure of the exotic, Ducrow devised *The Fair Slave, Alexander the Great and Thalestris the Amazon,* and *The Cataract of the Ganges.*

Mazeppa and the "Hippodramatic"

Ducrow's most spectacular and successful presentation, however, was *Mazeppa.* The close relation between stage pantomime and circus spectacle is shown nowhere more clearly than in the history of that "hippodramatic" production, which had first been worked out for the Coburg Theatre in Lambeth in 1823, four years after the publication of Lord Byron's poem. As adapted by Ducrow, *Mazeppa* became so popular a feature of the circus performance that it outlasted every other spectacle, and gave such an opportunity for showmanship that it was even played at one time by a woman—the beautiful American, Adah Isaacs Menken. For half a century, sensational depictions of the horse and helpless rider flared from circus heralds.

Byron tells the story of a young Polish page in the retinue of a count, who loves his master's wife unwisely and much too well, and is punished by being tied to an untamed horse and sent off across the steppes. Pursued by wolves, wild horses, and vultures, the horse races till it falls exhausted. Mazeppa is rescued by a Cossack, and is greeted on awakening by the Cossack's beautiful daughter. The exotic sentimentalism of all this appealed immeasurably to early nineteenth-century audiences—especially when the ending was changed to inject several notes of respectability. In the equestrian version, while Mazeppa lies unconscious, Abder Khan of Tartary arrives and recognizes him as his long-lost son. Mazeppa is crowned King of Tartary, goes into Poland with the cavalry, conquers the Count, and marries the lady.

In France, all through the years, audiences had roared with mirth at the Gallic version of *The Tailor's Ride,* which had become *Rognolet et Passe-Carreau.* That early vehicle for clowning was given in the faubourg for the first time in 1795, and had four in the cast—Rognolet, the tailor; Passe-Carreau, his clerk; the postmaster; and the postillion. Against *décor* representing the front of a shop, these characters enacted the troubles of Rognolet (here a powdered and frizzed Gascon tailor, speaking in strong dialect). After a series of absurd falls from a snapping horse led to him by the postmaster, the tailor was charged by the furious animal, and ducked under a bench. The horse turned the bench upside down, and Rognolet

112

The Great Emmett Kelly

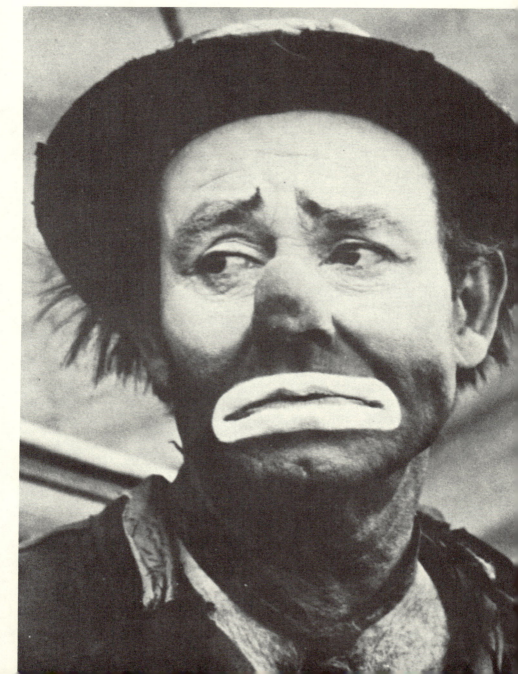

rushed into the shop to hide, with the horse following through a window. And so on and on, while the audience grew increasingly hilarious.

Pantomime had hit France at the end of the eighteenth century with as strong an impact as it had made on England, and pantomime's stepchild, the equestrian spectacle, first began to delight Paris when Astley's showed at the faubourg such hippodramatic numbers as *La Bataille et La Mort du Géneral Marlborough, L'Arrivée de Nicodème dans la Lune,* and *La Lanterne de Diogène.* In the early days of the Franconis at l'Olympique, Paris thronged to *La Prise de la Corogne ou les Anglais en Espagne, Le Pont Infernal,* and *Martial et Angélique ou le Cheval Accusateur.* With the advent of Adolphe Franconi, French revolutionary achievements were condensed into such spectacles as *La Prise de la Bastille, L'Empereur, La République,* and *L'Empire et les Cents Jours.* As many as 700 or 800 military figures would appear at once in the arena, coming in at one side and going out the other, while the circus resounded with almost constant military fire, beating of drums, and thundering of martial music. The audience took the whole thing so seriously that the ultrapatriotic sometimes forgot where they were, and rushed into the ring to participate in *la gloire de la France.*

At this time, the French spectacle began occasionally to change its nature by playing up themes in which animals appeared. In 1829 came *L'Éléphant du Roi de Siam;* in 1831, *Les Lions de Mysore;* in 1839, *Les Lions du Désert.*

In Great Britain, the circus spectacle was transformed by the Cookes into a sham sea fight, or some other action against an aquatic background. In 1804, Thomas Dibdin—he of the farces—had opened an aquatic theatre at Sadler's Wells, where he offered a bloodless adaptation of the Roman *naumachia,* which had been long forgotten, except for spasmodic copyings in Italian cities during the Renaissance. At Sadler's Wells, ships appeared, battles were fought, and all sorts of courageous rescues were performed in the 90-foot tank. Children could be thrown into the water, to be hauled out by a Newfoundland dog. Villains could be drowned, to the immense satisfaction of the onlookers, though everyone knew that the same villains would come to life for the next performance.

As soon as Thomas Taplin Cooke had built his amphitheatres, he proceeded to take over the aquatic spectacle for the circus. At first the ring was flooded, but with only enough water to carry ducks, swans, small boats, and a tiny steamer, which chugged around under bridges stretching from one edge of the ring to the other. In that setting, he presented a simple little comedy, which was so immediately successful that he built a sinking ring, deepened the water, and produced spectacles that attracted audiences from all across the country.

As early as 1818, two years after his Lisbon adventure, he was advertising "GRAND ACTION, Between Two Ships of War, A British Frigate and an Algerine Corvette, exchanging REAL RED-HOT BALLS," in the amphitheatre at Hull. An engraving depicts the ships tossing wildly in the wind and waves.

For those same evenings, horsemanship played an important role, with The African Youth going through "the whole of his much-admired Feats on the Single Horse," in addition to the "astonishing LEAPS over HORSES and Exquisite SOMERSETS" of a "Troop of Voltigeurs." Mons. Hengler is to appear on the tight rope, and Master Powell, the "Wonderful POLANDERIC PERFORMER," to exhibit his "Antipodean FEATS on the GEOMETRICAL LADDER." The wonderful pony is to mount a nine foot platform and fire a pistol, and the "Indian War Dance and Combat from the Pantomime of KANKO" is to be presented.

The aquatic spectacle was continued by Thomas Taplin Cooke's sons and grandsons, sometimes as a sea battle, sometimes as a melodrama. In one of those melodramas, the audience watched a fight between Indians and white settlers, heard the roar of water, the crackle of gunfire and the blasts of explosions, as dams were dynamited and dwellings, hills, and mills were swept away. Only a few circus directors tried to copy the Cookes by offering aquatic presentations, but the hippodramatic spectacle was continued with constantly more elaborate variations.

By the time the equestrian spectacle had been seated firmly in the saddle, and the clown had come of age, the entire scope of the circus as an institution had been immeasurably extended. Ducrow was directing Astley's. The Franconis were soaring high. Amphitheatres were opening in Germany. And across the Atlantic, a transplanted ring entertainment had taken root and begun to flourish, then died back, and given way to the true American circus.

10

Culver Service

Circus Comes

to America

THERE were, it seems, no jugglers or tightrope walkers on the *Mayflower,* but some descendants of mountebanks soon found their way to the new continent. The earliest report that has been unearthed, to date, tells of tight- and slack-rope walking in 1724 in the New Booth in an open area in Philadelphia known as Society Hill. The artists were a woman and a boy who came from abroad, and who apparently were not too skillful. It is 1780 when the next slack-wire performer is noted—a man named Templeman, who came to Philadelphia from England.

A Philadelphia Debut

Five years later, only fifteen years after Philip Astley set up his Amphitheatre Riding House in Halfpenny Hatch, the first establishment really resembling a circus was seen in America. This was in Philadelphia, where a dramatic company had given performances in 1749, and the first permanent theatre (curiously enough, called the Circus Theatre) was built on Walnut Street in 1766.

When, in 1785, Mr. Poole set up what has sometimes erroneously been called the first circus in America, he announced that he would be the "first American who ever exhibited feats of horsemanship on this continent." Perhaps he was the first American, but at least three Englishmen had been before him.

It is recorded that John Sharp, who arrived from England in 1771, gave exhibitions of riding in Salem, in the street near the burying ground, close by the almshouse. His pet stunts were to ride two horses, with one foot on each, and to control three horses galloping at full speed. In the same year, in Philadelphia, Mr. Foulkes showed his prowess on three horses. It was, however, Jacob Bates—he who made such a spectacular hit by his appearances before European crowned heads—who apparently impressed the Americans most deeply, and put on the most elaborate show. At the Bull's Head in Bowery Lane, New York, the spot where the Bowery Theatre was to be built a half century later, Bates in 1773 gave a performance that included *The Tailor's Ride to Brentford.* In November of the same year he appeared at Center Square in Philadelphia.

After Bates's tour, there was a hiatus brought about by a law passed by Congress in 1774 which forbade all theatrical entertainments and similar amusements. The law was not repealed until 1780, but once the path was cleared there was a swift acceptance of the new form of entertainment that had overwhelmed London and Paris.

Five years after the repeal, Mr. Poole set up his Philadelphia manège

*Van Amburgh's Triumphal Car passing the Astor House, April 20, 1846
—lithographed by N. Currier*

near the Center House and began to present the popular feats of riding one, two, and three horses. For a few months during the next year, he maintained a riding school in Boston. Mr. Poole owned three trained horses, and his program included a clown to "amaze" between the acts, and fireworks after the performance. In later programs, he paraphrased the doggerel Philip Astley had written, and worked it into a display number similar to the one Astley was using to show off his Little Military Learned Horse, Billy.

Thus Mr. Poole: "My horse lies dead apparent in your sight," and so on, concluding with, "Arise, now Billy; stop your sham and fun; Salute our *Nation's Hero, Washington*." Whereupon, of course, Billy rose and bowed.

At approximately the same time, there were other performers, English, French, Irish and Italian, in New York, Boston and Salem, and probably in Philadelphia. The stage was set for an established entertainment that would combine such skills in a single program.

George Washington Watched Him

John Bill Ricketts, an expert horseman, who had been a pupil of Hughes', arrived from Scotland in 1792 and at the southwest corner of 12th and Market streets, Philadelphia, built a structure that he opened formally on October 22. During that fall and winter, the place was used as a riding academy. The next year, on the same spot, Ricketts erected a

118

bigger and better building which would hold about 800. Doors opened at three o'clock, and exhibitions were given in daylight.

John Bill Ricketts opened the new building on April 3, 1793, to give what is now recognized as the first complete circus performance in America. He was assisted by his son Francis and another boy named Strobel, as equestrians, and by Mr. McDonald as clown. Before the season was over, he had added Signor Spinacuta, a tightrope walker, and Mme Spinacuta, a rider. Ricketts himself leapt over ten horses, danced a hornpipe on the saddle, and rode carrying a boy on his shoulders, in what was known as the *Flying Mercury,* an act that was to be a specialty for Andrew Ducrow at Astley's.

The Philadelphia Inquirer informed its readers that George Washington attended the first performance, which was given on the very day he issued his famous Proclamation of Neutrality. Later the paper ran an item to say that Washington had been present at the closing performance of the season, on July 22, when a benefit was given for Acadian refugees. It seems likely that Washington also attended the circus at other times, for he and Ricketts were good friends, and in the early mornings used to ride together out in the countryside.

Ricketts prospered. In 1794 he did so well that he established a fuel

fund for the city's poor, and today Bill Ricketts' money still helps the needy of Philadelphia. In the fall of 1794 the showman started to take his circus around the country, going first to New York, where he gave a winter season of equestrian performances with fireworks in some vacant lots on the west side of Broadway at Exchange Alley, near the Oyster Pasty, and then went on to Boston, where he appeared three times a week at the Amphitheatre. From New York the circus moved to other smaller communities.

Just what the Ricketts performances consisted of can be learned from the August 17, 1795, issue of the *Connecticut* (now the *Hartford*) *Courant,* which announced that the circus would be presented in Hartford on August 18, 20, and 22, down near the Connecticut River, a few rods south of the ferry landing. Obviously the lot was a temporary ring, set up in the open air.

There, says the advertisement, will be presented "Surprising Feats of Horsemanship," on one, two, and three horses. Assisting will be Mrs. Ricketts, Mr. F. Ricketts [John Bill's son, Francis], Master Long, and "Mr. Sully the Clown." Boxes were a dollar, and the "pitt" a half dollar, with tickets to be purchased at the circus, or at Messrs. Hudson and Goodwin's printing office.

Mr. J. B. Ricketts, it seems, was to make his appearance with a great display of mounting and dismounting techniques, at full speed, with and without a bridle, and to ride two horses at full gallop while he leapt over a cane backward and forward, and over a garter ten feet high. He would also ride a single horse, standing with his face toward the horse's tail, while he played with two oranges alternately in the air, throwing up an orange and catching it on the point of a fork.

Like Philip Astley himself, Mr. F. Ricketts would ride standing on his head on a galloping horse—though the pint pot is not mentioned. He was also to combine with Mr. Sully and Master Long in a great variety of feats of ability on the ground, *in the circus.* The word "circus" here was obviously used to designate the ring.

Mr. Sully, who had been a tumbler and singer at Sadler's Wells, seems to have been a popular figure. He gave the "Clown's Frolic between two horses," did a series of flip-flaps across the circus, and no doubt proved himself hilariously awkward and inept in *The Tailor's Ride to Brentford,* on a hunter and a road horse. Another feature of the performance was the "Two Flying Mercuries by Master Long, a child only five years of age, on J. B. Ricketts' shoulders, on two horses at full speed in the

Attitude of a Sweet little Cherub, who stands aloft, keeping watch for the Life of poor Jack."

During the month following the Hartford appearances, the circus reopened in New York, at the Broadway Amphitheatre, which had been undergoing alterations and acquiring additional scenery and machinery. Ricketts enlarged his program by putting in "ground and lofty tumbling," Signor Reano on the slack rope, and a song by Mr. Sully—"Four and Twenty Perriwigs," a parody on "Four and Twenty Fiddlers."

Meanwhile, a new headquarters was being built in Philadelphia at

Unloading the elephants

121

Sixth and Chestnut, which Ricketts named the Art Pantheon and Amphitheatre. There he opened on October 9, 1795. The building was circular, surmounted by a conical roof, and above its peak a "Flying Mercury" suggested the wonders within. The interior of the circus was horseshoe-shaped, and a ring occupied the pit in front of the stage, as in the Hughes' Royal Circus and in Astley's Royal Amphitheatre. Though the auditorium held between 1,200 and 1,400, it was crowded for the opening, which was in the evening.

Several pantomimes were included in the program, and the audience saw not only the customary performers, such as Signor Spinacuta, but others from London, including the Polander Dwarf or Warsaw Wonder, who darted through a blazing sun. John Bill outdid himself, somersaulting over the heads of thirty men and five horses with riders, riding two horses at full gallop, jumping twelve feet into the air to go over a garter, and controlling two galloping horses while standing on quart mugs affixed to the saddles. Sometimes he was carried on the shoulders of two riders, each on a separate horse.

On March 16, 1797, a new amphitheatre was opened on the east side of Greenwich Street, New York, which for that season and the next became Ricketts' headquarters in the city. At the same time, the circus made side trips as far as Albany; but Ricketts' luck was running out. He fell foul of the kind of disaster that was to ruin many a good circus man after him. In 1799, the Greenwich Street amphitheatre burned. On December 17, 1799, the Philadelphia amphitheatre was totally destroyed by fire.

There seem to be two versions of the cause of the fire in Philadelphia. One is that a drunken stagehand set it when he had to go into the loft over the stage with a lighted candle. The other has it that something went wrong while the pantomime *Don Juan,* in which stage effects called for a sea of flame, was being performed. At any rate, certain of the pious expressed their opinion that the fire was a judgment on the wicked entrepreneur. The $20,000 loss sent Ricketts into bankruptcy.

The Vessel Foundered

A benefit was given for him at Jaymond and Lailson's, a small French circus that had opened in Philadelphia two years before, and netted enough to buy him a ticket back to England. John Bill Ricketts embarked. The vessel foundered, and all on board were lost. His son Francis, who had stayed in this country, rode in circuses owned by other men, but never had one of his own.

122

The first circus in America had come and gone, a skyrocket blazing briefly and sinking into darkness. By its brief light, other foreign circuses and performers had found their way to these shores. Copies of Astley's, adaptations of Ricketts' sprang up here and there, though none of them had any prolonged success.

The time was near at hand, however, when America would develop its own indigenous circus.

11

Dever: Black Star

Elephants and Tents

A S AN institution, the American Circus is the perfect exemplification of the Yankee ability to take two bricks and a dream and build them into a skyscraper. There is probably no form of public presentation that has spawned more business genius and merchandising ingenuity, and brought forth more amazing personalities. In fact, its history is one of entertainment, transportation and advertising in the hands of men whose names still have a glamorous connotation for millions. Three characteristics distinguish it—mobility, the use of tents, and a love of elephants.

Of course circuses in other countries have always moved about somewhat, beginning with the one owned by Astley himself. As time has gone on, they have traveled increasingly. But in this country, ever since the early 1800's, they have always been wanderers, appearing in any given community usually once a year, for a few days at most. Once the tent had been used at all, it became as necessary a part of the American equipment as the horses, the tumblers, or the clowns themselves. As for the elephants—no American feels he has seen a real circus unless he has found in it at least a couple of elephants. They have been as much a part of the American circus as horses are to the English.

Elephants had been known in England, at the time of the Roman occupation of Britain. In the thirteenth century, Louis IX of France gave an elephant to Edward III; in the sixteenth, Henri IV sent one as a gift to Queen Elizabeth the First; in 1811, an elephant had been shown in a pantomime on the Covent Garden stage. In this country the animal was a stupefying novelty.

The very first elephant to reach these shores, so far as has yet been discovered, was an anonymous female who landed in New York on April 13, 1796. She was brought in by Captain John C. Crowninshield, and exhibited at various places for twelve and a half cents a look.

It is known that she was shown in York, Pennsylvania, in 1796, and in Newburyport, Massachusetts, and in Charleston, South Carolina, in 1797. Then there is a complete gap in the known records until April 2, 1806, when she appeared in Philadelphia in the yard of the George Tavern at Arch and Second Streets. In 1811, her owner showed her at Gettysburg, Pennsylvania, and thereafter the veil of silence falls. Obviously Captain Crowninshield's elephant toured up and down the eastern seaboard for at least fifteen years. So far as is known, however, she and her owner traveled alone, neither drawing to themselves nor joining any other entertainers.

125

Old Bet and Hachaliah

The movement that resulted in the mobile, tenting circus in this country really began with another elephant, named Old Bet. In the year 1815, Hachaliah (*sic*) Bailey of Somers, New York, bought an elephant. She was an African female called Old Bet, and he paid $1,000 for her to a sea captain who is supposed to have got her at auction in London for $20. The sea captain was probably Hachaliah's brother. History does not record what their relations were, after that little deal.

At the time Hachaliah Bailey bought Old Bet, he was living in New York City, where he was proprietor of the Old Bull Head Tavern at 23rd Street and Third Avenue. He put the animal onto a sloop and took her up the river to Sing Sing (now Ossining), and thence on foot to Somers. Using that town as headquarters, he toured the countryside. For a number of years, he and his charge went from town to town at night, traveling in the dark, probably in order to guard her from the eyes of the curious, who would not pay to see what they could snatch a look at for nothing. In the daytime, he exhibited her in barns and tavern yards.

The venture was an astonishingly lucrative one. Hachaliah made enough money to share; so for part of the time he either leased the elephant or took in as partners Nathan Howes and Aron (*sic*) Turner. Even

126

on part of the proceeds, Bailey did so well financially that he built a cara-vansery in Somers—a three-storied building of brick—which he called the Elephant Hotel. He opened the place with a grand banquet and ball in 1823, and four years later immortalized Old Bet by putting a granite shaft out in front, with a carved wooden elephant on top. The Elephant Hotel was on the main highway, and did a thriving business. After stand-ing there for more than a hundred years, in 1931 it became the Somers Town House. The monument to Old Bet still may be seen in front. Hacha-liah Bailey died in 1845, aged seventy, of a kick from a horse.

Only about five years after the opening of the hotel that Old Bet had helped build, she herself fell victim to the righteous wrath of certain New England villagers who still respected the Blue Laws, and thought that showing an elephant was almost as bad as going to the theatre. As she was being led into their town before daylight, they waylaid the party and fired a half-dozen shots that killed the offending beast.

"Witchcraft and Sorcery"

If it seems incredible that such bigotry should have lingered on into the nineteenth century, note an editorial in the *Weekly Recorder* of Chilli-cothe, Ohio, for August 2, 1815:

The principle object pursued by the conductors of the Circus is to enrich themselves at the expense of others. How far they have succeeded in their design in this place—what number of citizens have honoured them with their presence and favoured them with their support, we have not been particularly informed.

Believing that these men are prosecuting an unlawful calling—one that cannot be defended on Scriptural grounds, or on principles of sound reason and good policy, we presume the good sense of the citizens in general would lead them to treat their exhibitions with that unqualified neglect and contempt which they so justly deserve.

The good citizens of Sunbury, Pennsylvania, went somewhat farther. As the result of a performance there on August 19, 1829, six members of the circus company were individually charged with witchcraft. The bill accusing them said that they possessed

power of witchcraft, conjuration, enchantment and sorcery and being more-over persons of evil and depraved dispositions, and as magical characters having private conferences with the spirit of darkness, did . . . expose to the view of diverse and many people of this Commonwealth various feats, acts, deeds, exhibitions and performances of magic and witchcraft, such as:

Grand parade by the whole stud of horses; Young America hanging from his Horse; Leaping over a Horse through hoops, over Garters, and through a Barrel; Roman attitudes; Comic Still Dance, wherein the cloven Foot was palpably displayed; Flying by the Whole Company; Master Bacon riding upon his Head instead of his Seat of Honour; wonderful Somerset from a Horse at Full Speed by Mr. Downie; Dropping from the Rope and Coming to Life, to the Great Mortification of the Bystanders; . . . Officer and Recruit, or Double Transformation; Flip Flaps and Cobbler's Frolic, to the evil example of all kindred spirits, for the Promulgation of the Infernal Arts, to the General Scandal and Delusion of the Human Species—to the Evil Example of all others, in like case offending and against the peace and dignity of the Commonwealth of Pennsylvania.

The Sunbury protest would almost seem a publicity stunt such as Barnum himself might have thought up, if it were not for the records. These tell us that the Northumberland County jury ignored the bill, the circus folk were freed, and the county was directed to pay costs.

Such antagonism sometimes had more tragic results. In 1831, one Jim Bancker was charged with witchcraft and lawbreaking when he was performing in a small western town. As he was on the verge of arrest, he departed hurriedly. It was a rainy night and he lost his way, wandered around the countryside, was not found for two days, and died of pneumonia.

While circus performers in the British tradition were coping with these vicissitudes, the indigenous American circus was getting under way.

Cradle of the Circus

When circus addicts speak of the Cradle of the American Circus, they mean an area of about 20 square miles just north of New York City, on both sides of the line dividing New York from Connecticut, and thus in Westchester, Putnam, and Dutchess counties, New York, and Fairfield, Connecticut, all not far from the Hudson River. For many, many years, innumerable small industries and services connected with the circus helped nourish that whole region. Animals were bred and trained there. Acts were prepared and rehearsed. Tents, wagons, seats, and all sorts of small paraphernalia were built. Capital from cities and towns of the area controlled many of the larger shows. From the Cradle or nearby came scores of men famous in various aspects of the circus. Among them were Barnum, who was born in Bethel, three miles from Danbury, and lived much of his life in Bridgeport; Seth B. Howes, who became the wealthiest and most successful circus man of his time; Nathan Howes, another early promoter; and Elbert and Egbert Howes, Nathan's twin sons, who helped establish Howes' Great London Circus, one of the largest ever on the road. It was not until John Ringling took Ringling Brothers and Barnum & Bailey away from Bridgeport in 1927, to establish winter quarters in Sarasota, Florida, that the center of circus activity shifted from its earliest setting.

The American circus did not begin as an entity encompassing all the major features we think of as circus. Although for nearly a hundred years, anyone who has said "American circus" has meant a show made up of both ring acts and menagerie under tent, the two parts were not always inseparable. Both of them, however, did get their start in those four counties near New York.

The idea of exhibiting traveling groups of animals in America originated there. Even before Old Bet died, Bailey had added some other animals to his exhibit; and when Nathan Howes of Southeast, in Putnam County, leased the concession he enlarged the show, taking it on tour through the northeastern states with immense success.

Obviously animals could not be exhibited outdoors during a northern winter, and the problem of what to do with them for several months of each year became a pressing one. Three capitalists of North Salem, just northeast of Somers in Westchester County—John J. June, Lewis B. Titus, and Caleb Sutton Angevine—formed a touring menagerie combine. At first, during cold weather, they had to put the animals into country barns and cellars; but that was unsatisfactory in many ways. There-

Raising the tent

Nettie, "the champion leaping horse of the World"—one of the chief attractions of W. C. Coup's "New Show"

fore, in 1821, they established headquarters at 37 Bowery, New York, where in winter they could not only keep the animals but exhibit them. In warm weather they either leased them to other entrepreneurs, or went on the road themselves. Thus, on the Bowery, was born the scheme of showing odd and interesting creatures in permanent museums—a scheme that was to become a fine art with Barnum, on Broadway.

Traveling Curiosities

Not many years after the Bowery headquarters began to function, Messrs. Raymond and Waring set up another animal business, establishing an enterprise that was to be carried on with much success for thirty years.

As a traveling affair, the exhibition of curiosities of one kind or another probably had been going on in this country for a long time. On November 14, 1816, the *Boston Gazette* carried an advertisement for the last chance to see the MUMMY. "This week only," says the notice. "This extraordinarily preserved Human Body, which has excited the wonder, and gratified the curiosity of Philosophers and Antiquarians, will continue open for Exhibition during THIS WEEK, and no longer at No. 3, Cornhill-square (up stairs) from 9 A.M. to 9 P.M. Admittance 25 cents." Live animals were a much better drawing card than mummified remains or similar curiosities, and taking wild creatures around, to show them in one place after another, very soon became big business.

On January 14, 1835, several menagerie exhibitors and caravan companies—almost all of them from the region just north of New York City —got together and drew up a document forming "one joint stock company for the purpose of exhibiting wild animals belonging to them in company or copartnership for profit." The resultant organization was called the Zoological Institute. More than 125 men signed the agreement. Among the companies represented were such combines as June, Titus and Angevine, Raymond and Ogden, Lewis Bailey & Co., Purdy, Welch &

Co., G. R. and W. Howe, Jr., and Berry and Waring, and among the individuals such men as Seth B. Howes and Aron Turner. The menageries and other equipment were valued at $329,325.00 (a tremendous amount in the early nineteenth century) and the capital was divided into $100 shares. Almost all those who invested in the stock also lived in or near the strategic twenty-mile area.

To keep from antagonizing bluestockings, the Zoological Institute was advertised as scientific and educational, but even that did not protect its beasts, for two elephants were killed, and other animals were either shot or poisoned by fanatics. However, the project immediately began to pay enormous dividends. Expensive expeditions were now sent out to Asia and Africa, the Polar regions, and South America.

Among the earliest acquisitions they brought back were a rhinoceros, a hippopotamus, and a giraffe. Then came seals, whales, and all kinds of other odd sea creatures. It was not long until a lively market sprang up also in fakes, such as small sharks and whales made of leather, and "mermaids" and sea monsters concocted of whatever gave an appearance of authenticity.

By the middle of the century, the country was familiar with traveling exhibits under such names as the American National Caravan, the Animals of the Scriptures, the Association's Menagerie and Aviary, and Van Amburgh's and Driesbach's Trained Animal Exhibits. In the meantime, however, many things had been happening to the ring acts.

The Show Goes Under Canvas

Apparently Aron Turner not only was interested in animals but was a fan of the circus as it was then presented. He began to back performers who did trick riding, tumbled, vaulted, gave pantomimic entertainments, and beguiled with buffoonery.

Up to that time, circus acts here had been presented either indoors in more or less permanent buildings, or in the open air, with, at most, a fence or a temporary enclosure of canvas "siding" for protection and seclusion. Rain and hot sun were almost as much of a hazard for both audience and performers in summer as snow and ice had been for the animals in winter. Aron Turner, who was of an inventive mind, turned his attention to a solution of the problem. In 1830, he took his show out under a tent. It was a round tent, 90 feet in diameter—the first complete round-top tent ever used. With that achievement, the Danbury man established the future character of the American circus, and changed the whole course of its history.

12

Kirk Stephens: Black Star

The Flatfoots

HE BRAND of Yankee shrewdness and ruthlessness exhibited by such men as June, Titus, and Angevine, and later by their associates and business heirs, won for them the unflattering appellation of "Flatfoots." Numbered among the Flatfoots were many early investors in the Zoological Institute, who through an initial interest in traveling animals became involved in promotion of shows featuring ring acts, and participated in whatever combinations of public entertainment grew out of either type of enterprise. Sometimes these men actually operated shows; sometimes they merely put up money to finance them; but in either event theirs was the whip hand. The name "Flatfoot" is supposed to have come from their habit of accompanying the announcement of an intention to do this, or not to do that, with the incontrovertible statement, "I put my foot down flat!"

The fact that a comparatively few powerful men invested their money in innumerable shows, often maintaining anonymity behind show titles and unimportant front men, is one of the factors that make the American circus picture from 1820 to 1880 increasingly complex and difficult to define. For about sixty years, the Flatfoots imported, leased and sold animals, and managed circuses and menageries in their own names and those of others, bought in, sold out, lent money, foreclosed, and generally took advantage of the main chance, whatever it might be.

Sitting behind their desks hundreds of miles from actual operations, they could route shows into town ahead of their rivals, cut prices, spread slanderous tales about competitors, hire ruffians to intimidate them, cut down trees and burn bridges to delay rival companies, and otherwise exert an influence that was effective though largely covert.

Flatfootery can be said to have begun when Messrs. June, Titus, and Angevine, with Gerard Crane, first set out to exhibit birds and large and small wild animals in buildings and enclosures. Their operations very soon extended to the circus. In the beginning, Flatfoot activities were confined fairly closely to the Westchester-Fairfield area, but it was no time at all before Flatfoot shows were traveling all over the East and Middle West, and up into Canada. The peculiar combination of money, enthusiasm, and know-how that the promoters represented continued through various combinations, with the last important unit being made up of John J. Nathans, Lewis June (John J.'s nephew), Avery J. Smith, and George F. Bailey (a nephew of Hachaliah's).

George Bailey is a typical example. He was born in North Salem in 1818, and started as an employee of the Flatfoots, then joined Aron

Turner's circus, and married Turner's daughter. Gradually he took over the management, mounting the ladder steadily until he became a full-fledged partner in the combine. By 1858, Bailey and his associates had three circuses on the road—Sands and Nathans', George F. Bailey and Company's and the G. N. Eldred. When Bailey retired in 1880 (bowing out before the rapid ascendancy of the great Barnum and Bailey star), he was a very rich man.

During this period the circus and menagerie made tentative moves toward combining, moving gradually toward a more complex form that was to become the characteristic type of American tent entertainment.

According to W. C. Coup, who came into prominence as a manager in the 1860's, the circus and menagerie were originally set up as separate entities because more money could be made by that system. The menagerie was shown in the daytime, the circus at night, with separate admission tickets. Moreover, although circus acts were obviously spawned by the devil, thus suitable only for weekday presentation, the godly had collected animals ever since Noah, and it could be no sin to show them on Sunday. The first time a circus and menagerie were shown together, Coup says in his memoirs, *Sawdust and Spangles,* was in 1851, when George F. Bailey persuaded his father-in-law, Aron Turner, to buy six cages of animals from Titus and Company, and added those and several elephants to his arena show.

The Stupendous Camelopard

The original Flatfoots were the first to import jungle animals into this country on an organized basis. They had sent out an expedition to the great Kalahari Desert of Africa in 1835, under the direction of Stebbins June, which returned at the end of two years with numerous animals, including "the Stupendous Giraffe or Camelopard," first to be seen in this country. Doubtless its day was brief, for it was to be a long time before one of those fragile creatures could survive in this country for as much as two years. Thereafter, until the Civil War, expeditions to procure strange beasts became more and more commonplace.

Another of the important early touring menageries was the one owned by Colonel Joseph Cushing (1818–1884). Cushing was born in Dover, New Hampshire, and in his teens went to Gloucester, Massachusetts, to work in a fish market. When the circus came to town, young Joe followed the show, as thousands of boys were to do after him. He was a shrewd youth, and soon was able to buy the lemonade and candy concession (a

134

type of money-making scheme that apparently began to function almost as soon as the first tent went up), and then acquired the side show. Finally, Cushing became owner of the show, and in a few years had built it up into one with forty wagons, which for a number of seasons toured the eastern United States and Canada.

While this expansion was going on, two American performers directly sponsored by the early Flatfoots had already begun to achieve international reputations.

The Lion Tamer Met Victoria

As late as the end of the nineteenth century, people still sang about a man who "sticks his head in the lion's mouth and leaves it there a while; and when he takes it out again he greets you with a smile," as the band begins to play, and the boys around the monkey's cage had better keep away. The hero of that ditty was Isaac A. Van Amburgh. He was born March 11, 1801, in Fishkill, Dutchess County, New York, descended from one of the oldest families in that part of the country. Very little is known about his early life, except that he had a great interest in natural history. Legend has it that, at nineteen, when he was reading the Scriptures and came on Daniel in the Lion's Den, he decided to be a lion trainer—or "tamer." At any rate, Van Amburgh's first experiment in aping Daniel came at the Zoological Institute, when the animals were being exhibited on the Bowery. The young man walked into the cage, confronted a group of fearsome animals, controlled them with apparent ease, and brought forth thunderous applause. Immediately he became the talk of the town.

By the time he was twenty-three, Van Amburgh was traveling with a menagerie that bore his name, though it is possible that he was set up in business by the Flatfoots. Among his animals was an elephant named Hannibal, one of the largest ever seen in the United States at any time. With his show, Van Amburgh successfully visited major cities and towns, but this country offered insufficient scope, and in 1838 he took his show to England.

The young queen, Victoria, who was very fond of theatre and the circus, was fascinated by Van Amburgh's display. At the close of her first visit to the show she went on the stage to see the animals fed, and was so interested that she issued orders for a command performance at Drury Lane on January 29, 1839, with full court regalia. At the command event, after she left the royal box, Victoria talked for some minutes with Van Amburgh, thus publicly setting on him the seal of her approval. Receipts for the evening were 712 pounds, 17 shillings, and sixpence—the largest amount that establishment had ever taken in for a performance. Thereafter, the Queen watched the show six times in as many weeks. Such notables as the Duke of Wellington and the Marquis of Anglesea went back again and again.

Until his death, the public of both hemispheres looked on Isaac Van Amburgh as the "greatest lion tamer in the world." Incidentally, a report of his death was circulated in 1859, but the correct date appears to be 1865. On the basis of his own heralds, it seems certain that he was alive at least three years after that report was spread abroad. In a herald dated April 3, 1862, we read that he "stands before the world the confessed and acknowledged Prince of Showmen. . . . Recently, while absent in foreign countries, collecting animals for his menagerie, various reports of his death were circulated, but permit me to inform you that Van Amburgh still lives, and will visit with the Menagerie the place of exhibition mentioned on this bill below, and bear living testimony that he is not dead."

This is the word of Hyatt Frost, from whom comes the broad record of Van Amburgh's activities, and to whom he left his interests. After Van Amburgh's actual death, Frost became manager, but the great name went on. The interests Frost acquired were immense. By the mid-1840's, in addition to his American projects, Van Amburgh already owned the largest wagon show in England, and was leasing many animals to other menageries and zoos here and in Europe. By the time he died, his interests were even more extensive.

Hyatt Frost was black-bearded and piratical-looking. He had been born in Putnam County, New York, in 1827, and joined Van Amburgh in 1846. Originally he went ahead in a buggy to "bill" the show. Often he would find that his employer was in competition with bigger companies, which had arrived in town ahead of him and were passing out printed matter calling attention to their own magnificent enterprises, contrasting them with the picayune offerings of that upstart Van Amburgh. The story goes that Frost struck back by manufacturing a completely fictitious familiarity with the town and its people, asking about his "old friend" So-and-So and those others he used to know years ago. He is supposed to have prepared himself by surreptitiously investigating headstones in the local cemetery!

He carried on the business, under the Van Amburgh name, until nearly twenty years after his associate's death. Frost's final venture was with the Reiche Brothers, German importers of animals, with whom he or-

136

The side show has always drawn huge crowds of curiosity seekers

ganized a menagerie and circus that toured in 1885. After that venture, Frost retired, and lived in Amenia, New York, until he died in 1895.

Very few of Frost's early bills remain, because small organizations had their announcements printed locally, for local distribution, and immediately thereafter they went out of print and circulation. In one of his couriers (a kind of program somewhat more permanent than the usual herald) which has survived, Hyatt Frost opens with a tirade against the state where licenses are expensive, thus "rendering knowledge the manacled slave of gold." Moreover, he continues, "the proprietors of this Institute . . . many years ago commenced a work, which has been attended by the outlay of immense sums of money, unequalled risks, and a thousand scenes of personal peril and danger. To accomplish their designs, they have visited and traversed the burning sands of Africa, the wilds of inland Europe, the pampas of South America, and the forests and mountains and regions of eternal snow of the northern border of this continent," bringing "proof undeniable and impregnable of almighty wisdom."

Modern animal trainers who disapprove of Van Amburgh's methods and manners might agree that his animals gave proof of Almighty wisdom, but they would scarcely admit that the trainer did, though at this distance in time it is of course impossible to say just how much of Van Amburgh's vaunted cruelty was real and how much was showmanship.

Hyatt Frost, Van Amburgh's associate, let it be known that when Queen Victoria saw the lions fed they had been starved for thirty-six hours, and that when Van Amburgh was putting them through their paces they were so hungry that he literally had to lash them "into the most abject and crouching submission." It seems doubtful that any trainer would have starved valuable animals, but there is no doubt that in the cage Van Amburgh threatened them violently, at least appeared to be lashing them with the whip, deliberately created an atmosphere of noise, excitement, and cruelty designed to make the beasts act as savage and ferocious as possible.

The same year that Victoria first saw him, he made his debut in Paris in *The Daughter of the Emir,* in which he acted the part of an Arab who saved a little princess thrown to the savage beasts. The princess was hurled into the pit. The blond, athletic young man appeared among the lions, tigers, and leopards, seized her in his arms, and carried her out of danger. Among other tricks he performed were opening a lion's mouth, making tigers and leopards jump when he brandished his whip, and finally forcing them to approach and lick his boots as a sign of submissive obedience.

After Van Amburgh, the second American to achieve reputation in England was Richard Sands, born in 1814, no one knows where, of British ancestry, who in 1831 went out with Aron Turner's circus as a clown and general performer. Two years later, Sands left Turner and joined Nathan Howes, to remain with him for several years. Nathan Howes' young brother, Seth, ran the show, and Uncle Nate himself went on ahead to announce that something stupendous was on the way. In summer, the company toured in wagons; in winter, played a number of indoor stands, including Boston, Albany, Philadelphia, Baltimore, and Charleston—very much the same sort of route that Captain Crowenshield had taken with his anonymous elephant. Headquarters was in the old Richmond Hill Building in New York City. With Seth Howes, one of the most famous of the Flatfoots, Sands received training not only as a performer but as a manager—two fields in which he was to shine.

Seth Howes, who has been called "Father of the American Circus," was a close-mouthed, astute businessman, who was born in 1815 and lived to be eighty-six. When he retired in 1870 his fortune was estimated at twenty millions, and he had the reputation of being the richest circus man of his time in America.

At first he worked as equestrian director in Flatfoot shows, but soon demonstrated his remarkable aptitude for management. He saved more than one near-bankrupt circus and at one point had great success touring with a museum and menagerie for which Barnum let him use the great name.

Seth Howes took Joseph Cushing into partnership in 1856, and carried a hand-picked show to England, where it stayed for seven years. When in 1858 that circus responded to Victoria's command for a performance at the Royal Alhambra, it included a number of performers who were to become exceptionally famous. Among them were John H. Murray as equestrian director and Joe Pentland as clown. The Queen was so delighted with the company that she gave Howes and Cushing a purse of 500 pounds.

Sands left the Howes show in 1838, and went as a performer with the Miller and Yates Great American Circus, which almost immediately became Miller, Yates and Sands. After various other reorganizations, Howes and Sands traveled farther west for four years. That venture was at first uncomfortably primitive, for the circus moved around in good

Ralph A. Brant: Black Star

The parade of the Carl Hagenbeck Greater Shows through Canton, Illinois, August 23, 1906.

weather and in winter holed up wherever it could—in warehouses with little or no heat, or in barns. After a while, the company built its own home locations.

In 1840 Sands joined a combination made up of the same old Flatfoot trio—June, Titus, and Angevine—with General Welch. The company played in the most populous cities in the eastern part of the country, and in winters filled long engagements in theatres. Lewis B. Lent, who came from Hachaliah's home town, was hired as business manager, and very soon there was another reshuffling of names and responsibilities.

In 1842, Richard Sands and Lewis Lent, backed by L. B. Titus, made a landmark in American circus history by taking their equestrian show to Great Britain, and proving that they were at least as good as those performers who were direct descendants of Philip Astley. For three years Sands drew thunderous applause from English audiences, who favorably compared his riding with that of Astley and Ducrow.

England had already brought a circus to this country. In 1836, Thomas Taplin Cooke had invaded the Western Hemisphere, coming to the United States with 130 performers (many of them Cookes), 42 horses, 14 ponies, and numerous servants and helpers. Soon after his arrival, he built an amphitheatre in New York, seating 2,000, and proceeded to cap-

140

ture the American public. When fire destroyed that amphitheatre and everything except the horses was lost, Cooke gathered himself together and started on the road, while another amphitheatre was being constructed for him in Baltimore. Not long after he opened in Baltimore, his new building there burned too, with the loss of all the horses. Then, as circus proprietors had already done before him and will doubtless do until the circus is no more—he picked up the pieces and tried again.

Despite his courage and pertinacity, however, bad luck pursued him until, overcome by homesickness, he went back to England, where he took part in hippodramatic spectacles until he died at eighty-four. In this country he left a stimulating tradition and a son and daughter. The daughter was to become mother of one of the great figures in the American field, and the son, also Thomas, was to stay in circuses in the United States until he died in 1897, at the age of ninety-six.

During the next half-dozen years after Sands and Lent returned from England, they played from New York to New Orleans, with months of tenting in the summers, and had few serious rivals. The menagerie was becoming a more and more inevitable part of any circus, and their old posters indicate that their show carried four elephants, twelve camels, many horses and ponies, and mules trained for riding acts.

Richard Sands' name has a prominent place in the history of circus promotion, for he invented a new kind of poster—the first ever to be printed in color—made of rag paper, and intended to be used over and over.

After the London trip, in 1852, Sands, Seth B. Howes, and Henri Franconi built a large hippodrome in New York, at Broadway and 23rd Street, and on May 2, 1853, the building was opened with an equestrian performance by the Franconis from Paris. Interchange of talents across the ocean was in full swing. Capital put up by Sands, Seth Howes, Avery Smith, and probably other Flatfoots, brought from Europe the best acts obtainable there. The promoters made money in the cities and lost it on the road, but the intake must have more than compensated for the outgo, because the field of travel was continually enlarged.

In Havana in 1861, Richard Sands and a number of his company died of yellow fever. For two more years, the show continued as Sands and Nathans'. Then Nathans retired to devote himself to other interests, and the name of Sands passed into obscurity. There are some names, however, that will blaze in colored lights as long as written history remains, or as folklore exists. One of them is Barnum.

13

Harold M. Lambert: Frederic Lewis

Barnum Runs a Side Show

NE OF the strangest anomalies in the entire annals of the ring entertainment is that Phineas Taylor Barnum, whose life in show business covered more than a half century, was a circus man for only twenty years.

Ask anyone what name most immediately suggests the circus, and the chances are ten to one the answer will be "Barnum." Yet Barnum had virtually nothing to do with the true circus until he was sixty years old, and then his contribution was chiefly that of promoter. He depended on others to take care of the practical matters of management, while he acted as idea man.

The establishment in New York to which he gave approximately thirty years was known as a museum, but was actually a glorified side show. Astley's and other early circuses had had a few freaks. A waning interest in monsters lingered on in nineteenth-century England from Renaissance times, but a far more intense enthusiasm for oddities developed in the United States. For nearly a hundred years, the side show, as an institution, has been an almost indispensable adjunct to the American circus.

During the twentieth century, the interest has somewhat diminished, probably because of increasing familiarity and more general understanding of the scientific causes of physical abnormalities. When a giant or a midget is known to be the result of malfunctioning of the pituitary gland, a good part of the excitement of seeing one is gone. There are, however, still side-show tents alongside the big top, catering to much the same curiosity as that aroused and assuaged by Barnum in his American Museum.

Barnum: The Skyrocket

From its earliest days, the circus in this country has fostered peculiarly dramatic personalities. Barnum was the most dramatic of them all. The circus has also created geniuses who worked more or less behind the scenes. Barnum was associated late in life with two such geniuses—W. C. Coup and James Anthony Bailey—who were content to leave the fireworks to him. Barnum was the skyrocket, the roman candle, the cannon cracker, that enlivened the action they organized and the scenes they created.

It was inevitable that innumerable legends should grow up around the name of P. T. Barnum. He was always a figure larger than life, whose natural element was the bizarre. Some of the legends are exaggeratedly commendatory. Most of them are equally disparaging or even damning. One of the most unfortunate is that he was a trickster, a perpetual liar, and an unscrupulous cheat who perpetrated a series of clever deceptions on a public he looked on as fools. As late as 1955, an article in a national magazine bore the caption, "How Barnum Took the Suckers."

There is no lack of available material on his life, methods, and convictions. In 1855, he published a long and detailed autobiography. It underwent numerous revisions, the first in 1869, and after that date an appendix was added each year. In all, a least a half-million copies were sold. Barnum's contemporaries wrote voluminously about him. There have been plays and fictionized versions of his life. Despite all that, the man himself remains an enigma.

One thing is certain, he was one of the most remarkable promoters of all time. By instinct, Barnum established rules of thumb that advertising men have followed ever since. Long before the layman ever heard the word psychology, Barnum knew that in order to attract public attention you have to arouse curiosity, and that there is no more effective appeal to curiosity than through the strange and bizarre. He understood the value of repeating a phrase, a slogan, a method, an idea. He recognized the importance of association. He discovered that, when you are trying to draw public attention to something new or obscure, any publicity is better than none. But he also realized that the public must get its money's worth, in some manner at least, even if not exactly in the expected way. He also established the all-too-popular thesis that if a thing is bigger it is necessarily better.

Although Barnum's name is traditionally associated with the cynical epigram "There's a sucker born every minute," the chances are he never said it. On the other hand, there are those who believe that he invented the adage usually attributed to Lincoln: "You can fool all of the people some of the time. . . ."

To be sure, P. T. Barnum called himself a "humbug," by which he seems to have meant a practical joker, and he often used the same expression for the jokes themselves. The dictionary says a humbug is "an imposition under fair pretenses." Barnum would have contended that, except for two or three instances, of which he was far from proud, the pretenses surrounding his practical jokes were always fair. The majority of his contemporaries seem to have agreed with him.

The practical joke has had no more prolific expression than around the cracker barrel and spittoon in early New England, and it was there that Barnum had his initiation.

Phineas Taylor Barnum was born in Bethel, Connecticut, on July 5, 1810, into a family of small means and few pretensions. His father, Philo, was an ineffectual rolling stone, who was never able to give his family more than the barest necessities. The boy had to turn his hand to earning pennies at a very early age, and his brief schooling was interrupted by work on his father's farm and all kinds of odd jobs. From the time he was twelve until he was fifteen, he sold lottery tickets (then legal) to workmen in the hat and comb factories in and around Danbury. Even then, his precocious advertising ingenuity emerged in the use of big gold signs and posters, in writing doggerel, and in putting on oyster suppers after the lottery drawing.

In 1825, Philo died insolvent, after borrowing all the money his son had saved up. The next step for the boy was clerking in a store in Grassy Plains, a village not far from Bethel. There he saved enough to take a flier by opening a porterhouse in Brooklyn. The new project prospered moderately, and he was able to go often to the theatre, acquiring a love of the amusement world that was never to leave him.

Grandfather Phineas Taylor, for whom he had been named, wrote asking him to come home and open a store. So Phineas went back, invested his whole capital of $120 in a fruit and provision store in Bethel, and on the side took to selling lottery tickets again. He had forgiven his grandfather for a rather cruel practical joke. For years, the old man had held out the prospect of a lordly inheritance, a piece of ground he called Ivy Island. Then one day he took the boy out and showed it to him. It was a swamp covered with ivy.

Perhaps it was from Phineas Taylor that Phineas Barnum inherited his own love of practical jokes, but it was in the country store in Bethel that he learned the techniques of perpetrating them. There, too, he met no less a person than Hachaliah Bailey, who told stories of experiences with Old Bet and of operating steamboats on the Hudson. One of Hachaliah's favorite witticisms, it is reported, was to say that he had sold a half interest in the elephant, but things were not going so well since that, and he guessed he would shoot his half of her.

In 1829, Phineas married Charity Hallett, an attractive young "tailoress." For the next few months, in addition to his lottery business, he published a paper he called the *Herald of Freedom*. Even in those days of slanderous recrimination, he was too outspoken to avoid libel suits, and one of them landed him in jail for sixty days. When he got out, his friends put on a celebration that must have warmed the cockles of his showman's heart. Speeches were made, and an especially composed ode was sung in the courtroom. Dinner was served for several hundred friends and admirers. A parade of forty horsemen, with a marshal carrying the American flag, followed by a band and P. T. Barnum in a coach, traversed the three miles to Bethel and returned to Danbury.

Barnum was a remarkable mathematician, but he hated picayune bookkeeping. Disgusted with petty returns and unpaid accounts, and yearning for broader fields, he sold his store and took his wife and baby to New York. He had almost no money but was full of energy and self-confidence. He was twenty-four years old.

It was not a propitious time. In December, 1835, the city was almost destroyed by a fire that raged for three days, and unprecedented hard times followed. The only work to be found was selling workmen's caps, and the Barnums were desperately poor. However, when things looked blackest, several hundred dollars came in unexpectedly from debtors in Bethel, and the young couple opened a boarding house on Frankfort Street, where they did a thriving business. Later, they bought into a grocery store. The outlook was more encouraging, but the small-town boy in the great city was still looking for his true *métier*.

A Hoax and a Gamble

He heard about a Negress named Joice Heth, who was being shown in Philadelphia. She was said to be a hundred and sixty-one years old, and to have been George Washington's nurse. Barnum went to see her, bought her for $1,000—$500 of which he borrowed—and took her back to New York to exhibit. Receipts grossed $1,500 a week, and after a while he took the old woman on tour. Phineas Taylor Barnum had found his life interest.

The affair of Joice Heth is one of the comparatively few actual frauds with which Barnum can be charged. At the time, there was a great deal of controversy concerning her age, and when the old woman died within the year the autopsy proved that she was not much more than eighty. It is hard to imagine that even a young man from the country could have been quite so naïf as to think the woman could have reached the age that had been claimed for her. Yet, he says, he believed that the papers he got with her were genuine, and she was so crippled and helpless that she might have been any age at all. At any rate, he was attacked savagely about the hoax, often by the very newspapers that had heralded the old woman as a true phenomenon. Later he wrote that "the newspaper

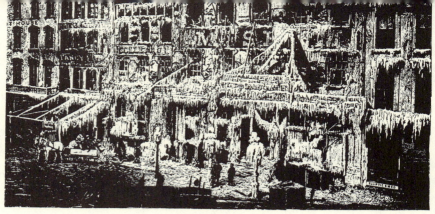

The destruction of Barnum's American Museum, between
Prince and Spring Streets in New York City, March 3, 1868

and social controversy on the subject" served his purpose as a showman by "keeping my name before the public." He had had a taste of notoriety, and from that day never lost his need for the drug.

In 1836, after a brief and unsuccessful tour with an Indian juggler he called Vivalla, Barnum met Aron Turner, and had his first close contact with a real traveling show and an opportunity to study the early type of entrepreneur. Acting as ticket seller, secretary and treasurer of Turner's company, he traveled with it, receiving $30 a month plus 20 per cent of the net profits. The program included a blackface comedy role which Barnum took over, including singing and dancing, when the Negro quit without notice.

When the company disbanded, Barnum bought a little equipment and went out with his own show, which was of a similar type. To the company, composed of a ventriloquist, a sleight-of-hand performer, a comic named Joe Pentland, to be known to posterity as the first great American clown, and himself as Negro singer and dancer, he gave the resounding name of Barnum's Grand Scientific and Musical Theatre. It lasted only a few months, but taught him a great deal.

After Barnum gave up the show and went back to New York, he invested $2,500 in the business of a German manufacturer of waterproof blacking, cologne, and bear's grease, who soon disappeared with the money. Not long afterward, Jack Diamond, a Negro dancer whom he had taken on tour, absconded in New Orleans with the cashbox. Despite these

147

and innumerable other experiences of human cupidity and dishonesty, Barnum was an old man before he could accept the fact that it is dangerous to be too trustful. "I hope," he wrote, "I shall never so entirely lose confidence in human nature as to consider every man a scamp by instinct, or a rogue by necessity."

In 1841, having tried numerous roads to success, usually ending in failure, Barnum took the gamble that was to make him famous. By using every cent he had in the world, borrowing all he could (putting up as collateral his grandfather's joke, Ivy Island), and taking advantage of every possible device to play the owners one against another, Barnum bought the thirty-two-year-old Scudder's American Museum on Broadway and Ann Street in New York. He himself said he bought it with brass. Promptly, of course, it became Barnum's American Museum. Although he is known to our world as a circus man, for thirty years he was first of all the owner of that extraordinary institution.

There, you could see almost everything that ever was, and a few things that never were. For the museum, Barnum created his most original promotion schemes, devised some of his most spectacular advertising, and set up exhibits and activities that occasionally fooled, and always delighted, millions of customers.

Many of the advertising stunts familiar today were invented by Barnum. He sold at auction the tickets for Jenny Lind's first concert, and thus created the original ticket scalpers in the city. He put on baby shows and contests, dog shows, poultry shows and flower shows, with prizes in numerous categories.

Though perhaps he did not start the ball of exaggerated terminology rolling down through the century, Barnum was of course a pioneer in the creation of "circus language." He reveled in etymological distortions, and heterogeneous, multilingual atrocities such as echo even today in the pallid enormities of beautician, lubritorium and their ilk. In his early handbills and advertisements, there seem to be comparatively few of them, except hippotheatron, hippodromical and elephantus-hippo-paradoxus, but he helped to establish a mode.

During the later years, when American circus promoters were crying their wares in extravagant superlatives and magnified misrepresentations, there were to be some wonderful evidences: equescurriculum, hippocollosculum, cirqzoolodon, hipposoonomadon, athelolypmimanthem, hippo-olympiad, quadrapantheon and octoplexzara! Before the end of Barnum's life such adjectives as mammoth, monstrous, gigantic, colossal,

148

elephantine, amplitudinous, stupendous, marvelous, magnificent, glorious and superb were to have lost virtually all meaning.

Albinos and Industrious Fleas

When he opened the museum, on January 1, 1842, Barnum offered relics and curiosities from all over the world. There were not only such strange sights as albinos, "industrious" fleas, and "educated" dogs, but ropedancers, a ventriloquist, jugglers, automatons, models, dioramas, and living statues. The first Punch and Judy show in America was a featured entertainment.

To get a crowd around the building at the opening, he had a man walk about solemnly out in front, putting down a brick here and a brick there, picking them up, replacing them, interchanging them, standing off and looking at them, and occasionally entering the building—all without a word or an answer to questions. It took no time at all to collect a crowd, and whenever the brick artist went inside scores of the onlookers bought tickets and followed him, trying to discover what he was up to. Huge painted panels, showing strange animals, were placed all over the outside of the building. An "ice cream garden" was set up on the roof. A band played on the balcony. Calcium lights—the first seen in New York— shone from the roof, illuminating the entire area "from the Battery to Niblo's Garden," a famous summer theatre on the east side of Broadway, between Prince and Houston Streets.

At this period Barnum showed in the museum two kinds of flying fish, one from the Gulf Stream, and the other from the West Indies; a "Siren" or mud iguana, presented as an intermediate animal between the reptile and the fish; the "Ornithorhincus" from New Holland, "being the connecting link between the seal and the duck"; the "Paddle-Tail Snake from South America"; and the "Proteus Sanguihus," a "subterraneous animal from a grotto in Australia—with other animals forming connecting links in the great chain of Animated Nature." This was seventeen years before Darwin published his *Origin of Species*.

All the records show that, when it came to business, Barnum was scrupulously honest. Throughout his life he refused to lend his name to any shady get-rich-quick schemes, and his word was even better than his bond. In the entertainment field, he thought of himself as an educator (which he undoubtedly was), but he also was playing a game, and it delighted him to mix reality and whimsy. If he did not know the correct name for a thing, he made one up. If he did not know its origin, he simply

149

invented one that seemed exciting. If he did not know how to spell a word, he guessed at it.

Before the year 1842 was out, with an admission of 25 cents, the museum was the most popular place of entertainment in the city. In fact, on March 17th of the first year, such a mob of Irish celebrants went in with their lunches, prepared to spend the day and evening, that Barnum had to think up a way to get them out again. There were crowds waiting on the sidewalk who could not get in. He called his painter and had him concoct a big sign, which he put near the rear door. TO THE EGRESS it said, with a hand pointing the direction. Anxious to miss nothing, the revelers went through the door and found themselves in the street. Barnum had gauged correctly the appeal of the practical joke, for those who had been fooled merely waited to see the next suckers emerge.

The "Fejee Mermaid"

One of the earliest added attractions at the museum was the "Fejee Mermaid," which Barnum, of course, knew was faked, and which was actually the worst swindle he ever perpetrated. The "Mermaid" was a horrible dried-up monster, three feet long, made of a meticulously joined monkey head and fish body, which had been bought in the Far East by a trusting sea captain with $6,000 of the ship's funds. That outlay was so little appreciated by the captain's employers that he was told he must work out the amount. He had not finished paying when he died, leaving his son nothing but the monster. The son sold it to the Boston Museum, which also contained a collection of more or less legitimate curiosities, and Barnum bought it from that institution.

Such faking had been going on for centuries. In China, in Marco Polo's time, "pygmies" were manufactured and sold. These fakes, with human-looking faces, shaved except on the chin, were dried, preserved in camphor or other drugs, put into wooden boxes and sold to traders who carried them all over the world. Marco Polo says sternly that there are no pygmies so small as that anywhere. "This is merely an imposition."

Stories of mermaids, Nereids and Tritons, long accepted by even the most intelligent, probably originated in sailors' glimpses of seals and other marine creatures. A New York audience of the 1840's was slightly more skeptical, and the problem of promotion, as Barnum saw it, was to "modify the general credulity in the existence of mermaids, so far as to awaken curiosity to see and examine the specimen." He started his publicity from a distance, arranging for the papers to receive carefully planted letters from Alabama, South Carolina, Washington, and way stations. Barnum's partner, Levi Lyman, posed as Dr. Griffin, agent for the Lyceum of Natural History, London, and gave a preview and some come-on interviews in Philadelphia. By the time he and the mermaid arrived in New York, thousands were agog, and the American Museum was mobbed. During the first four weeks after Barnum acquired the mermaid, the receipts were $3,341.93, whereas for the four preceding weeks he had taken in only $1,272. In three years, the gate amounted to $100,429.43.

In 1843, Barnum began unwittingly to do his bit toward initiating the Wild West Show—a form of entertainment that was to become tremendously popular by the end of the century. His first public recognition of the lure of the West was to buy fifteen half-starved young buffaloes, park them in New Jersey, and trick the newspapers into running stories about a free buffalo hunt in Hoboken. The hunt was free, but Mr. Barnum had bought the rights to the ferry fares, and some 24,000 persons paid to go to Hoboken to see the frightened, cowering animals, which finally ran away into a nearby swamp. He made $3,500 in that one day, and repeated the stunt in Camden.

New York saw its first group of wild Indians shortly after the buffalo hunt, when Indians from Iowa whooped through their war dances in the museum. The public was fascinated by these visitors from the still-mysterious plains and mountains, and interest continued to such an extent that in 1864 Barnum bribed an interpreter to let him show some dignified chiefs who had gone to Washington to visit Lincoln.

Toward the end of the century, the Wild West Show was to evolve a form peculiarly its own, although reminiscent of Astley's early riding-school exhibitions and even of the Roman *desultores*. Such an enterprise as the Buffalo Bill Wild West and Congress of Rough Riders of the World gave its performances in an open-air arena, surrounded by grandstands with canvas shade. There the audience saw the wildest kind of riding by cowboys, gauchos, vaqueros, and Cossacks, with rope twirling, lassoing and sharpshooting, plus romantic spectacles. In 1898, for example, the program offered *Custer's Last Stand,* an attack on a mail coach, a Virginia reel on horseback, and shooting at glass balls by Annie Oakley.

Innumerable western riders had got into the game, usually calling themselves Bill—Buffalo, Pawnee, Oklahoma. Their shows made such an appeal that circus men began to put on Wild West stunts for the "concert," which by that time had come to be an accepted addition to the regular performance. A Wild West concert is said to have been seen first in 1912, on Hunt's Silver Plate Circus and Oklahoma Bill's Wild West.

Even now, some of the smaller circuses still carry such a concert, and contemporary variations on the rough rider have invaded the circus ring even during the regular performance.

Affair of the Woolly Horse

Back in the 1840's, an aura of broad plain and untrammeled forest also surrounded Barnum's other famous hoax, that of the Woolly Horse. The horse was a strange-looking object, having body and legs covered

152

with tightly curled hair, no mane, and almost no hair on its tail. It was real enough and, presented in straightforward fashion, it would not have won more than a second glance. Barnum bought the little horse in Cincinnati, and kept it under cover in Bridgeport until the papers reported the safety of Colonel John Charles Frémont, who had been lost while exploring in the Rocky Mountains. Immediately, other dispatches began to arrive from the West, saying that the explorer had found on the Gila River a very strange animal, etc., etc., which was being shipped East. Two days later, an advertisement in the New York papers announced that the horse Frémont had found was in New York and would be exhibited for a few days at Broadway and Reade Street.

Frémont was not at hand to deny the story of the discovery. Nobody suspected Barnum. The Woolly Horse went on tour without mishap until it reached Washington, where Frémont's father-in-law, Senator Benton from Missouri, sued Barnum's agent on the grounds that the latter had obtained 25 cents from him under false pretenses, insisted that Frémont had not told him a word about such an animal, and informed the world that he was sure it was another hoax. A cautious court dismissed the case.

The Woolly Horse had served his turn. It was sent back to Bridgeport to graze in a field near the railroad tracks—a field that Barnum was to use later for a spectacular piece of publicity. Looking back on the scene he had woven around the little horse, the showman was not too proud of it. "It was the only feature of the show," he wrote, "that I now care to forget."

By the power of his imagination and the resourcefulness of his pen, Barnum transformed innumerable otherwise comparatively commonplace objects into curiosities the world rushed to see. When a natural oddity appeared on his broad horizon, he exploited it to the tune of millions. Of all his promotions, none was more successful than that by which he converted a small unknown Bridgeport boy into an international celebrity.

14

Of Triumphs and Tribulations

ONE DAY in 1842, Phineas Taylor Barnum's brother Philo told him about a midget he had discovered in Bridgeport. The boy was five years old, weighed 15 pounds, and was only 25 inches tall. His name was Charles Sherwood Stratton.

The Midget and the Giant Promoter

Midgets are very rare, and Barnum quickly came to the conclusion that this one offered the opportunity of a lifetime, for he was a bright little fellow, pert, a good mimic, quick-witted and adaptable. Looking for a name that would suggest Lilliputian dimensions plus dignified importance, Barnum hit on "General Tom Thumb." The child's miniature stature was emphasized by advancing his official age to eleven; and, because imported curiosities were more appealing than indigenous ones, he was said to be English. Like everyone else of his day, Tom Thumb's manager spoke of all midgets as "dwarfs," and it was as a dwarf that this prodigious midget was advertised.

Tom Thumb was put into a uniform, taught a few songs and dances, and patiently coached on what to say and how to conduct himself. In December, 1842, he was taken to New York, to work at the museum for $3 a week, plus expenses for himself and his mother. Before the first appearance, while masterful publicity and advertising were building up eagerness to see the curiosity, the child was dressed in baby clothes, and Barnum carried him back and forth between the museum and the lodgings. That trick was so effective that, two years later, when showman and midget got off the ship in Liverpool, the precious freight was concealed under a shawl.

To call on the newspaper editors in New York in 1842, Tom Thumb and Barnum wore identical costumes—tight grey trousers, grey chesterfields with capes and deep pockets, grey beaver hats, frilled shirts, flowered satin waistcoats, and high stiff stocks. In grey-gloved hands each carried a gold-tipped walking stick. Barnum was six feet two inches tall. Needless to say, the papers filled their columns with stories about the showman and the tiny creature.

Tom Thumb was the second midget to be publicly exhibited in this country; but nobody remembered much about the first one, Major Stevens, who was now forty years old and had grown to be 40 inches tall. He had not had P. T. Barnum to promote him.

Crowds packed the museum to see little Charlie Stratton. Watching an exhibition fight between giants, from where he stood in the wings, the

155

child got so excited he rushed out onto the stage. One of the giants picked him up and deposited him out of harm's way. Naturally, Barnum immediately introduced a regular feature called *The Dwarf and the Fighting Giants*. The small actor also danced, sang, did imitations, posed as Cupid, offered "Grecian Statues," and let the ladies kiss him. It is estimated that at least 80,000 persons saw him during his first engagement, and he himself said ruefully years later that he bet he had been kissed by a million ladies.

Tom Thumb's next contract was for $7 a week, plus a bonus. Very shortly afterward, he was advanced to $50 a week and all expenses. He was soon counting his money by the thousands.

Tours in the United States could no longer satisfy the great promoter. In 1844 Barnum decided that it was time to cross the Atlantic. By that time, the interchange of entertainers of all kinds was both customary and popular, and Barnum expected to be greeted in England by a figurative, if not literal, band. Upon his arrival he was disheartened to find that nobody in London seemed to know he was around.

Command Performance

Nothing could keep him down for long, however. He rented a luxurious house, and drove around the city with Tom Thumb sitting beside him in a brougham. Before long, they received an invitation to entertain for the Baroness Rothschild, who gave them a generous purse. The ball of fortune had begun to roll. Barnum engaged Egyptian Hall in Piccadilly for a public display, and the show was a sellout. He still was not happy. He wanted to present his midget before royalty, and not a word had come from Queen Victoria.

When the discouraging silence continued, Barnum decided to do something about it. At last he got the ear of the Master of the Queen's Household and confided to that dignitary that Louis Philippe wanted Tom Thumb to go to Paris. Almost immediately Victoria sent an invitation. Royalty was completely charmed by the little fellow, who (despite previous orders not to address the Queen directly) greeted the company with his customary salutation, "Good evening, ladies and gentlemen." He is also said to have told the Queen that she had a "nice place here," and to have asked her where her little boy was. Tom sang, danced, gave some of his imitations, and at the conclusion enchanted everyone (except Barnum, who was uncharacteristically nervous) by backing out a few steps, turning around and running to catch up with the long-legged adults, and repeating that process until he reached the exit.

156

A second audience followed, at which the Prince of Wales and the little princess were present, and a third in which Leopold of Belgium participated. During the second visit, the Queen gave Tom Thumb a jeweled pin, bearing the initials V. R. When he appeared for the third time, he hinted for a pony and got a pencil case; but Victoria later sent other gifts, and Queen Adelaide, widow of William IV, gave him a watch and chain. Barnum himself was very soon to provide the pony.

They were making $500 a day in public appearances, and had just begun. Performances were given for the King of Saxony and the Viceroy of Egypt. The Duke of Wellington became a Tom Thumb fan. A play called *Hop o' My Thumb* was written especially for the diminutive actor, and given at the Lyceum for charity.

Now that the midget was a public personage, it was fitting that he should travel like royalty, and Barnum ordered a coach made to size. It was 34 inches high, painted silver and red, white and blue, lined with yellow silk, and drawn by four matched ponies. While the midget was at the height of his popularity, Barnum decided—before the marvelous became commonplace—to leave England and investigate fresher fields. They went to Paris. According to a story that may be true, Tom Thumb was playing in the Luxembourg gardens when a nice unknown gentleman came along and helped him sail a boat. It was Louis Philippe. The King received the small American three times, gave Tom Thumb an emerald and diamond stickpin, and granted permission for "Le Général Tom Pouce" and his manager to drive to the Longchamp Races by way of the Champs-Élysées, which ordinarily was reserved for the court and the diplomatic corps. In addition to his other accomplishments, the gifted midget learned to speak French, and to play the piano and violin, and very quickly he became as much the rage in Paris as he had been in London.

During a tour of France, the entourage consisted of three vehicles, twelve horses, Tom Thumb's coach and four ponies, and a party of twelve persons, including Tom Thumb's father and mother. After delighting audiences from Rouen to Bordeaux, they went to Madrid where the boy performed for Queen Isabella, and thence across France to Belgium, where he also appeared before the royal family.

Truth and legend are so inextricably mixed in anything touching the life of P. T. Barnum that it is impossible to be sure whether Tom Thumb was actually abducted in France on the way to the Belgian border, and, if he was, just what happened. One version goes that brigands met the party in the forest, took the coach and the jewels, and carried Barnum and

Mrs. Tom Thumb and a borrowed baby

Mr. and Mrs. Stratton with them. Tom escaped into the woods, and walked until he reached the castle of Count Julien de Manon, who immediately set out on horseback with his men and the midget. At a farmhouse in the depths of the forest, they found the coach and ponies in the stable. Barnum and the Strattons were released from a cellar, where they had been hidden, after having been bound and gagged. The count caught the bandits and retrieved the jewels. Barnum's version was that Tom Thumb himself also had been captured, and that $10,000 had been demanded for ransom. After long negotiations, this amount was paid to gypsies, and a shepherd who was looking for lost sheep found the boy in a cave in the mountains.

Numerous European papers certainly carried stories about the kidnaping, and all Europe was exceedingly excited about it. As a result, Tom Thumb drew still bigger crowds.

158

After the European tour, which lasted three years, the travelers returned to the museum. By this time they were in partnership. Some estimates have it that the entire tour brought in 150,000 pounds; others that, during the last two years alone, each partner made a million dollars. Be that as it may, Tom Thumb built a house in Bridgeport for his parents, and Barnum built there a circus man's dream palace, costing $150,000, which he called "Iranistan." Its domes and minarets, copied after those of the Pavilion at Brighton, rose in more than Oriental splendor above the placid New England landscape, until the structure burned to the ground in 1857. Barnum later built two other Bridgeport houses, Lindencraft and Waldemere, but his heart was in Iranistan.

Tom Thumb to the Rescue

In 1849, with Sherwood Stratton, Tom Thumb's father, Barnum organized Barnum's Great Asiatic Caravan, Museum and Menagerie, a peripatetic animal and side-show exhibit. The following year, agents were sent to Ceylon to obtain elephants. On their return still a year later, after terrific difficulties, they brought back twelve. To announce their arrival, ten of those elephants were harnessed in pairs to a chariot and paraded through the New York streets.

After traveling in the United States for four years, the Caravan was disbanded and all the equipment except one elephant was sold. He was put down in Barnum's Bridgeport field near the railroad tracks, and a mahout in Indian costume was instructed to start ploughing with him whenever a train drew near. Passengers nearly leapt out of the windows, and P. T. Barnum got many columns of free publicity. Every time the elephant was mentioned in print, the editors (who were not yet wise in the ways of press agents) let the story carry the information that it belonged to that P. T. Barnum who owned the American Museum in the city.

Barnum invested the proceeds from the Caravan sale in various schemes, almost all of which turned out badly, and when a clock company in which he was interested failed he was forced into bankruptcy.

In the meantime, as soon as Tom Thumb became eighteen years old, he had started off as his own manager. When the midget now heard of his friend's difficulties he offered to renew their association. Gratefully, Barnum accepted, and in 1857 the two men again toured Europe, making a great deal of money for both of them. The results of the European tour (during which Barnum himself paradoxically lectured far and wide on "The Art of Money Getting") were so satisfactory that in 1859 he was able to pay his debts and take back the American Museum, which had been lost in the bankruptcy.

A certain amount of confusion still clings to the events that ensued after Barnum found and engaged another "dwarf" in 1862. He himself said that her true name was Mercy Lavinia Warren Bumpus. Actually, it was Mercy Lavinia Warren Bump. For the sake of euphony he dropped both the first and last names. Lavinia Warren and Tom Thumb met and, after a courtship complicated by the fact that another of Barnum's midgets, Commodore Nutt, fell in love with her, she and the General were married. Barnum resisted all temptations to make a Roman holiday of the wedding, and on February 10, 1863, it was held in Grace Church with great elegance.

Of course the showman could never resist stretching the truth to make it fit his purposes. For nearly a hundred years, there has been an almost universal conviction that Tom Thumb and Lavinia Warren had a baby, which at two and a half died of "inflammation of the brain." A great many persons have seen a photograph showing Lavinia with the baby on her lap. The sad truth is that one day Barnum snatched a baby out of the audience, popped the infant into the midget's arms, and had a picture taken. Thereafter he sold copies for 25 cents each. Mr. and Mrs. Tom Thumb never had a child.

For Barnum's little people there were a few more years of travel, including a trip to Australia by way of Japan, Shanghai, and Singapore. On his return, the General retired. By that time he wore a wispy beard and a straggling mustache, and was a portly figure 27 inches tall, trying belatedly to be a playboy. He bought a yacht and race horses, and in other profligate ways squandered almost all the money he had saved. So, when he died of a stroke at forty-five, he was again poor. Yet at one time he was reputed to have owned one of the largest collections of jewelry in the United States, and is supposed to have kept the valuables in a 1,000-pound safe, the door of which was so heavy he was unable to open it.

Lavinia remarried, but her life with another midget, the Count Primo Magri, was unhappy. She and her second husband ended their professional careers in the "kid show" at Coney Island, and she died in 1919, at seventy-eight, a very advanced age for a midget.

Through the years, Barnum had been increasing the exhibits in the museum, collecting every conceivable type of wild beast and more and more odd human creatures. In the years around 1860, curiosities poured

160

in. Barnum bought an interest in the California Menagerie owned by one Grizzly Adams, whose head had been torn open by one of his pets, and who was dying slowly, but refused to quit because he wanted to build up for his wife as big a nest egg as possible. Adams's new partner put up a tent at Broadway and 13th Street, and in order to advertise the show the animals were conveyed down Broadway and up the Bowery, preceded by a loud band. Adams himself, wearing a hunting costume, topped by a wolf's-head cap trimmed with tails, rode at the head of the parade on a wagon with three uncaged grizzlies. After a few months, Barnum bought out the other half interest, and reluctantly let Adams go out with the bears into Connecticut and Massachusetts. The trainer continued until he died. Thereafter, the bears and other animals from his collection went into the museum and were exhibited by a trainer known as Herr Driesbach —the same Driesbach whose name had earlier been paired with Van Amburgh's. With the exception of Neptune, a sea lion that remained in New York in a tank, the whole group eventually went into a traveling menagerie.

In 1861, Barnum advertised the "first and only" hippopotamus in America, to be seen in its own special tank at the American Museum. In search of other impressive curiosities, Barnum himself went up the St.

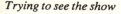
Trying to see the show

Culver Service

161

Lawrence to get two white whales, sent them 700 miles by train, and put them into a tank with fresh water. In a few days they died. He piped bay water into the basement, built a 24-foot tank of slate and "French glass" on the second floor, and tried another pair. They too died. Not to be deterred, he acquired two more, which not only lived but were shown along with a certificate from the great Harvard biologist, Louis Agassiz, saying that they were what they purported to be. To the collection were added sharks, sea horses, porpoises and exotic fish, some of which perished of cold. The contents of the Aquarial Gardens in Boston were annexed, and each summer the exhibit was replenished by sending a ship to the Gulf of Mexico. The first true aquarium in America was being developed.

The Bearded Lady

Human curiosities had always delighted the thousands who visited the museum, and until he closed it in 1868 the showman's reputation was enhanced consistently through such headliners as the Bearded Lady, the What Is It? (really a strange-looking Negro boy), a double-voiced singer, a pair of Siamese Twins, the Albino Family, and Anna Swan, the Nova Scotia Giantess, who was seven feet eleven inches tall, and weighed 413 pounds.

On July 13, 1865, the American Museum burned to the ground, and the only animals saved were the "educated" seal, one bear, some birds, and a few monkeys. The loss was $400,000, and the insurance was for only $40,000. At least 150 employees were thrown out of work. It took Barnum just four months to remodel and move into the five-story Chinese Museum building at Broadway and Prince Street, which he stocked with new curiosities gathered from all over the world. For the New American Museum he bought several entire museums and hundreds of small collections.

At approximately the same time he went into business with the Van Amburgh interests. This was probably not Van Amburgh himself, but Hyatt Frost, who inherited the business sometime in 1865. The collaboration, to which Barnum did little more than lend his name, was called the "Barnum and Van Amburgh Museum and Menagerie Company." It was on exhibition at the museum in the winter, and became a traveling show in the summer.

For many years, Connecticut had recognized P. T. Barnum as one of its most remarkable citizens. He had had such resounding success with

Jenny Lind's 1850–1851 tour that the next year he was offered (and refused) the nomination for governor of Connecticut. Barnum had been responsible for much foresighted and practical development in Bridgeport. He served in two sessions of the Connecticut legislature, and there so distinguished himself that he was nominated for Congress in 1867. When he lost that election, he gave even more time to the improvement of Bridgeport. During the next two decades Phineas Taylor Barnum raised the city and the whole area around it to an eminence such as it had never enjoyed, and in 1875 he was elected mayor. A statue stands in the municipal Seaside Park, still proclaiming him as one of the greatest of city fathers.

In 1868, on a biting cold day when water turned to ice in the hose, the New American Museum was destroyed by fire. Almost all the animals, including Van Amburgh's lions and tigers, perished in the flames. The aging Barnum, whose career had been a series of melodramatic ups and downs, attempted to retire, but a new and even more exciting adventure was beckoning. Undoubtedly P. T. Barnum thought then that his reputation had been established for all time. He could not possibly have imagined that he would be remembered not as the owner of the American Museum but as the father of "The Greatest Show on Earth."

Long before the day came when he ceased to be a museum man, however, an especially bright and romantic chapter of the American circus had been developed against the background of the Mississippi River.

15

Parades and Showboats

N O OTHER lost aspect of the circus is so much regretted as the passing of the circus parade. None calls up such a surge of nostalgia. The gaffer who long since may have forgotten his first wife's name can still remember standing beside the dusty road watching the approach of the band with its brass instruments gleaming in the sun, the gaily painted and gilded cages in which lions drowsed and tigers perpetually paced, the elegant riders on their cavorting steeds, the beautiful ladies in strange and wonderful costumes swaying in howdahs atop the elephants, the calliope shrilling its tunes, the clown stumbling along beside the horses, turning occasional flip-flaps, and pausing every now and then to bow right and left with impressive mock solemnity. A lifetime later, the man who was that boy can still smell the reek of animals, breathe the scent of wood and cloth and metal heated by the sun.

There are those who say that Philip Astley invented the modern circus parade when he drove around London with his Little Military Learned Horse, Billy, beside him in a carriage. That, however, seems to be considerably stretching a point. As a matter of fact, if one forgets the Egyptians, the Romans, and the Italians of the Renaissance, whose purpose was entirely different, the first circus parade was seen in New York State in 1837, when the short-lived Purdy, Welch, Macomber and Company got together a band of men, playing wind instruments, put them on horseback, mounted a couple of drummers on elephants to bring up the rear, and streamed through the streets of Albany on the first of May.

From that time on, for almost exactly a century, no circus could open its tents without first giving the expectant public at least a preliminary glimpse of the delights to come. Large or small, the American circus parade was, of course, primarily an advertisement. As the years passed, exhibitors tried harder and harder to impress their potential customers, and in the end the circus parade succumbed to its own enormity. Except for an occasional procession, it is now virtually a thing of the past. Although since 1952 a few of the more important American truck shows have paraded, and the results have been greeted with tremendous excitement, these processions are pallid copies of the mighty pageants of the great days.

"Here Come the Elephants!"

As the circus grew in size, parades became more and more important and elaborate. Soon the cry "Hold your horses! Here come the elephants!" was ringing down American streets. By the early 1850's the parade always

165

included a band wagon, and occasionally also a platform wagon or two decked out with banners and colored bunting, carrying dogs and other small animals, and men and women in bizarre costumes. Then along in the line came cage wagons, with removable sides painted with Biblical scenes such as Daniel in the Lions' Den, Jonah and the Whale, and the Lion and Lamb lying down together. These structures were usually light but very strong. There was no telling when they might have to be dragged through streams and swamps, or even through drifts of unseasonable snow. And always there was mud.

The music from trumpets and horns, no matter how loudly they blared, became thin and petulant in the open air and, consequently, mechanical instruments were invented, to give depth and body to the music and to assist the overworked bands.

By the middle of the century, a parade of some kind was an accepted concomitant of any promotion in which it could be used. When Jenny Lind landed in New York on September 1, 1850, Barnum put on a midnight parade that moved down Broadway to her hotel, while at least 20,-000 men, women, and children packed windows and roofs, and hung to lampposts and the frames of awnings. There were no elephants, but 300 firemen, in red shirts made brighter by the flaring light of torches, escorted the Musical Fund Society to a place beneath the singer's window, under which the musicians played various instrumental numbers. The crowd cheered, and Jenny waved her handkerchief. Barnum was not yet a circus man, but he was using circus techniques.

At approximately this time, the circus team of Spalding and Rogers built a big parade wagon which the owners called the Apollonicon. It was a mechanism for producing music as if from 1,000 instruments, and was manipulated by Carl Fuhrman who, according to the custom of the day, called himself "Professor." This wagon was not a calliope, which is a different genus altogether, invented almost simultaneously, but not used in parades until several years later.

Remember the Calliope?

The calliope, usually said to have been invented in 1855 by Joshua Stoddard, was made with a large charcoal-burning boiler at one end, which had to be stoked continuously to provide constant steam for the whistles (originally perhaps only eight, but certainly increased almost immediately to either twenty-one or thirty-two). One hundred and twenty pounds of pressure, going through a cylinder, were required to start the

166

e elephants, on their way to New ork's Madison Square Garden, march down Broadway

Underwood and Underwood

whistles squealing. If pressure dropped, the valves controlling the pitch could let it go off as much as a full tone. Brass carried the sound farthest, but in the early days most of the whistles were made of copper. By a series of wires and arms, the valves were connected to a keyboard, at which the man who sent forth the thrilling music—inevitably a "professor"—sat, playing the contrivance as if it were a piano. The first time the calliope was used in a parade was probably in 1859, by Sands, Nathan and Company's American and English Circus.

The Apollonicon, creation of Henry Green of New York, must have been more intricate than a mammoth pipe organ. From the console, Fuhrman operated bellows which brought forth the sounds of organ pipes, whistles, reeds, and horns; and pulled levers which controlled the tympani —drums, triangles, gongs, and cymbals.

The wagon was a great boxlike affair, so high and heavy that forty horses were required to pull its weight. It is as driver of the Apollonicon that we hear first of J. W. Paul, who was to distinguish himself for years by driving forty-horse teams for other companies, with other parade

167

wagons, some of which are still in existence. To conduct such a huge and unwieldy structure as the Apollonicon up and down hills, around corners, and through mud was an almost insuperable task, and very soon Spalding and Rogers transferred the ungainly contrivance to a place where it could stay quietly in one position, and where its music could be amplified and romanticized by water—a river boat. Spalding and Rogers put a floating circus onto the Mississippi River, and actually invented the show-boat.

Spalding was an Albany druggist, always called "Doctor," who anticipated the modern drug store with its diverse stock by carrying a side line of paints and oils, in which he did very well. Sam H. Nichols, a successful touring circus owner who in 1840 built the town's first amphitheatre, got so far into debt to Spalding for items from the drug store's side lines that in 1843 his creditor took over both amphitheatre and show.

Continuing success in the American circus business has always demanded persistence, inventiveness, and an intuitive knowledge of what the public will accept at any particular time. At the outset, Spalding followed a more or less conventional pattern, and for spectacles relied chiefly on such old equestrian standbys as *The Cataract of the Ganges, Timour the Tartar, The Naiad Queen,* and *The Forty Thieves.* Almost immediately, however, he decided that audiences were tired of such spectacles and began to search for other attractions.

When he needed a partner, he was unbelievably fortunate in finding Charles J. Rogers, son of a famous English "scenic" rider, who had some money to invest. After the company of Spalding and Rogers came into existence, for almost two decades the men made a perfect team, with Rogers running the show and Spalding making the plans. The ex-druggist was to put his stamp on the circus in several ways, both practical and romantic.

In 1847, the partners leased a big river steamer, the *Allegheny Mail,* to take their show to St. Paul and down the Mississippi to New Orleans, going ashore with a tent to play all stands *en route.* Although other circus men had preceded them over the route, their first season was so successful that Spalding decided to enlarge his circular tent. To make a larger tent practicable, he invented props that are used today in all tenting circuses, and are still known as "quarter poles."

Aron Turner's tent was just a round pavilion, 90 feet across. When more area was needed, the obvious next step was to enlarge the diameter. But such enlargement is not feasible beyond a certain point. In addition to

168

other complications, if seats are too far away from the ring it is impossible to see the action. An excellent compromise seemed to be to split the canvas down the center and spread it sidewise by inserting "middle pieces," exactly as our grandmothers used to enlarge the round table when company arrived, by putting in extension leaves. The more company, the more leaves. However, the question then arose of how to support the elliptical structure. Gilbert Spalding's quarter poles take up the slack between center and side poles, so that the roof will not sag.

Spalding also invented a stringer-and-jack type of seat, which is still orthodox equipment for almost any circus, and has not been wholly discarded even by Ringling Brothers, who several years ago introduced the more mechanically elaborate seat wagons. In the interest of safety, Spalding installed oil lamps to replace the candles that used to be lighted in clusters around the center pole. Although he is largely forgotten, his imagination and ingenuity helped to turn a simple one-horse show into the three-ring circus.

Back in the late 1840's, encouraged by his successful river tours, he decided he would like actually to present the circus on a boat, and not go ashore at all for performances. His first thought was to put the whole affair onto a steamer, that might churn up and down the river under its own power. He discussed his idea with Captain E. N. Shields, a Cincinnati boat designer, who persuaded him that such a plan would not be practical, and that he would better put the show onto a barge and tow it. The result of the conference was the *Floating Palace,* a barge built by Shields at a cost of $42,000, and two light-draft towing boats that cost approximately as much more. All three were delivered in 1852.

The *Floating Palace,* forerunner of the Mississippi showboat, had a 42-foot ring in the center, with a mirror at each side, giving the impression of multiple rings. There was a dress circle of 1,000 cane-bottomed chairs, each numbered; a family circle of cushioned settees to hold 500; and a gallery for 900 more. The sources of hot-water heat and gaslight were set up on the towboats. Not even a cigar was permitted on the *Palace.* Old timers used to tell of seeing *Floating Palace* employees perched on docks or rails near the river, gratefully pulling on the cigars they had been waiting for all day.

"Showboat's Comin'!"

The menagerie was shown on the deck of one of the towboats, and the public passed across that deck on the way to the big barge where the

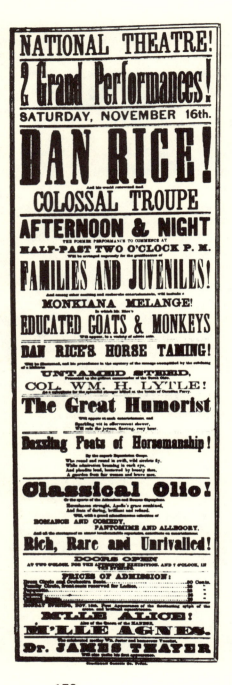

ring acts were to be seen. Both the *Floating Palace* and its attendant barges were decorated in cream and gold, with carvings, mirrors, paintings, carpets, and draperies. Many a yokel's eye must have popped at such elegance, as the fleet moved serenely down the river. There was always lively tooting to announce the arrival, and in the great days a cannon was shot off.

Spalding's inventiveness was repaid by success from the start. Understanding audience reaction, he changed either the program or the performers before playing any place the second time.

In 1853, when Spalding arrived in New Orleans several weeks earlier than usual, he learned that Mobile was anxious to see the show. Despite the advice of rivermen, he decided to satisfy that interest. The *North River* towed the *Floating Palace* out into the Gulf, and then up the Mobile, Alabama, and Tombigbee rivers, drawing enormous crowds in Mobile, Montgomery, and other centers. On the way back, the fleet ran into a storm, and the helpless *Palace* reached the Mississippi only after a desperate struggle. Tremendous publicity resulted all over the country.

After that narrow escape from disaster, Spalding and Rogers toured up and down the river for several years, adding attractions one after another. In 1854, they leased Van Amburgh's menagerie, and appar-

170

ently the great trainer himself presented his animals on the *Palace,* while the ring show went out on wagons under Rogers. The following year, the *Palace* became temporarily a floating side show, with an exhibit of curiosities from Barnum's American Museum, and others that came from Albany. At that time, the ring features went out as two wagon shows—one under the direction of Rogers, the other with Spalding. The Apollonicon was used to call attention to Spalding's section. After that season he decided that moving the unwieldy instrument from place to place was too difficult, and set it up as a feature of the *Palace* flotilla.

Minstrel shows also were added to the program, and were greeted with such enthusiasm that in 1856 the partners bought another steamer, the *Banjo,* which had a stage and performed the double duty of towing the *Palace* and carrying the minstrels.

In those days, the advent of the showboat and its attendants was announced by the Apollonicon installed on the advance steamer, which also carried posters and copies of a little newspaper, *The Palace Journal.* The paper contained items about what was happening on and around the *Palace,* and was used as a kind of herald. Next around the bend came boats carrying the menagerie and towing the *Palace* (with the performers). It is hard for anyone today to imagine the excitement

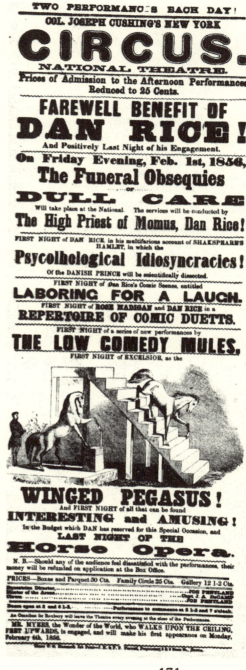

171

that was aroused in isolated communities by the appearance of this world of magic and romance.

When the Civil War tore the country apart, it interfered so seriously with circus business on the river that, in 1862 and 1863, Spalding and Rogers took their show to South America. On the way back, the vessel in which it was traveling was wrecked and much of the property was lost. The company soon recovered, however, opened in New York, and later returned to the river and the *Palace*. Then, early in 1865, at New Albany, Indiana, the *Floating Palace* burned to a charred wreck. The season was finished in wagons, but in October of that year the partnership was dissolved. Rogers retired. Spalding continued to manage theatres in New Orleans, and occasionally circuses at home and abroad; but the days of his bright glory on the Mississippi were over.

Uncle Sam in the Ring

The great river formed, too, the stage for much of the career of the greatest clown America has ever seen. His name was Dan Rice.

No aspect of the circus has gone through such profound modifications as those surrounding the comic, who has responded like a weather vane to social, economic, psychological, and even political changes, tempering his manner to the prevailing wind. Dan Rice was much given to topical songs and recitations, which he made up himself—naïve bits of doggerel, notable for their monotonous rhymes, halting meter, and too obvious humor. His most famous acts were those in which he appeared in a stars-and-stripes costume, with an Uncle Sam goatee wiggling on his chin. The minute he appeared the audience went into paroxysms—not at what he did but how he did it.

Dan Rice was born Daniel McLaren in New York in 1823, but took his mother's maiden name for professional use. His stepfather taught him to ride, and he was expert at seven, and a jockey at eight. After a roving adolescence, during which he raced horses and worked as a pedlar, Dan found his way into the entertainment world in 1839, when he danced in blackface in a benefit at the so-called St. Louis Museum. His first appearance in a circus amphitheatre was in Pittsburgh, where he danced and sang, performed as the "Young Hercules," and began to invent his famous topical jingles. In Philadelphia, in 1841, he showed feats of strength and other numbers in Masonic Hall, where P. T. Barnum was displaying a mechanical contrivance called *The Battle of Bunker Hill*.

Overnight, Dan Rice became the vogue. For five months he toured

Europe to great acclaim, then did a bit more roving in this country before he actually made his debut as a clown in 1844, with the Bowery Circus in Galena, Illinois. There he appeared as an equestrian comic, in the old Astley tradition, and for a number of years continued to make a hit in that capacity.

The next step for Dan was his own circus, which he took out on the *Allegheny Mail,* going ashore to show at all towns on both sides of the river. For almost twenty years, he chiefly played the river towns, either with his own circus or with others.

All their lives, the Ringling brothers cherished memories of seeing Dan Rice's circus at McGregor, Iowa, when they were boys. Rice led the parade in a shiny buggy with snow-white horses. He was followed by two men on horses carrying flags; a band wagon drawn by twelve dappled horses; four open dens with lions, tigers, hyenas, and three leopards (each with its trainer); nine men and six women on horseback, dressed as medieval knights and ladies; the famous trained blind horse, Excelsior; an elephant; and last, a clown in a cart, who would appear later calling out, "Whoa, January!"

Dan Rice's career was very erratic, seesawing between wealth and poverty. He was a stubborn, tempestuous man who resented authority, had little business sense, and got himself into financial hot water with distressing frequency. For years, Rice seldom made less than $1,000 a week on salary (an unheard-of amount for those days), and from his own circuses he often drew lordly returns. Yet he was forced into bankruptcy, lost his shows, started over again, repeated the process, and died in his seventies in utter poverty.

Despite his temperamental peculiarities, he was much beloved by his contemporaries, and noted far and wide for his great personal courage. In those days, when feelings ran high, altercations were likely to end in violent action; yet Dan Rice could face an angry audience without flinching, and the story goes that, once in Memphis when a man strode up to the ring edge and threatened to shoot him, the comedian not only stood his ground but in an extemporaneous song ridiculed the rambunctious gentleman so effectively that the latter retired in abashed confusion.

A "Learned" Pig

Among Rice's most valuable assets was a "learned" pig, which he christened Lord Byron. Such pigs have often made gentle and mysteriously clever companions and have been popular with innumerable clowns, from Billy Hayden to Felix Adler. We have it on the authority of "Lord" George Sanger, who trained them in his youth, that a circus pig is taught to respond when the trainer makes an audible click, and very soon the pig will respond to a mere click of a fingernail. Once it has learned to listen for its master's signal, the pig can mystify bystanders by picking out cards, telling fortunes, answering questions, and otherwise appearing to have a lively intelligence.

Two other prize attractions were a performing rhinoceros and an elephant named Lalla Rookh, which Rice taught to walk a tightrope just as an elephant had once done in the Circus Maximus.

When Dan Rice's show reached New Orleans in 1848, the owner came down with yellow fever, and was taken to Baton Rouge to be nursed, while the boat steamed on. After a bankruptcy following the yellow fever episode, Spalding and Rogers became silent partners to help Rice get onto his feet, and he organized a new small circus, which he called "Dan Rice's One Horse Show" in wry homage to his trained horse Excelsior.

Spalding and Rogers had engaged the English "Shakespearian Jester," William F. Wallett. When by chance the tents of their show and Dan's were pitched close together, the two comics made friends. As soon as Wallett's contract was up, he joined Rice, and they immediately began to play to tremendous business. In their dialogue, alternating roles, one became the ringmaster and the other the comic, and the public could not get enough of them.

The new partnership with Wallett initiated the decade of Dan Rice's greatest prosperity. In warmer months he and Wallett played the river system, and during the winter gave programs in an amphitheatre Rice built on Charles Street, New Orleans. In another building he had a "museum."

The New Orleans amphitheatre project seems to have been successful for only a few years afterward, and Rice flitted from one thing to another. After two engagements in a circus promoted by Forepaugh and O'Brien and another big enterprise of his own, he bought the steamboat *Will S. Hayes,* and toured from St. Paul to New Orleans, making a net profit of $125,000 in the 1869 season. Two years later, he ran the Great Paris Pavilion show up and down the river, as the most spectacular venture of his entire career.

Shortly thereafter, Dan Rice's star began to fall. His health failed. He had business reverses, went into bankrupty again, and in a fire in 1879 lost everything but Excelsior. Three years later, Rice went to San Francisco, where he was greeted with an acclaim that gave him back his old assurance. When the banking house of Jay Cooke failed, he lost $80,000. Still he bounced back. He lectured, and built a floating opera house, and toured the river again; but nothing was successful, and his last years were full of bitterness and self-pity. When, at the turn of the century, he died in a New York lodging house on 23rd Street, the world had long since passed him by.

While Dan Rice and Gilbert Spalding were carrying their gala delights up and down the Mississippi, a French artist was making headlines about another American river.

16

The Intrepid

Funambulist

THE MOST spectacular circus feat that has ever been performed in the United States was not presented in the circus.

In 1859, a French funambulist who called himself Blondin walked across Niagara Falls on a tightrope.

Through a century we can still hear echoes of the incredulity with which the country received the announcement of his intentions, the excitement and apprehension with which the crowds watched him balancing high above the sinister current, and the shouts of applause with which the onlookers greeted his achievement.

In the middle of the nineteenth century, the mighty falls had already become to the American public a symbol of incalculable primitive power and romance. When Barnum opened his American Museum, almost the first additional attraction he acquired was a scale model of Niagara Falls, for which he paid $200. The falls fell 18 inches, with real water, which was pumped up again and again. The showman advertised the mechanism as "The Great Model of Niagara Falls with Real Water," and achieved some unexpected free publicity when the Croton Board of Water Commissioners got the impression that he was depleting the new reservoir. They informed him that they could not possibly furnish water for Niagara Falls for $25 a year, but had to retract, albeit with chagrin, when he proved that a barrelful would take care of the model for an indefinite period.

Years later, when the great funambulist announced that he would cross the falls on a tightrope, Barnum arranged excursion trains to the scene, adding to the crowds that watched from the bank of the Niagara River.

Blondin, whose real name was Émile Gravelet, had learned his art from a scion of a long-famous dynasty of wire walkers. The first known member of the family was Jacques Ravel, who in 1605 presented his skilled posturings in Danzig. More than two hundred years later, his descendant, Jean Ravel, who called himself Blondin, came to this country with his troupe in 1855 to perform at Niblo's Garden. Jean Ravel-Blondin was a shining luminary in his own time, but today he would be forgotten if it were not for his greatest pupil, Émile Gravelet.

According to an eyewitness account of the fabulous crossing in the New York *Daily Tribune* of July 1, 1859, Gravelet assumed the Blondin pseudonym because there were two brothers named Javelli in the troupe at Niblo's Garden, and his true name was confused with theirs. A more probable explanation is that he took it in homage to his master.

177

Émile Gravelet had been born in 1824 in Saint-Omer, France, and was to die in London in 1897—another of those acrobats who lived to an advanced age and continued to demonstrate his skill until a time of life when normal muscles become stiff and normal bones grow brittle.

When he announced that he would attempt to conquer Niagara, Blondin already had been in this country nearly four years, and was famous in most of the principal cities of America. He was a fair-haired man, with very light eyes, slightly below the average height and weight, who wore a mustache, and a little tuft on his chin. Wherever he appeared, he was "the wonder of all who beheld him," noted for his "ease, precision and extraordinary grace." Nevertheless, much of the world refused to believe that even he could accomplish this unthinkable feat, and a furor of publicity resulted.

Specialists in the art of the tightrope say that, ordinarily, no greater acrobatic skill is required to maintain one's equilibrium on a rope stretched hundreds of feet in the air than on one strung two feet above the ground. The chief difficulty is always psychological, although the turbulence of air above Niagara did create an especial hazard. To attempt such a crossing, a man needed not only superb technical skill and miraculous adaptability to the demands of the moment but an absolute assurance in his own power and invulnerability. Émile Blondin possessed all those qualities in full measure.

At Niblo's Garden, he had demonstrated that he could approach the most difficult problem with incomparable *sangfroid*. One day at rehearsal, Antoine Ravel (perhaps Jean's son) had fussed for an unconscionable length of time over the placing of the various units, preparatory to somersaulting over a group of Bedouins standing with fixed bayonets. Émile, who had been lounging around at the rear of the stage, impatiently tapping his boot with a little switch, suddenly walked up the inclined plane and with the utmost nonchalance threw a complete somersault over the Bedouins, their muskets and bayonets, and over Antoine himself, landing on his feet with effortless ease.

Early in June of 1859, Blondin went to Niagara to make his preparations. His first idea was to make fast one end of the rope on Goat Island and to carry it "right across the jaws of the Horse Shoe Falls." At last he decided instead on a spot halfway between the falls and the suspension bridge, and spent several days getting a rope stretched 1,100 feet in the air. The rope was three and a quarter inches in diameter and 1,300 feet long, and was finally hauled into place by attaching it to a smaller cord

that had been taken across the river by boat. Every 18 feet all the way across, a guy rope was fastened to the hemp on which Blondin was to risk his life, and was carried to rocks and trees on one shore or the other. In addition, four ropes nearly as heavy as the major one went out 200 feet apart to huge rocks on the edge of the river. Even at that, the whole thing dipped nearly 60 feet in the center.

Blondin supervised every detail, and by the end of the month the whole country around was in a state of great excitement, which grew more intense when bad weather made the crossing impossible on June 28, originally scheduled for the attempt, and there was a postponement of two days.

Suspended Between the U.S. and Canada

Thursday, June 30, dawned fair, with a few hazy clouds and a refreshing breeze. The crowd began to collect at an early hour, and trains kept coming in from every direction until four in the afternoon. The

179

Tribune reporter estimated that by five o'clock there were 8,000 on the Canadian side (where admission was free) and 4,000 on the opposite shore (where each one had to pay 25 cents to get into an amusement park). Many of the observers were ladies.

Precisely at 4:30, Blondin appeared in the "pleasure gardens" on the U.S. side, where he warmed up on a short tightrope. At 5:15 he stepped out onto the fateful cord, bareheaded, dressed in pink tights with a yellow spangled tunic, wearing buckskin moccasins, and carrying a long balancing pole. After talking coolly to his friends for a moment or two, he addressed the crowd, "Gentlemen, any one what pleases to acrors, I carry him on my back." No one accepted. Blondin then walked out firmly and rapidly, took several steps, balanced on one foot, went forward a few yards, lay down, turned over, raised himself with apparent ease, balanced astride, bounced up and down, made numerous other passes and elaborate turns and, at last, reached a point midway between the United States and Canada. There he stopped and lowered a light cord to the *Maid of the Mist,* which had steamed out to a place beneath him. The captain attached a bottle of wine to the cord. Blondin drew it up, bowed to the crowds on each bank, drank the wine, threw the bottle into the river, and walked on to Canada. The crossing had taken eighteen minutes.

After resting for a half hour, the intrepid funambulist calmly made the transit back to the United States in a little less than half that time, stopping only once, to lie down for two minutes. Shouts and delirious cries, shots from large and small guns, and the swelling blare of martial music greeted the conqueror as he stepped back onto the earth few persons had thought he would ever see again. He was driven through the streets in triumph. Blondin was the hero of the day, the "king of the rope."

He appeared to be not very exhausted, and had "manifested no more fear or nervousness than any ungymnastic novice would at eating his breakfast," according to the *Tribune* writer, who concluded, "Thus was accomplished one of the most daring and useless feats that even this fast age has ever witnessed."

Newspapers all over the world proclaimed the supreme artist, and during that summer Blondin made four more crossings. At one time, he went out to the middle of the rope, sat on a chair, made an omelette on a portable stove, and ate the omelette. He went over blindfolded. He carried an unsung hero, his manager, one way on his back, and made the return trip on stilts. Dressed as an ape, he pushed a wheelbarrow. The Prince of Wales (Edward VII) watched one crossing.

180

Harold M. Lambert: Frederic Lewis

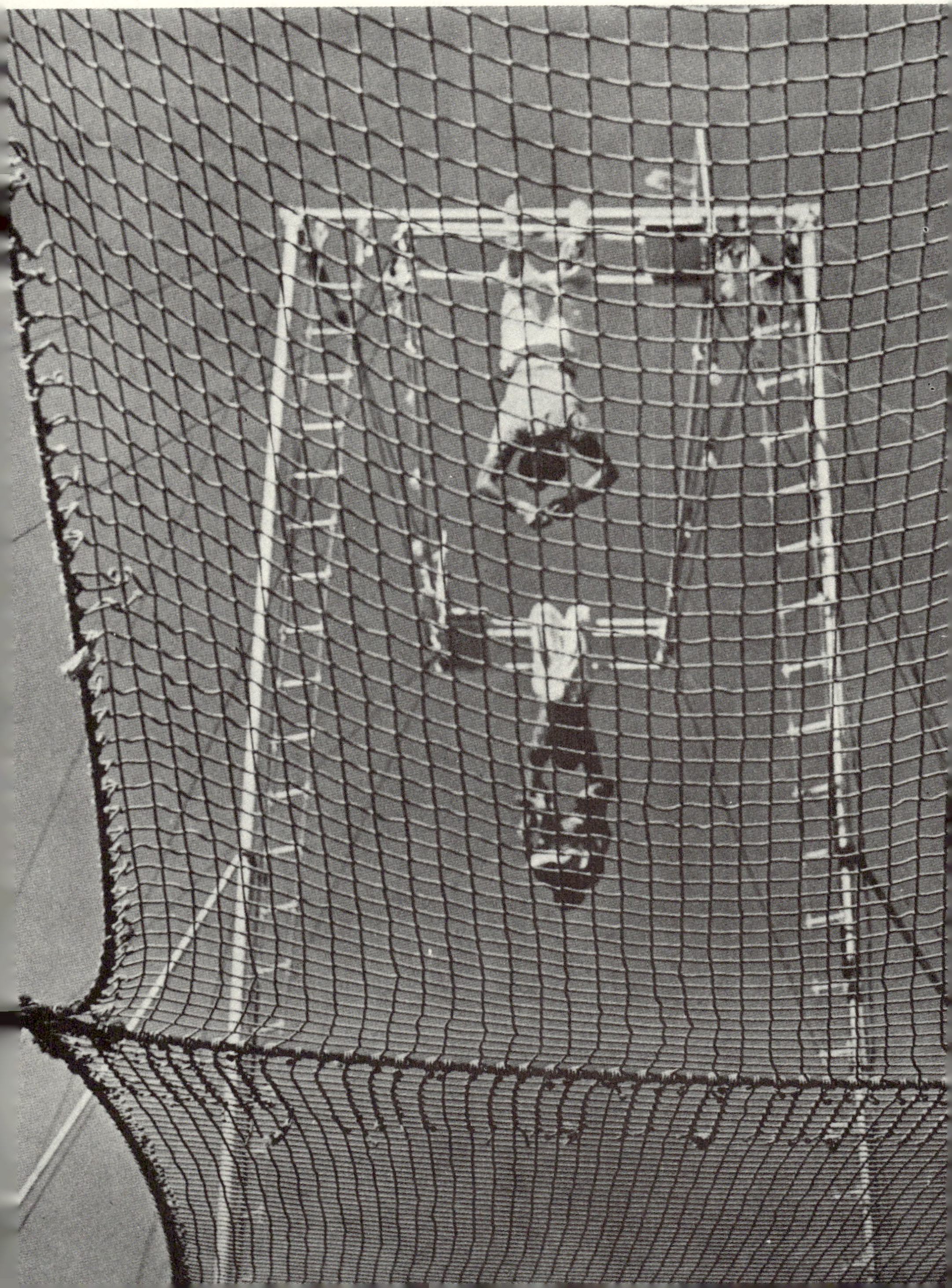

"There Oughta Be a Law Against It"

In a day when transportation was slow and difficult, the curious traveled from far-distant places to see those incredible feats. William Dean Howells went up to Niagara and saw Blondin make one crossing with his feet in wooden buckets about as big as butter firkins. Those remarkable feet, which seemed to Howells to have a life and wisdom of their own, were completely encased in wood, and it was wood only that touched the rope. Moreover, for one of the three transits that day, the funambulist dropped his balancing pole and merely stretched his arms. One harrowing trick terrified Howells as it has terrified many another onlooker since the time men first began to walk ropes. The figure stopped above the gulf and swayed deliberately as if it were losing its balance. Howells came to the conclusion that the whole thing should have been prohibited by law.

Loaded down with gold, medals, and honors, after more than a year of continuing success in this country, Blondin returned to Europe. In 1861, at the Crystal Palace in London, he strung a rope 170 feet in the air across the central transept, and turned somersaults on stilts. During a tour of the Continent, as befitted a great celebrity, he appeared on the streets wearing pantaloons coming down over varnished boots, and carrying a gold-headed cane that had been given to him by an admirer.

At the invitation of Arnault, director of the new Paris Hippodrome, Blondin performed in that famous arena in 1867, and an old print shows him there, far aloft on an intricate construction of poles and guy ropes. Another print gives nine vignettes of his most famous exploits. There he is, carrying the stove, cooking, ropewalking in a dressing gown, balancing on a chair, lying on his back, carrying a man on his shoulders, sitting with one leg stretched along the cord, standing on his head, and riding a primitive-looking velocipede. At that time he liked best to appear in red tights, red sequined tunic, and a shining copper helmet with red plumes.

During the International Exposition, the great funambulist gave Paris a hint of the Niagara thrill by walking high in the air across the Seine. In 1880 and 1881 he was back in this country, where, after attempting to obtain permission to appear in Central Park, he went out to Staten Island. There he performed additional feats such as walking a high rope with his small son on his shoulders.

The last public appearance of Émile Blondin was in Belfast, Ireland, in 1896, when he was seventy-two years old.

In this country, numerous copyists were springing up. A woman,

Maria Speltarini, crossed Niagara in July, 1876, with a 30-pound weight attached to each ankle. The most famous imitators of all were Signor Farini and Harry Leslie. Farini, who used a slack rope, and walked with his feet in a sack or sacks, was later to invent a machine that would propel a human projectile across a circus arena. Leslie, who called himself the "American Blondin," added excitement to the Niagara scene by making the transit in a more than slightly inebriated condition, wavering terrifyingly but never slipping. It was Leslie who set the style for walking between tall buildings as an outside attraction for the circus.

For years after the Niagara achievements, in any American town of even moderate size, every now and then some usually unknown performer would appear, stretch a rope from one tall building to another, and pass the hat in advance. Then he would step forth in tights and spangled trunks, seize his balancing pole, walk out onto the rope, and scare the onlookers half to death. Often he would hang a trapeze from the middle of the rope and, when he got to that point, stop for a terrifying routine. Only infrequently did one of those foolhardy gentlemen fall and break his neck.

All through the first part of the nineteenth century, the cord—high or low, tight or slack—had been exceptionally popular in Europe. The

The Last Night
of Performing here.

Circus, Hull,
FRIDAY, December 18th, 1818.

The Amusements to commence with

HORSEMANSHIP,
Polanders, Tight Rope, Still Vaulting, Feats of Strength, Sagacious Pony: Indian War Dance and Combat, from the Grand Serious **Pantomime of KANKO.**

Admission :——The Boxes 3s.——Pit 2s.——Gallery 1s.——Standing Places 6d.

Doors to be open precisely at Half-past Six, and the Performances to commence at Half-past Seven.

The African Youth
Will go through the whole of his elegant and much-admired Feats on the Single Horse.

THE WONDERFUL PONY
Will mount a Platform, NINE FEET HIGH, and Fire off a Pistol at the Word of Command.

Mons. HENGLER's unequalled Evolutions on the

Tight Rope,
Indian War Dance and Combat,
From the Pantomime of KANKO.—With the RUINS of TROY.

In the course of the Evening, there will be a GRAND

Pony Race,
By favourite Ponies of HULL, for a Sweepstakes, the best of three Heats, (each Heat five times round the Ring.)—The Second-best will be entitled to a handsome Hand-whip.—Ponies to be entered previous to Four o'Clock on the Day of Running, at the LONDON TAVERN.—Three Ponies are already entered at 5s. each.

Olympic Contentions
BY THE WHOLE COMPANY.

Master POWELL, the Wonderful POLANDERIC PERFORMER, will exhibit his Antipodean FEATS on the

GEOMETRICAL LADDER.
Director of the Ring, · · · · · Mr. COOKE.——Clown, · · · · · Mr. GARBUTT.

After which, Mr. GARBUTT will throw innumerable FLIP-FLAPS and SOMERSETS, &c.

Troop of Voltigeurs,
Who will exhibit their astonishing LEAPS over HORSES;

And introduce some Exquisite SOMERSETS, *not to be equalled.*

A PRINCIPAL ACT OF

HORSEMANSHIP
By Mr. POWELL, in which he will Leap over Whips, Handkerchiefs, and Garters, &c.

TO CONCLUDE WITH THE

TAILOR's Journey to BRENTFORD.

Messrs. C. & P. return their grateful thanks to the Public of Hull for the patronage the Circus has received this Season.

• Tradesmen having demands on Messrs. COOKE & POWELL, are requested to send them in immediately, for the purpose of their being discharged.

Robert Peck, Primer, Pocket Office, &c. Scale-Lane, H—"

German Wilhelm Kolter, whose father had been a famous rider, made an unparalleled sensation in Aix-la-Chapelle at the Congress of Monarchs in 1818. A few years later, another wire walker, Jack Barred, stretched a cord between two high windows and set out to cross the gulf. As Barred emerged from one window, Kolter arrogantly came out of the other without a balancing pole. The men walked to the middle of the rope, and each refused to give way. Barred knelt on the rope. Kolter grabbed Barred's pole, jumped over his adversary's head, and went calmly on his way.

But of all cord dancers of any time or place, none was more extraordinary than Saqui, daughter of one Jean-Baptiste Lalanne, called Navarin le Fameux, who was celebrated for a somersault over a blazing plank. Saqui was born during the French Revolution and never stopped exhibiting until just before she died in 1866. Napoléon Bonaparte was so enchanted by the young Saqui that he let her follow the encampments of the Imperial Guard. She progressed from one triumph to another during the Restoration, made a vast amount of money, lost much of her popularity in the time of Louis-Philippe, later earned a pittance at little outdoor carnivals, and died in poverty. An old Italian woman who had loved and admired her to the end had a mass said for Saqui's soul, asking that the great artist might be forgiven for the sacrilege of having once walked between the towers of Notre Dame.

Saqui's art was that of the ballet, with graceful and elegant posturings, pirouettes, arabesques, dancing on the toes, all transferred to a tight wire usually high in the air, with only her arms for balance. If we can believe the enthusiasts who saw her, she was incredibly skillful.

In the same year that Blondin electrified the world at Niagara, another Frenchman created the only truly new feature of circus acrobatics in a thousand years. Inadvertently, he also gave his name to a costume for dancing and acrobatics which is as commonplace for our day as an elasticized swim suit.

Daring Young Man on the Flying Trapeze

In 1859, Henri Maîtrejean was recruiting acrobatic and gymnastic acts for Louis Dejean, who had become the supreme authority in the French circus world. Maîtrejean heard of a handsome young fellow in Toulouse who had set up an act in his father's gymnasium that was novel, wonderful, and startling in the extreme. Maîtrejean went to Toulouse to look it over, and reported that here was a real find. The young man's name was Jules Léotard.

184

Up to that time, all aerial work had consisted of more or less intricate turns on a fixed trapeze, and even those were rare. Young Léotard and his father had developed a routine by which a person could appear to be flying. Léotard was the original, and at that time the only, daring young man on the flying trapeze.

He and his father had rigged up in Toulouse an apparatus consisting of two trapezes and a pair of triangular holds like rings, hanging at some distance apart, from a beam. Underneath was a padded board, and at one end of the board there was a platform for the athlete. At the other end stood Papa Léotard, who could thus swing the trapeze toward his son. The son threw himself from one hold to the other, maintaining perfect balance with his muscular but slender body, and going through all kinds of passes, including a pirouette and a somersault.

In November of the year Maîtrejean discovered him, Léotard made his debut at the Cirque Napoléon, and all Paris rushed to see him. His act was so impressive and he was so elegant that it was no time at all before he was inordinately famous, and was engaged for a grand tour of European circuses and the Alhambra in London.

Inevitably, anybody who could turn a somersault on the parallel bars tried to imitate the master. Flyers, good and bad, graceful and awkward, male and female, sprang into the air all over Europe and America. The routine developed. The primitive apparatus changed. A mat replaced the padded plank, and another platform was added. At least one partner, who was also a flyer, came on to assist the star. The catcher became an integral part of the act. After 1875 there were to be no great changes in the display itself, and development of the art was dependent on the skill and imagination of the individual. Thus at last came such incomparable artists as Codona and the Concellos.

In the mid-nineteenth century, when Blondin was startling the world, when Léotard was still supreme in the spectacular feat he had invented, and when, in the more generalized circus picture, the menagerie tent was being tied constantly more closely to the big top, a change was coming about in the training and exhibition of jungle animals. Van Amburgh and his ways were no longer accepted without question. New figures were entering the cage.

17

Taming the
Beasts

AFTER Van Amburgh's early triumphs, many years passed before the world at large began to realize that wild animals could be trained by any method except one based on fear and brutality. The mighty exponent of the moderate point of view, Carl Hagenbeck, seemed to appear on the scene totally unheralded. Nevertheless, other modern trainers for years had been preparing the way for Hagenbeck, though they usually were little known beyond a comparatively restricted *milieu* and did not pass on the methods they had developed.

Such a trainer was Henri Martin. Martin was born in Marseilles during the French Revolution, ran away to be a sailor, traveled the world, returned to France, became a gymnast and rider, toured Central Europe with an equestrian troupe, and arrived in Rotterdam. In the Dutch city he saw the Van Aken menagerie, at that time the best in the Lowlands. He also fell in love.

The young woman to whom he gave his heart was Nelle Van Aken, daughter of the menagerie owner. As a somewhat stern method of proving his affection, Nelle told Martin that she would marry him if he would go into the cage with Atir, a dangerous Royal Bengal tiger. As Antonio Franconi had done, and as Isaac Van Amburgh was to do, Martin went in at once, and found that he too possessed that indefinable something that makes wild beasts obey.

When Henri and Nelle were married—in the menagerie, no less—the guests (other show people) gave them a superb leopard, a Borneo monkey, and a parakeet that could speak several languages. While working for his father-in-law, Martin constantly studied animals, talking to them, making friends, trying to understand them, before he began to exhibit as a trainer. Then, as the caravan traveled from city to city, he perfected his technique. By the time he opened his Ménagerie Royale in Paris in 1829, he had learned to control the animals with apparent nonchalance—a most unusual manner which caused a great sensation.

Henri Martin was a handsome man, who worked in the cage in his shirt sleeves, wearing a colored waistcoat and tight trousers. One scene was played against a background representing a garden at night. He showed a hyena. Then in came Carlotta, a lioness, who turned rhythmically, licked Martin's hands, growled gently, and held one end of a baton, emitting dramatic groans during a tug of war. Atir, the tiger, and Neron, a lion, appeared, were introduced as "my two best friends," and went through their paces.

Saved—By a Tiger

Atir proved his right to the title. During the performance one day, when Neron was in a bad mood, the lion seized Martin's leg. Another lion, seeing his chance, threw himself onto the trainer. Atir leapt at the animal's throat, and saved Martin by driving off both the lions.

If we can believe the records, it was not a new thing for a ferocious beast to show protective affection for a human being. In the winter of 1709, which was bitterly bleak in Lorraine, a little Savoyard boy, perishing of cold, crawled into the bear pits in the gardens of the court of Leopold II, and crept into the den of a bear named Masco. Masco took the boy between his legs and held him against his body. Next morning the boy went off for the day, but slipped back again that night, to find that Masco had saved some of his own food for him. This procedure continued night after night, until one morning the youngster overslept. When the animal did not come out to get his food, and the keeper investigated, he found the boy asleep, and the bear watching over him.

When Martin appeared at Franconi's Cirque Olympique in 1831, it was the first time that savage beasts had been seen in a modern circus arena. In a tremendously successful pantomime, *Les Lions de Mysore*, the trainer, dressed as an East Indian, struggled with serpents and staged a mimic chase with lions and tigers.

A man named Herbert, who had built a big menagerie at Le Havre in 1830, never used a whip, but had a peculiar method of his own to subdue his animals. When one misbehaved, he gave it a violent kick. Either that gesture was sheer window dressing, or Herbert was very lucky, for the lions would lie down at his feet or put their paws on his chest, or let him stick his head into their mouths. Almost nothing is known about him, but his contemporaries said that, as a trainer and exhibitor, he rivaled Martin and the Pezons and the Bidels.

Pezon Trained Wolves

The first Pezon, Jean François, was a genius who in the time of Louis XV trained wolves. The story goes that shepherds were terrified by great packs of wolves that descended on their flocks. Pezon went out into the country at night, and often used to stroll back into a town in the morning, leading a wolf on a leash. He taught those supposedly unteachable animals to do all sorts of tricks, and took them with him from village to village. He was equally successful with other animals, eventually building up

188

the largest French menagerie of the time, which contained at least 100 beasts. With his white hair, white shirt, well-cut breeches and red sash, as he tenderly caressed his favorite lion, Brutus, Pezon cut a dramatic figure. When he retired, his menagerie went to his son, and from him to later generations. Not all of the descendants of Jean François had his good fortune with predatory beasts, for in 1940 his namesake was killed in the arena by a lion.

Bidel was a gentleman of great elegance, with long hair and mustaches, who conducted himself in the ring with a nonchalance comparable to that of Martin. A troupe of Royal Bengal tigers, numerous black and white leopards, plus hyenas, bears, wolves, monkeys, camels, and a solo artist lion named Milady made Bidel's one of the great traveling menageries of all Europe. For many years, no one could visit a fair on the Continent without seeing animals owned by either a Pezon or a Bidel.

All over Europe the fair had played a tremendous part in the development of traveling menageries. Such organized perambulating exhibits were seen in England long before there was one in the United States.

Among the earliest English traveling menageries of which there is a record were Pidcock's, Polito's, and Ballard's. The pioneering Pidcock's started out in 1708. Polito's, active a half century later, was lost while crossing to Ireland. Ballard's is best remembered because one of its lions attacked a lead horse on the Exeter stage coach, in 1816, and later was on display at Salisbury Fair, where it attracted tremendous crowds.

Originally, any such traveling exhibits went chiefly from one of the established fairs to another; but after a while they stopped anywhere they could find a public.

One of the best known of the British menageries traveling in the early nineteenth century was that of "Captain" George Wombwell, who had started forth in 1807, when he was thirty years old. Wombwell's first exhibit was two boa constrictors, which he bought on the London docks for fifty pounds. He soon owned a large collection of exotic animals picked up from foreign ships. With his animals he wandered from one end of Great Britain to the other, and eventually his show became so large that it was divided into three units.

Such traveling menageries as Wombwell's delighted the countryside with a group of brightly painted wagons, usually showing jungle scenes on the sides. The wagons pulled into a town, deployed around three sides of a square, leaving the fourth for an entrance screened by a painted show front, got out the band, and started the spieler. There might be two or three wagons big enough to hold the great carnivora, and several smaller ones for such animals as wolves and monkeys. Elephants, giraffes, and camels were picketed in the center. Admission was a shilling. Elephant rides were extra, and sweets and programs sold for a couple of pennies. It was all rather like a specialized fair.

A German circus

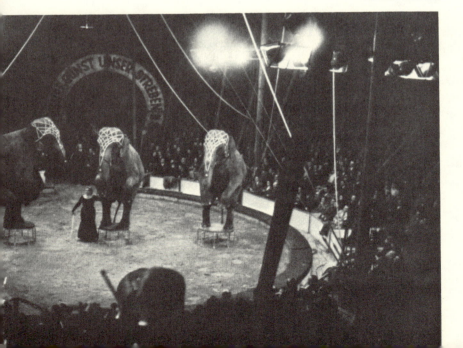

After George Wombwell's death in 1850, his shows continued for many years in the hands of nieces and nephews, some of whom were named Bostock. The Bostocks were among the most noted of all animal men of the period—a time when animal men flourished. E. H. and Frank Bostock, grandnephews of George Wombwell's, were to be famous not only throughout the last half of the nineteenth century, but well on into the twentieth.

During a long career, E. H. Bostock—a shrewd, dapper, determined man—ran three menageries, opened hippodromes, owned circuses, variety shows and cinemas, exhibited freaks, and sent his shows to France and South Africa. He was, in fact, a psychological cousin to P. T. Barnum. Frank Bostock became a famous trainer of wild animals—another "lion king," who was to spend the greater part of his life in this country. Two of his special attractions were an orangutan who played billiards, and a lion who rode on a horse.

Great jungle animals were not the only ones being trained in the nineteenth century for traveling entertainment in England and on the Continent. Clowns made a habit of incorporating small creatures into their acts. The first "educated" pig appeared at Bartholomew Fair in 1816, and was followed by many others. Most famous was a pig owned by Billy Hayden who, though English, was a fixture at the Cirque d'Hiver. Donkeys, cats, geese, pigs, and poodles were taught tricks by the beloved pantomime comic, Whimsical Walker, known to generations as "Whimmy." One of Whimmy's donkeys would turn over pages of music on a stand, and "sing"—on one occasion for Queen Victoria at Windsor. Walker taught a few tricks to domestic cats, but during the first performance they all disappeared and never were seen again. Other trainers had better luck. A comedian named Dicky Usher exhibited what he called "a stud of cat"; and one Bisset developed a Cat's Opera, and made a fortune.

Even into the late nineteenth century, no matter how the training was accomplished, the exhibition of great jungle cats was still very often a matter of scaring them into a state of hysteria by firing guns, beating gongs, cracking whips, and prodding them with red-hot irons as the Romans had done. The beasts then roared and raged enough to satisfy the onlookers. Audiences were so bloodthirsty that accidents were sometimes even faked, though there were a shocking number of occasions (as there still are, and probably always will be) when the trainer actually was torn to bits.

The Remarkable Hagenbecks

Thoughtful men began to decide that such exhibition tactics were not fair to either animals or trainers. A *dompteur* could control his beasts more effectively, and had a better chance of emerging from the cage in one piece, if the animals were not constantly in a state of unnecessary tension. Moreover, starving, beating, and otherwise torturing a valuable animal was not only cruel but uneconomic. Certain trainers came to the conclusion that audiences could be induced to prefer acts emphasizing the cleverness of the animals rather than their ferocity. The trainer who achieved the most remarkable effects by working on that assumption was Carl Hagenbeck.

Hagenbeck's father was a Hamburg fishmonger, and the boy acquired his first exhibition experience at four, in 1848, when some fishermen delivered six seals they had caught in their nets. The seals were put into wooden tubs, and the small Carl exhibited them at a penny a head. When he was twenty-one, his father (who was engaged in a small way in buying and selling animals) turned over the business to him, and he set out on a career that was to end only with his death.

After making a fortune in exhibiting wild animals of all kinds, running a menagerie, and sending out ethnographic exhibits, Hagenbeck bought an estate on the outskirts of Hamburg and set up a zoological park. The great modern zoos where wild animals are kept outdoors in conditions that offer some approximation of freedom owe their existence to Carl Hagenbeck, who proved that all kinds of animals, including the great jungle beasts, will thrive best in the open air.

Hagenbeck began also to change the accepted methods of training. Working on the theory that cruelty will result in hatred, that an animal's intelligence develops best if it spends a great deal of time with a human being it respects and likes, and that each beast must have individual attention, Hagenbeck substituted praise and rewards for punishment and deprivations. With Deyerling, who assisted him, he astonished the public by the response his methods evoked from savage beasts.

Hagenbeck also modified the entire manner of presentation. Animals had originally been exhibited in the arena in their traveling cages. After 1875, it became the custom to build up a cage in the ring, on a small platform surrounded by grilles. In 1887 or 1888, the Hagenbecks invented the kind of big cage-arena that is always used now, in which high grilles rise around the entire ring. This cage-arena enlarged the trainer's scope by

192

giving space for bigger groups of beasts, with pedestals, ladders, seesaws, etc., and made it possible to control the animals during the first training by having assistants outside the cage, holding them on leashes.

By the time Carl Hagenbeck was forty, he was exhibiting tigers, bears, and cheetahs at the Crystal Palace. Soon he was sending groups of gentled animals all over the world, and he himself came to America for many engagements. It was during one of those trips that he set up a collaboration with Benjamin Wallace, resulting in the Hagenbeck-Wallace circus combination.

Carl Lorenz Hagenbeck, son of the original Carl, an even more remarkable trainer than his father, was especially fond of tigers, and made a pet of one named Alexander, which rode around with him in his car. Such men as Richard Sawade, Julius Seeth, and William Peters were also to become famous by using Hagenbeck's methods.

The life of any trainer of jungle beasts is inevitably as dramatic as it is dangerous. In the late 1880's, when Julius Seeth's reputation reached Abyssinia, he went out at the invitation of the Emperor, Menelik II, and stepped into a cage with twenty-eight newly captured lions, all of which, to the astonishment of the Emperor and his court, slunk back when they saw the trainer approach. Seeth picked out four lions that looked teachable, and in eleven days trained them to go through a number of simple tricks. As reward, Menelik gave him a gold cuff, set with precious stones, and $30,000 worth of lions. With the lions, Seeth traveled the world, until one day in Moscow a butcher gave them rotten meat, and they all died of ptomaine.

During the early days of Hagenbeck's experiments, the menagerie in the United States was just becoming an integral part of the circus. Animals were still confined in tiny cages, which not only were drawn into the ring but also carried the beasts in the caravans that traveled the still-primitive roads.

18

Peter Kamm: F.P.G.

Wagons on the Road

DURING the Civil War many small circuses disappeared altogether. Larger organizations, even those that had been established for some time, encountered almost insuperable difficulties, and some of them succumbed. Throughout the war years there were almost no parades of any kind. When peace came, however, a war-weary public yearned for recreation and forgetfulness. Old circuses flourished. New ones sprang up. The parade came into its own.

Toward the end of the Civil War, the Howes and Cushing Circus, which had been started in 1845, returned from a seven-year tour of Great Britain. This show now became Seth B. Howes' Great European. In the 1870's, under the name Howes' Great London, it was to support Barnum's entrance into the circus field.

An old herald of 1867 indicates what Howes then showed in his Great European parade. The big attraction was "a LIVING LION, loose unchained, free, untrammeled, CARRIED AT LIBERTY in the Streets! AMONG CROWDS OF PEOPLE." That large ferocious animal, we learn, is to be summoned from his den, "led up a steep inclined plane by MR. PIERCE, and placed on his elevated seat on the MAGNIFICENT Allegorical Car!" before the procession moves. Moreover, at the conclusion of the march the lion will be "AGAIN LED TO HIS CAGE in the presence of the spectators," who are advised to take their places at either the beginning or the end of the march, if they want to see "this NOVEL, DARING AND IMPRESSIVE sight."

The richly wrought car for the Great European's silver coronet band was drawn by "Elegantly Dressed and Caparisoned CAMELS!"—twelve of them, if we can believe the picture—and bore a "GOLDEN HORSE" rampant. The camels, it seems, had been imported a few years before by the United States Government "to test their availability and utility as a means of transportation across the south-western plains," for a "Camel Post." Howes had prevailed on the Government to let a few of these animals be seen in his "GRAND DIURNAL PARADE."

Preparations had been in the making for a year or so, and the Great European soon owned a group of the most elegant parade wagons known in the history of the circus. Some were vertically telescoped, with sections fitting inside each other like those of an old-fashioned drinking cup, so that for storage or long-range travel they could form a compact nest, and for the parade be lifted by windlasses to a great height. The new wagons were enlivened by colorful painting, and by a good deal of carving surfaced with gold or silver. Considerable ingenuity was evidenced in the choice of draft animals.

Among the most famous creations of the time were: the Chariot of India, 10 feet high, 35 feet long, weighing 10 tons, drawn by African and Asiatic elephants; the World Chariot, 12 feet by 25, which could be extended to a height of 35 feet, and was drawn by 20 Flemish horses; the Lilliputian Chariot, hitched to 20 Shetland ponies; and the massive Car of Jerusalem, with 8 spotted Jerusalem donkeys. All these wagons were imported.

Yankee Robinson's Grand Parade

Yankee Robinson, a circus man who many years later was to play a strategic role in the life of the Ringling Brothers, was another pioneer in the presentation of gorgeous parades. Since 1857 he had been running a wagon show, which faded out of existence in 1873. His greatest years were those immediately after the Civil War, and in 1868 he offered a parade that presaged some of the most elaborate pageants of later decades.

Fayette Lodawick Robinson had been born in New York State, in 1818. He was another original character, a genius at advertising and organization, and one of those circus men who knew how to make money but not how to keep it. As a boy in West Richmond, New York, he was apprenticed to a shoemaker, and took part in amateur theatricals even while he was learning to cobble. In his twenties, he started out as a showman with a secondhand curtain depicting a Grecian urn, and two paintings of the life of Christ. Those he loaded onto a wagon, and set off to make his fortune.

During the next few years, Robinson tried everything from blackface to high tragedy, went out with two different circuses, leased a museum in Cincinnati where he billed himself for the first time as Yankee Robinson, and for several years toured with his own *Uncle Tom's Cabin* show, under canvas.

By 1858 he owned two circuses, and went out himself with one of them. The other, known as the Burt and Robinson Circus, was probably the first show that arranged for the entire company to camp on the lot, instead of boarding everyone in town. Camping on the lot was so unusual a procedure that as late as 1875 the English Thomas Frost, in *Circus Life and Circus Celebrities,* commented on the arrangements then in operation by Van Amburgh:

196

Van Amburgh and Co. own two menageries, one of which accompanies the circus. It will surprise persons acquainted only with English circuses to learn that the staff of the combined shows comprises a manager and an assistant manager, advertiser, treasurer, equestrian director, riding-master, band leader, lion performer, elephant man, doorkeeper, and head ostler, besides grooms, tent-men, &c., to the number, all told, of nearly a hundred. The number of horses, including those used for draught, is about a hundred and forty.

In 1870, the management adopted the plan of camping the horses and providing lodgings and board for the entire company, so as to be independent of hotel and stable keepers, whose demands upon circus companies are said to have often been extortionate. To this end, they had constructed a canvas stable, and two large carriages . . . to form a house eighteen feet by thirty. This is their hotel, and the cooking is done in a portable kitchen, drawn by four horses. Fifty men are lodged and boarded in this construction, which is called, after the manager, Hyatt Frost, the Hotel Frost. Among the cooking utensils provided for the travelling kitchen is a frying-pan thirty inches in diameter, which will cook a gross of eggs at once.

Just how Yankee Robinson managed the details of his organization is unknown, but he prospered and shortly combined his two circuses into one. While he was traveling with that show, in Raleigh, North Carolina, John Brown raided Harper's Ferry. Perhaps because of Robinson's unfortunate *nom de guerre,* a committee called on him with malevolent intent. Warned of the coming visitors, he dashed twelve miles into the woods and, following the advice of his friends, shortly departed that region. Never again did he see stick or stitch of the circus into which he had put all his savings.

With the courage and persistence of his kind, he refused to be downed, organized a small dramatic company, and seven years later bought the Australian circus of Neville and Mabie. The manager was P. A. Older, later to be heard of in his relations with Barnum. Business was remarkably good and, when they closed in Chicago in the fall, Robinson built a Coliseum and Zoological Garden, where he gave semitheatrical programs during the winter.

In the spring he created a parade that was to act as a stimulus for the circus industry. Robinson built his parade around a mechanical musical instrument which he called the Polyhymnia. It was a colossal organ, 15 feet high, 13 feet long, and 8 feet wide, mounted on wheels. The front of the instrument was exposed at one side, in a deep panel, ornate with gilding and big mirrors. On each end and on the opposite side were gaily painted pictures. Blasting out tunes that sounded as if they were coming from an enormous hand organ, the Polyhymnia led the parade. Then along came the great Golden Dragon, a kind of sea serpent with claws and tail, glittering with gilt.

The most startling novelty was a big tableau wagon, drawn by six matched horses and driven by a man dressed as Neptune, holding a trident. In the center of the car stood Amphitrite with Nereids around her, and the Spirit of Darkness just behind. Long arms, ending in ornamental seats, projected from each corner of the car, holding the Four Seasons. The symbolism and even the names may have been a little scrambled, but the crowds along the way gasped in delight, and reporters grew lyrical. Farther along in the pageant, there was a "gorgeous" band wagon, carrying a full corps. Then, according to the *Daily Republican* of Quincy, Illinois, where the parade was seen on May 2, along came a camel led by an Arab, with a Persian lady on his back. There were also 25 knights in burnished mail, 24 maroon-clad horsemen with white feathers in their caps; about 20 richly painted wild-animal cages; and a fantastic group on horseback in costumes resembling a rooster, frog, monkey, mule, and bear, all in mammoth proportions.

At that time, W. C. Coup (who was to be Barnum's first circus partner) was assistant manager of the Yankee Robinson show, and much of the new equipment must have been acquired with $60,000 that had just been invested by one M. Smith of Philadelphia. The parade was described as "a stream of gold and glitter, a mile long." Performances came completely up to expectations. This achievement was the high point of Yankee Robinson's career.

198

Then suddenly he decided that his show was big enough to send out in two parts. When he took one section into Canada, it lasted there only twenty-three days and immediately thereafter his fortunes began to go downhill rapidly. First he became agent for W. W. Cole. Next he managed to get together a small wagon show; but that left him broke at the end of a few months. It was when he was in his seventies that he had his last circus fling, and the one that made his name familiar to many who otherwise would never have heard it. He tied up with five young men from Baraboo, Wisconsin, who were just starting out. In 1884, when he was about to give those five boys their initial training in running a traveling circus, old Yankee Robinson predicted: "I tell you, the Ringling Brothers are the future showmen of America. They are the coming men!"

Others hastened to imitate Robinson's elaborate parades. Before the century had run its course, competition in tableau wagons and other original features was to reach such a pitch that any owner who could not produce a procession at least a mile long was hopelessly out of the running.

During the days of travel by wagon, big parade cars added immeasurably to the difficulties. Roads were rough and narrow, dusty in dry weather and muddy in wet. Bridges were of light construction and could easily go hurtling downstream if the water got too turbulent. Road curves were not banked, and there were no fences or posts on the edges of declivi-

199

ties. Dwellings were often few and far between, and there were many miles of country where not even the faintest light beckoned. Even in towns, gaslights on the lampposts flickered sparingly. The circus moved through the dimness, mysterious and almost silent.

Back in the early years, the then much smaller circus had almost always traveled as an entity. By the 1850's, shows began to be divided into sections, so that the slowest-traveling equipment could get a head start. Organization of schedules was already a major operation, with the executive known as the boss hostler in charge. Until railroad days, there was no radical change in routine.

The boss hostler first sent off a baggage train. Not long after midnight, as soon as the show had been torn down and reloaded, this section went along with canvas, baggage, supplies, and heavy equipment. Supposedly the teamsters had got most of their sleep during the day, around the lot, but they often drowsed as the heavy wagons creaked their way slowly toward the next stop. The men whose work it was to put up and take down the tents promptly curled up in the wagons and slept until they reached the new lot. As soon as they got there, everyone began to unload the wagons and set up the background for another performance.

In the meantime, perhaps two or three hours after the first section left, the "cage train" followed. This included the band wagon, the animal cage wagons, the elephants with their keepers walking at their heads, the ring horses, and all the light carriages, carts, and carryalls in which officials and performers were transported.

Old-Fashioned Cavalcade

The cavalcade moved through the countryside by the light of its own torches, with the wagons rolling steadily or lurching along, at a horse's pace. Ahead went a guide carrying a lantern, planting flares to indicate the turning at any puzzling fork or intersection. The elephants shuffled on majestically, sleepy mahouts at their sides. Drivers dozed. Wheels and bodies of wagons creaked. Occasionally an animal roared.

This second section, unlike the first, stopped somewhere just before it reached town—in a tree-shaded meadow, in a grove, on the edge of a stream—some place where at least water was available, and where there was a certain amount of seclusion. There the animals were watered, the parade wagons were washed, brass was polished and leather cleaned, flags and banners were put up on the band wagon, and plumes on the horses.

Meantime, performers had dashed into town to find rooms where they

200

could dress and nap. There they changed into costumes and rejoined their companions. After Van Amburgh and others set the style for quartering performers on the lot itself, everybody stopped together on the edge of town, and there prepared for the parade.

Canvasmen and drivers, who doubled in brass, picked up their battered instruments. The clown got into his little carriage and took up the reins of the mule he always drove.

With wagons, animals, and human beings in place, usually not later than 9 A.M., the cortege started on its way, to give the expectant public a tantalizing taste of the wonders that later would be seen inside the tents. The glittering pageant swung into town, progressed along a prearranged line of parade to the lot where the tents were already up, unless the heavier first section had been held up by the weather or accident.

Catastrophes on the Road

Accidents were distressingly frequent. Even when the equipment was at its lightest, a heavy rain was almost sure to cause trouble. Wagons often were mired over their hubcaps and the elephants had to be deployed to pull them out. Bridges collapsed, and men and animals were injured. In their nodding lethargy, drivers up in front sometimes passed flares without noticing them and, before someone discovered the error, the whole caravan would have gone astray. Whenever there was a wreck or blockade of any kind, the mighty and usually tractable elephants were called in to clear it up. If elephants had not been an inevitable part of the American circus from the time it began to travel, the whole story of its development might have been very different.

As the heavier parade wagons came into more common use, transportation difficulties increased. It was literally impossible to convey an immensely tall structure, weighing many tons, through a covered bridge, around a hairpin turn, or up and down a very steep incline. On October 30, 1871, the big Howes band wagon fell over a precipice between Barnes Corners and Millerton, New York. There were other equally bad accidents. At best, touring with such huge affairs meant taking safer but roundabout routes, and even avoiding certain districts altogether.

It was time to find an answer to these problems, and travel by rail was very soon to provide the solution.

Meantime, as the American circus was building toward the mammoth enterprise it became in the 1870's, across the Atlantic a comparable phenomenon was being developed by other giants of the entertainment world.

19

Charlotte M. Estey: F.P.G.

From Caravan to
Buckingham Palace

THE BRITISH "Lord" George Sanger is a superlative example of the rags-to-riches tradition—one of the amazing number of poor boys who became circus multimillionaires. Sanger's boyhood was spent in poverty much more stringent than any Barnum or the Ringling Brothers ever knew.

"Lord" George Sanger

From the time he learned to talk, George Sanger was a showman, who literally never knew any other kind of life. By middle age he was famous all over the world, and had already made a tremendous fortune. Gentle, kindly, beloved of all who knew him, he lived to be eighty-four and then died in a moment of brutal melodrama.

His father, James Sanger, who comes to us through the admiring words of his son, was a handsome, hard-working man of great character. At eighteen, he had left his home in Wiltshire and gone up to London for a two weeks' holiday. He did not get back for ten years. On London Bridge he was seized by ruffians out to gather cannon fodder, and impressed into the Royal Navy. When eventually he was invalided out into civilian life, after being wounded at Trafalgar, aside from a pension of 10 pounds and his own talents, James had only one asset. On the ship he had learned a fair amount of sleight of hand from two brothers who had made their living as conjurers before they too were impressed.

Peep Show on His Back

When James reached home, his parents were dead and his brothers far from enthusiastic at his return. With a tiny peep show, which he carried on his back, the independent young man started out to make his fortune. Very soon he married a girl who had been a lady's maid. Needing some kind of dwelling, James built a caravan, with a roof and sides of tin, and in that they ate and slept as they traveled the highways and byways.

That caravan must have stretched like a fairy-tale purse. It was only 12 feet long, a bit more than 7 feet wide, and about 7 feet high; yet a time was to come when, inside and out, it would carry the man, his wife, their household equipment, several children, the peep show, and the horses and frame of a small roundabout (merry-go-round).

From time to time, the peep show waxed more impressive, with new pictures. Other attractions were added. The first was "Mme. Gomez, tallest woman in the world," who, although fairly tall, was given an illusion of greater height by the ingenious use of heels, platforms, and draperies.

Two small mulatto boys were easily persuaded to play the parts of "Tahmee Ahmee and Orio Rio, savage cannibal pigmies of the Dark Continent," and drew good crowds until someone notified the authorities.

Times were usually pretty thin for the Sangers, with only occasional interludes of comparative prosperity. Children were born—ten of them. There was sickness and death. But through it all, James and his wife managed, and the family was close-knit and happy.

The life they lived was only a slightly modernized version of one that had been familiar in England, and all Europe, since the Middle Ages. The Sangers and others of their kind were mountebanks, carrying entertainment around the countryside, moving whenever possible from one fair to another.

In general, as they have done from time immemorial, the show people of Sanger's time got along well together in a sort of esoteric fraternity that lived in a world of its own. Ordinarily they moved in groups, for protection as well as companionship. Often they met with antagonism from townspeople, and frequently hoodlums attacked them, considering it great sport to upset a caravan in a ditch, or attack some lone showman with fists or cudgels.

When such treatment befell the Sangers, James was always among the first to respond to the cry for help—as his ancestors had responded to the medieval "À moi!" and American circus folk of the time rushed in when they heard the rallying cry "Hey, Rube!" He was a strong man, as well as a courageous one.

James's son George was born in 1827, and at five was already an experienced barker. His earliest real memory was of standing near the peep show and pouring forth a spate of patter about a gory murder scene that was one of the attractions of the show. As he grew up, he and his brothers continued to help their father in any pitch he was working.

Sometimes the Sangers were threatened with actual starvation. Troubles of many kinds beset them. When George was in his teens, the family acquired the old roundabout. It required a good deal of mechanical attention, and when George was climbing about on it one day he slipped and tore his leg so badly that the whole calf was hanging loose. James rushed him three miles to a doctor, who said there was nothing to do but cut the leg off, though of course he couldn't guarantee that the boy would not die anyhow. James replied that his son might die, but it would be with his limbs on him. Thereupon he picked George up, galloped back to the caravan, laid him down, threaded a curved needle with strong white silk

204

and, while the boy tried to keep from screaming, sewed the calf back on—sixteen stitches "in good sailor fashion." The wound grew together so that the leg was as good as new, and George never forgot to give thanks to his father for saving him from being crippled for life.

When smallpox struck one of the children, James remembered what he had heard about the Turkish inoculation, and vaccinated his family in primitive but effective fashion. Other people came begging for the same treatment. With a courage that might have got him into serious difficulties in those superstitious days, he vaccinated hundreds. It seemed to George ironic that, when he himself was only twenty-three, his wonderful father should die of cholera.

The epidemic to which James Sanger succumbed was a long way in the future when George began to extend his activities outside his father's small project. He went to work at Richardson's Theatre, where there was a freak show. There he became closely acquainted with fat men and women, a Hottentot Venus, dwarfs, a two-headed woman, a living skeleton, a learned pig, and "Madame Stevens, the Pig-Faced Lady." Madame Stevens was a nice brown bear who was strapped into a chair and seated close to a draped table. Her face was shaved, and the rest of her was covered by a dress, shawl, poke bonnet, and gloves. A boy under the table would prod her occasionally to make her grunt—obviously the proper mode of communication for a pig-faced lady.

After a brief interlude with a juggler, by helping his father again with the peep show, the boy made enough money to start off in a small way on his own. Like Antonio Franconi, he began as an exhibitor of birds and tiny animals, training five hen canaries, two redpolls and six white mice. The canaries rode in a coach; the redpolls fired a cannon; and the mice climbed poles and brought down flags. Obviously Sanger had never heard of Franconi's birds, for he says that his own exhibition was one of the first of its kind. His personality and patter stood him in good stead, and he did very well at parties and meetings, though in one village an onlooker announced, "Them be witch-taught, them be!" The boy also trained two hares to do tricks with hoops and drums.

During an especially difficult winter, George made and sold toffee and peppermint rock candy, and tried his luck with a few conjuring tricks. Soon his brothers, William and John, joined him, and they set forth as a traveling exhibit. Mrs. Sanger made a Hamlet costume for her handsome son George, who was billed as the "Wizard of the West." He recalled many years later that he was a great favorite, especially with the girls.

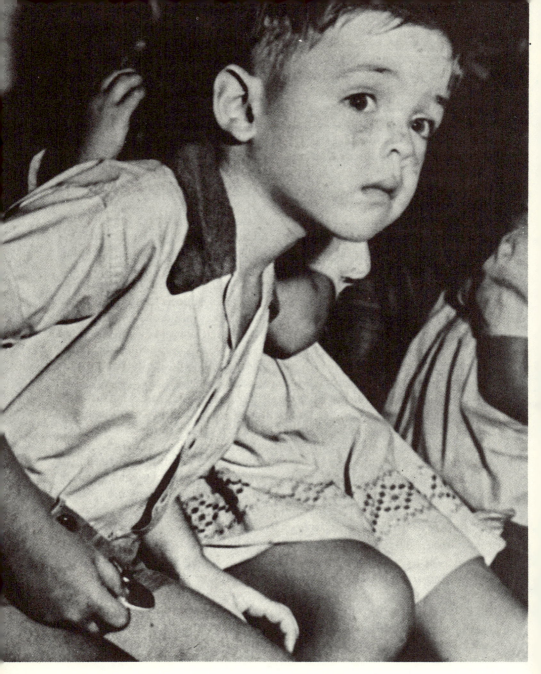

Carroll Seghers: Black Star

The boys did very well financially. In addition to the historic fairs, new ones were being started all over Great Britain, and the young men went from one to another. They would rent a vacant lot, and stay at the fair from three to six days. By the time their father died, they had developed a good business. A couple of years before, John had married a girl who specialized in thought reading and second sight. George now married Nellie Chapman, the "lion queen" with George Wombwell's show. They went up to London, where they fitted up an empty building and gave a series of acts, including a Christmas pantomime, *The Ice Witch,* in which George played Harlequin.

All sorts of untoward things happened to George and his wife. While they were making a magic-lantern show, a stove exploded in the van, burning them badly, and George lost most of his hair. While a doctor was treating them they were robbed of all their money. Broke and very discouraged, they gathered themselves together for a tour of Scotland. Their first child was born and died. As they grew even more desperate, George developed an ingenuity worthy of his father. He set up a shoal of "Performing Fish" and a "Smoking Oyster," which mystified all onlookers and brought in the shekels in rare fashion. With the proceeds, he bought a pony and trained it, acquired a new tent and show front, and bought another horse to use as a rosin-back. George Sanger was ready to start his first circus.

The company consisted of himself, his nieces and nephews, Watty Hilliard, a clown, William Kite, who could do almost anything, and one other man. Not many years later, Sanger's company was to consist of 1,100 persons, with 180 horses, 18 lions and innumerable other animals, presenting acts and spectacles of extraordinary magnificence. Now, in the early 1850's, he offered juggling, ropedancing, trick riding and a few other numbers. Like the Astleys in the early days, the Sangers passed the hat at the conclusion. Out of that venture they made 500 pounds. Sanger was now truly a circus man, and remained one to the end of his days.

Little by little he added to the stud, the company, and the equipment. In 1854, on lowly Bannister Street, Liverpool, he built a show place with a canvas top and boarded sides, in which the company presented what he later called "semi-dramatic-cum-circus" entertainment at a penny a throw. The Cooke circus was then playing in Liverpool at the amphitheatre, not too successfully, and many of its well-known performers switched over to Sanger.

At that time, the highly popular *Mazeppa* was still a novelty in the provinces. Sanger took it to them. For the purposes of romantic verisimilitude, it was necessary for Mazeppa's horse to buck. Sanger, who in his memoirs gives away all sorts of trade secrets, says that you persuade a horse to buck by sticking a pin into it.

Within a decade, the rising young manager owned sixty horses and employed many of the best artists. To the company he added ten Red Indians. He had developed them out of some conveniently available Negroes, to compete with what he insists were fake Indians carried across the Atlantic by Howes and Cushing to astound the British. The Sanger Circus also contained numerous wild animals, including six lions, with which he and his wife put on a spectacle of the Martin and Van Amburgh type, called *The Condemned Preserved,* about a rajah who condemned a poor African boy to the lions because he had the temerity to love the rajah's daughter. When the youth was thrown into the den, the daughter jumped in after him, while the rajah wrung his hands. The boy quelled the lions, saved the girl, and of course married her and lived happily until the next performance.

George Sanger was now a circus proprietor to be reckoned with. He had made a great deal of money, and more kept pouring in. In 1871, for 11,000 pounds, he bought from William Batty the Astley amphitheatre on Westminster Bridge Road, and renamed it Sanger's Grand National Amphitheatre. He also took a three-year lease on the Agricultural Hall in Islington, and built circuses in Manchester, Birmingham, Liverpool, Glasgow, Dundee, Aberdeen, Bath, Bristol, Exeter, and Plymouth. At Manchester he maintained a show that ran continuously for five years. By this time, in Great Britain as in the United States, anyone who went to the circus expected to see a menagerie as part of the show. Sanger had the biggest collection of exotic animals and the most important circus-plus-menagerie in the United Kingdom. In fact, he was the true popularizer in Europe of the circus with menagerie added.

For three decades thereafter, Sanger's story was to be one of phenomenal success, with bigger and better companies, added attractions, and more elaborate spectacles. As time passed, his circus became an institution firmly entrenched in the hearts of his countrymen. None of the success was due to chance. Sanger did it by determination, hard work, clever advertising, and making the most of every opportunity.

Just before Sanger acquired Astley's, William Cooke had lost 16,000 pounds there when he rented it from Batty. Others had previously come to grief. Sanger redecorated the building, showed all sorts of wild animals, and as his Christmas pantomime gave *Lady Godiva*. Performances were a combination of stage and ring, of legitimate and equestrian drama. Success was immediate, and beyond his expectations.

"The Marvel of All Beholders!"

The parade he presented at that time was the marvel of all beholders. Its most spectacular feature was an elaborate, very high "telescope" tableau wagon, on the top of which sat Mrs. Sanger as Britannia, with a pet lion at her feet. By careful planning and judicious finagling, Sanger managed to get his parade involved with a royal procession given in thanks for the recovery of the Prince of Wales after a bout of typhoid. From his landau drawn by four horses, Sanger bowed and smiled as if the whole thing were in his honor. He made the most of the publicity, and after that, when he repeated the pageant, he called it "Sanger's Royal Thanksgiving parade."

He cut an elegant figure in a black frock coat, black trousers, a tall top

Lawrence D. Thornton: Frederic Lewis

209

hat, which he wore constantly, elastic side boots, and a satin tie that became the nesting place for a pin given to him by Queen Victoria. As his mustache, chin beard, bushy eyebrows and what hair he had left on his head grew grey, George Sanger touched it up with coal-black dye.

Up to this time, his brother John had been with him. Now they divided 100,000 pounds' worth of property, and John left to found his own circus. George decided that the time had come for a tour of the Continent. He set out with 46 carriages, 160 horses, 11 elephants, 12 camels, and 230 persons and all their equipment. The start was not auspicious, for the circus went across the Channel in an unseaworthy boat, which was caught by a furious storm just as it drew alongside the quay at Le Havre. Getting ashore took seven hours, while horses screamed, elephants trumpeted, and women and children shrieked. Thousands watched from the quay, and the newspapers carried lurid stories. George Sanger played to unexpectedly big business all over France.

That venture was the first of eleven such summer tours, during which his circus went to France, Germany, Bohemia, Spain, Switzerland, Denmark, Belgium, and Holland, playing all capitals, and appearing before ten crowned heads.

Sanger was the kind of man who accepted melodrama as a natural atmosphere. In 1878, in Paris, eight lions he had rented for use in a jungle love scene got loose in the theatre, and some of them hid in the cellar. Nobody would go after them, but Sanger showed himself his father's son. After one of the beasts had knocked him end over end, he went into the cellar alone in almost total darkness, and made a great show of whacking about with a stick. The frightened animals ran around until they were glad to crawl back into their cages. Meantime, the colored performer who was hero of the love scene had failed to show up; so, as Barnum had once done, Sanger blacked up and played the part. He made such a hit that later, with a real Negro, the piece played for sixteen months.

"If Your Majesty Pleases!"

In his memoirs Sanger divulges how he came to call himself "Lord" George. He got tired, he says, of hearing Buffalo Bill called "the Honorable," and decided that if the American Wild West showman could be "the Honorable William Cody" he could be "Lord George Sanger." He added the title to his old bills and had it printed on his new ones, and Lord George Sanger he was to the end of his days. His brother John also adopted a title, on the assumption, no doubt, that if one member of the

210

family was aristocracy, the others were also. Toward the end of his active career, the older man was commanded to appear before the Queen. She said to him, with a twinkle, "*Lord* George Sanger, I believe?" "Yes, if your Majesty pleases!" replied the sturdy old showman.

Sanger wore his hat so consistently that, when he was about to have an audience with the Queen, he was reminded that he would have to take it off. Legend says that he appeared, hat on head, leading two Shetland ponies, and explained to Her Majesty that he would like to take off the hat but was afraid the ponies would run away if he let go of them. Supposedly the Queen laughed. Such an anecdote is too much out of character to be credible. Sanger makes it clear that he was deeply impressed by the honor of an appearance before royalty.

Lord George was never unduly modest about his achievements, however, and he was proud of the place he had in the national picture. Whenever possible, he waved the British flag. "There is nothing American showmen have ever done," he says, "that Englishmen have not done first and done better."

Until he retired in 1905, his circuses went on under his personal direction, continuously elaborated by his lively and uninhibited imagination. One of the high lights long remembered was the presentation at Astley's of *Gulliver's Travels,* as a sort of Swiss Family Robinson mélange which Dean Swift would scarcely have recognized. On the stage at one time were 300 girls, 200 men, 200 children, 13 elephants, 9 camels, 52 horses, plus an ostrich, several emus, pelicans, deer, kangaroos, buffaloes, Brahma bulls, and two lions that were led into a group by collar and chain.

In 1889, Sanger was ordered to make extensive alterations in the amphitheatre. He complied, but the results were unsatisfactory, and four years later he reluctantly relinquished the famous old shrine to the authorities, to be torn down. At that time, too, his beloved wife died.

When he was almost eighty, Sanger retired to his farm at Finchley, and wrote his charming and colorful book, *Seventy Years a Showman.* His life was quietly drawing toward its close, when one evening in 1911 he was sitting at ease, listening to a guest reading the news. In rushed a man who had taken leave of his wits, brandishing a hatchet. In another moment, old Lord George was dead.

Not only had his personal achievements been tremendous. In England he formed a vital link between the old equestrian form of circus, with its emphasis on the riders, and the modern, in which interest is focused almost equally on a great variety of acts.

20

Trail-Blazing Continentals

WHILE Sanger was becoming a significant force in Great Britain, while Spalding and Rogers were rousing the river echoes with their Apollonicon, and while Dan Rice's One-Horse Show was preparing the American public for the gigantic productions of Forepaugh and Barnum & Bailey, the French circus had already attained a robust maturity. By the middle of the century, Paris had become the vital Continental center.

The Colorful M. Dejean

The great French producer was Louis Dejean, who had stepped in when the Franconi dynasty threatened to collapse, fostered the enterprise, enlarged its scope, put up new circus buildings, and maintained a force of artists of such quality that any number of them were to go forth from under his parental care and establish organizations of their own.

Dejean started his career as a butcher's boy, and then became a butcher, with headquarters on the property the Franconis had bought in 1835 for the new Cirque Olympique. When Adolphe Franconi failed, he bought the business for 500,000 francs.

Dejean was a colorful and paradoxical figure, noted for both parsimony and generosity, ruling his great property and his performers with an iron hand, but occasionally dispensing largesse with paternal benevolence. He grew richer and richer. As a builder alone, he has never been surpassed, for three of the great circuses in Paris came into existence through his enterprise. In 1838, Dejean established the Cirque des Champs-Élysées; in 1841, the Cirque d'Été; and a decade later, the Cirque Napoléon. Meantime, he had sold the old Olympique, which thereupon became a lyric theatre.

By the time he built Cirque d'Été, the pantomime had moved into the regular playhouse, and a fickle audience had followed it. To lure back the crowd, Dejean put up a circus-theatre, much like the old building in the faubourg. In 1852, when he built the Cirque Napoléon, he reversed himself. The plan used there—a single ring surrounded by seats—became the typical French circus. In large measure because of the compact homogeneity of that single ring with the seats close all around, the types of acts and the kind of clown most pleasing to the French have differed greatly from those to which Americans are accustomed, in our elongated, multiple-ring tents.

Throughout imperial and republican regimes, Dejean carried on, offering entertainment of immense variety and elegance, including elaborate *naumachiae* in the flooded arena of the Champs-Élysées. The years around 1841 were especially spectacular, featuring at least a half-dozen performers who later were to found their own dynasties. In the epoch from 1847 to 1852, considered the greatest for the French circus, Dejean employed many non-French artists, and himself invaded the foreign field. In 1847–1848 he sent a company to London and Liverpool which was so successful that it returned the following year. It was, however, in Berlin in 1850 that Dejean scored his most remarkable triumph, when he entered into competition with the fabulous Ernst Renz.

The Terrible-Tempered Mr. Renz

Renz was born in 1815 of a circus family, and as a child had trained with a noted cord dancer. He learned riding from Brilloff, one of the early German directors, and, as his assistant, went with the company to Berlin, touring Germany with it under canvas in the summer. Though Renz was then only twenty-one, he was the star of the show. One of the numbers was a modification of Astley's *Tailor's Ride to Brentford,* which in Germany became the adventures of a drunken peasant. In it Renz played the lead, ending with a forward and a backward somersault. He also rode in *poses plastiques,* in the manner of Ducrow, and danced on a rope. In a concluding pantomime, depicting the death of Captain Cook, he carried six persons on his shoulders, and did a back bend with a 140-pound weight in each hand.

When Brilloff died in 1842, Renz became director. Two years later, his company was a force to reckon with, and very soon the new director controlled an immense enterprise, with a permanent arena in Berlin, and buildings in Hamburg, Breslau, and Vienna, in each of which he showed for part of the year.

Renz knew nothing whatever except circus and, it is said, could neither read nor write. In his own great domain, he insisted on rigid discipline, and if he was thwarted went into terrible rages. Many an underling felt his fist, and one day he picked up a wagon shaft and chased his advertising man all over the lot. All his employees naturally enjoyed jokes at his expense. Once, when he was giving the *Nibelungen* as a pantomime, someone remarked that the Opera was then presenting the same thing. Next day, Renz announced to his associates that he was going to sue the Opera, because it had not only stolen the title of his pantomime but had also used all of his *haute école* music.

Yet, despite his cultural deficiencies, Ernst Renz was so successful a manager that when he died in 1892 he left a fortune worth three million dollars.

When Dejean visited Germany in 1850, he gave that country its first true glimpse of the romantic spectacle, presented with the utmost magnificence—a prodigious entertainment with luxurious equipment and costumes such as Berlin had never seen. Renz was completely outclassed. Fortunately for him, Dejean returned to Paris in 1852, there to manage his circuses until he retired in 1870, leaving his son as director.

By the time Dejean built the Napoléon, which is still functioning as the Cirque d'Hiver, several of his companies were touring Europe. In fact, most of the traveling circuses on the continent were being supplied by France.

The oldest of these was founded by Jacques Tourniaire. In 1815 Tourniaire went to Russia, where he became director of the first Russian circus. When he died in 1829, his sons Benoît and François inherited the Russian enterprise, but had even more roving feet, and in 1846 came to America, leaving the Russian circus to other brothers.

Roustabouts raising the tent

215

Shortly after Jacques Tourniaire went to Russia, he was followed by Paul Cuzent, a trick rider who, with his three famous sisters, left Dejean's company and founded a circus there that made a vast fortune before he died of cholera in 1856.

Claude Loyal (who called himself Blondin after that Jean Ravel-Blondin who also taught the hero of Niagara) traveled in France and Germany during the mid-nineteenth century. He left as many descendants as Thomas Taplin Cooke, and they went out into circuses all over the world to shine in innumerable specialties, carrying on the tradition even in our own time.

In 1956, the French Napoléon Rancy circus marks its centenary. The founder, born in 1818, was son of a man who went about with a little traveling theatre. At thirteen the boy ran away to join Dr. Tollet, who gave free entertainments in order to attract patients, in the tradition of the nostrum-selling mountebank. Théodore soon left him and showed up in 1850 at the Champs-Élysées with a new formula for *haute école,* directing his horse without either saddle or bridle. In the course of wide travels, Rancy founded his own circus in Rouen, his headquarters until his death in 1892. From there, the Cirque Napoléon Rancy went out all over Europe; it also gave the Egyptians their first view of a circus in 1868, at the inauguration of the Suez Canal.

In Italy, permanent circuses have never been so important as in England, France, and Germany, and when the nineteenth-century companies gave performances in Rome, Florence, or Milan, they usually appeared in rebuilt theatres. Many great circus families, however, had their origin in the land of the Caesars, and today there is not a company, here or in Europe, that does not contain star performers whose ancestors came from Italy. Among the early names were Guillaume, Pianni, Pieratoni, Ciotti (who established himself in France), Sidoli (in Rumania), Truzzi and Ciniselli (in Russia), and Guerra (in Germany).

Genius on a Galloping Horse

Most dramatic of all was the career of Alessandro Guerra, born in Italy in 1790, and a man of such terrible temper that he was called *Il Furioso.* Guerra's personal hippodramatic stunt, which no one has ever equaled, was to play a flute, violin, or guitar on a galloping horse. In 1826, he and Jean Ravel set up a manège in Berlin, where for years they presented the topmost artists, and offered pantomimes like *Mazeppa* and *The Last Days of Pompeii.* However, in 1848, Renz gave him such in-

216

tense competition that the Italian had to leave Berlin before the end of the season. He went back to Italy, where an economic crisis sent him scurrying to France. Ironic bad luck followed.

Il Furioso, now a sick old man, was obliged to break up his circus, and Louis Dejean went down from Paris to Bordeaux to buy the four best horses in the show, getting them for a song. No sooner had the magnificently trained animals fallen into Dejean's hands than Guerra heard from his former partner, Ravel, who had started his own circus in America and wanted Guerra to take his whole troupe across the Atlantic. Obviously the trip was now impossible. Putting his terrible pride into his empty pocket, *Il Furioso* appealed to Dejean to let him buy back the horses. In an arrogant letter, Dejean refused and countered by offering to hire the Guerra family for his own circus. Upheld by the last of his pride, Guerra refused that charity, and went to Spain, where he died before another year was out. His children dispersed into troupes all over the Continent.

In Germany, after the great contest with Dejean, the herculean, illiterate, efficient bulk of Ernst Renz sat firmly on the circus throne for more than two decades. In 1876, in the Berlin Karlstrasse, Renz built one of the most luxurious arenas ever seen. Lackeys in knee breeches, silk stockings, and powdered wigs supervised the seating. Incense was burned in the stables. To add to the elegance, much of the program was printed in French. A feature was made of elaborate pantomimes, which some historians say contributed to the collapse of the Renz circus in the 1890's, after Ernst's son, Franz, succeeded his father, as had happened with the Franconi dynasty a half century before.

The Great Krone Empire

The great Krone empire did not really begin until the 1880's, but has endured beyond any other in Germany. It goes back to Fritz, who in 1870 founded a little menagerie to go from fair to fair. Fritz's son, Carl, whose name was to become known all over the Continent, was a sixteen-year-old student in Munich when his father was killed by a polar bear. The boy left college to take over direction of the menagerie, by that time the largest in Europe. With the sensitive foresight of a great showman, Carl Krone soon realized that the old fairs were on the way out. Therefore, shortly after the turn of the century, he added a three-ring circus to his menagerie, with which he toured from city to city in the summer, and which he showed in a permanent building in Munich from December to March.

After struggling through the years of the First World War and the resulting inflation, Carl Krone flourished again in the 1930's, with a collection of animals said to be unrivaled, even in America. He himself directed his great enterprise through the evil days of the Second World War, and re-established its prestige before he died. The great Krone circus, its tents decorated by the familiar symbolic gold crowns, in 1956 is again the greatest traveling company in Europe.

Other great entrepreneurs established themselves in Germany or went out into other European centers, sometimes to build empires that endured for decades. There were, for example, Hans Stosch, called Sarrasani, whose amphitheatre in Dresden was the largest in Europe; Paul Busch in Berlin; Albert Schumann, who took over the Renz interests when they fell from the hands of Ernst's son; William Carré, who set up headquarters

218

first in Belgrade and then in Holland; and Magnus Hinne, Ducrow's brother-in-law, who traveled with his circus in Turkey and Greece, and built luxuriously in Petrograd, Moscow, and Copenhagen.

In Switzerland, the future Swiss National Circus was evolving in the hands of the Austrian Knie family. The dynasty began with Friedrich Knie, born in 1784, who at the age of eighteen was lured away from the medical profession by the charms of an equestrienne in a troupe of traveling riders. He became a rider and ropewalker, and in 1808 started his own circus, with a dozen fine horses. Then he fell in love with Tonia Stoffer. When her father put her into a convent to keep her out of his way; Knie proceeded to affix a cord to a wall of the convent, walk up it, and carry Tonia down the cord in his arms. A few years afterward, when his horses were requisitioned in the Napoleonic wars, the young people were so hard up that, with their three small sons, they existed all one winter in a Moravian village by eating corn the farmers threw to the chickens.

The next generation of Knies walked tightropes, and gave performances in the open air, chiefly in Switzerland and South Germany. Carl, one of Friedrich's sons, who did the most to perpetuate the family circus, went up onto the cord when he was seventy, had a terrible fall, recovered, and lived to be ninety. Members of the fifth and sixth generations of Knies are now learning the literal and figurative ropes.

In Great Britain, a hundred years ago, when the Cookes were still attracting immense crowds to their amphitheatres, and Sanger was becoming a force to reckon with, three other circus families were achieving a certain renown—the Ginnetts, the Henglers, and the Fossetts. Two of these dynasties had their roots in Astley's, and sent shoots around the world, including the United States.

Jean Pierre Ginnett, who established the family name, is of interest in the story of the circus chiefly because it is generally believed that he was the first person in England to make use of the full round-top tent, shortly after Aron Turner invented it in 1830. Ginnett was exceedingly adept at training horses, and his small son had ridden with Ducrow as an infant prodigy. That son, John Frederick Ginnett, prospered so inordinately after he became head of the family that he was able to leave to his three sons a circus business centered around three buildings—in Brighton, Belfast, and Torquay—and 80,000 pounds in cash. The show and the fortune still continued to grow for a half century, and the family received the accolade in 1893 when Queen Victoria ordered a command performance at Balmoral, and paid all expenses out of her private purse. She also gave Fred Ginnett 100 gold sovereigns and the usual jeweled tiepin.

The first known Hengler, Henry, who had been a tightrope walker at Astley's, was billed with Cooke's in 1818 as "Mons. Hengler," and finally joined the traveling circus of Price and Powell. Powell, a rider who seems to have been in partnership with Cooke in 1818, married a Hengler daughter. Consequently, when Price and Powell went bankrupt, the Hengler brothers bought the show, and began to put on programs made up largely of acts produced by members of the family and their in-laws. In summer they moved around under canvas, and, as fortune smiled, first built temporary wooden buildings for winter, and then replaced them by stone structures. Eventually the whole business fell into the hands of Charles Hengler, who by that time owned amphitheatres in England, Scotland and Ireland, and had become a formidable rival of Andrew Ducrow's. In his rings, Hengler presented any number of world-famous performers, and on his death both business and tradition passed into the hands of his son Albert.

The Fossett Circus, still an important English entertainment, goes back to Robert Fossett, who, like Sanger, began as a small, peripatetic showman, going from fair to fair. It took a long time for the Fossett show to become a successful circus, for bad luck followed it persistently; but by the last years of the century (in the hands of the original Robert's grandson) it was the biggest on the road.

The first Robert had left nine sons, and the eldest, a second Robert, one of the best bareback riders of his time, married into the Yelding circus family, and took in his in-laws as performers. After various ups and downs, when the show went into bankruptcy it was bought by George Sanger, who offered it back to the Fossett family. Three of the sons accepted, but Robert insisted on starting out on his own, and it was his circus that became Sanger's great competitor. Fossett also assumed a title, and became "Sir" Robert.

The equestrian career of Robert the Third began before he could ride, for his mother used to strap him onto a pony and lead that living pram in the processions. At eleven, Robert ran away to join Frank Bostock's Circus and Menagerie, and toured Ireland with it. He was so versatile that, after he went back to his father's company, he showed the elephants, rode, worked on the bar, and became a clown whenever one was needed. One of his most famous tricks was to put his head into a sack and his feet into wicker baskets and, thus impeded, run across the ring and jump onto the horse's back.

220

Today, the enlarged Mammoth Jungle Circus of Sir Robert Fossett, directed by the latest Robert's widow, two sons and a daughter, travels with a four-pole tent seating approximately 3,000, and carries a large collection of animals.

While these great circus empires were being set up across the Continent and in England, circus in the United States was reaching the time when it would quite literally become the Greatest Show on Earth. To be sure, the eldest of the Ringling brothers was still in his teens, and Barnum and Bailey were just two separate names, but Phineas Taylor Barnum at last had reached the epochal crossroads of his life.

21

The HUMAN CANNON Ball

"LOYAL"
FIRED FROM THE CANNON.

Bettmann Archive

Barnum Finds

His Destiny

T HE TIME had come for Barnum to take up the career toward which, for almost sixty years, destiny surely had been directing him.

He had learned something about circuses from Arón Turner, and a great deal about traveling shows through those he himself operated. He had watched the phenomenal growth of the circus as a form of entertainment on its way to becoming very big business. His fingers must have itched to manipulate levers that would propel such a multiple enterprise; and his agile mind must have toyed with the possibilities circus would offer for the bizarre advertising and promotion schemes that were as natural to him as the breath he drew.

The fateful moment arrived in 1870, when Barnum went into partnership with William Cameron Coup, a little-known showman twenty-seven years his junior. In his autobiography, Barnum says he suggested the collaboration. In *Sawdust and Spangles,* Coup says it was his own idea. However it came about, it was a natural. Barnum had the money, and was known all over the world as an alchemist who could transform a tuppenny bit of glass into something resembling the Kohinoor, or turn some wretched human abnormality into a million-dollar attraction.

Though Barnum described him as "my very able but too cautious manager," from all other accounts Coup was a gambler, of great personal charm if unfortunate impetuosity, who was given to taking long chances, which sometimes paid off. At the same time, he was an inventive genius of a very practical turn of mind.

When he was a young man, Coup joined Barnum's traveling freak show as a roustabout, and for several years learned the essentials the hard way. Before he was twenty-five, he took over the side-show privileges with the Mabie Brothers, and five years later joined the Yankee Robinson show, becoming assistant manager. After a year at Robinson's, Coup married and settled down on a Wisconsin farm. He might have remained a farmer if in Chicago one day he had not run into the clown Dan Castello, who had a scheme for putting a circus onto a steamer and playing points on the lake. Coup joined Castello in the venture, and they did very well. After that, Coup could not rest until he had a show worthy of his mettle.

"World's Fair on Wheels"

Barnum was in retirement in Bridgeport. Coup went to see him and, it would appear, finally charmed and argued the great showman into agreeing to his proposal that they start a circus together. Coup himself became general manager and director. Barnum's son-in-law, S. H. Hurd, acted as equestrian director. Barnum put up money and property, and added the tremendous drawing power of his name. The "P. T. Barnum Travelling Exhibition and World's Fair on Wheels" took to the road in 1871.

Barnum had announced the forthcoming enterprise at length in an 1871 issue of the *Advance Courier,* a tabloid newspaper he printed to inform the public about exhibits and activities at the American Museum. Like many a man before and after him, once he had succumbed to retirement, Barnum did not care for it. He wrote:

> After thirty years' active career in the Museum and Show business, I undertook, at the end of two disastrous conflagrations, to retire permanently from business cares, taking Horace Greeley's characteristic advice, "Go a-Fishin'," for the balance of my days.
>
> But neither ease nor fortune itself furnishes a comfortable content; and being stimulated by energies that will not abate, by a constitution unimpaired, and a desire once more to gratify the demands of an anxious public, I have absolutely become "restive" under "rest." . . .
>
> I am therefore prompted to undertake a new Mammoth Enterprise, by collecting, equipping, and putting in actual operation a great NATIONAL MUSEUM, MENAGERIE CARAVAN AND HIPPODROME combined . . . which I can transport, by means of 500 MEN AND HORSES, to every important neighborhood, township, and city of my native land.
>
> I intend it to constitute in the aggregate . . . the LARGEST GROUP OF WONDERS EVER KNOWN. . . . Everything will be *new*. The exhibition will contain more startling and entirely novel Wonders of *Creation* than were ever before seen in one collection, as I expect to make this the CROWNING SUCCESS OF MY MANAGERIAL LIFE.

He did it, too.

The new circus had its premier performance in Brooklyn on April 10, 1871, with the greatest amount of canvas ever used for a circus, and more men and animals than had ever been brought together in one. The tent covered nearly three acres, and held 10,000. The ensuing wagon tour took in the Eastern and Middle Western and Western states from Maine to Kansas.

During the first season, Barnum was on hand in every major city, and sometimes seized the opportunity to give a lecture on temperance, which had become an obsession with him. Coup plastered the route with bills, sometimes to a distance as great as seventy-five miles from the destination, and arranged for excursion trains. Receipts for the first season exceeded $400,000.

Circus or no circus, Barnum was still a museum man. He took the show back to the Empire Rink for the winter season, and augmented his menagerie by giraffes, sea lions, and barking seals. The big side-show novelty was the four Fiji Cannibals who, according to Barnum's story, had been educated and converted by missionaries. He showed also Alexis, an Italian goat who had been taught to ride, leap through hoops, and jump onto a running horse.

Financial returns were fabulous, but Coup was not satisfied. Thinking toward the future, he decided that, as three times as much business could be done in a large town as in a small one, the best system would be to skip the little towns, even if it meant making long jumps between centers. It was of course impossible to take such jumps when the show moved in the old-fashioned way, by horse-drawn wagon. There was no doubt that travel by railroad would be much more satisfactory, if it could be managed. Coup gave the problem a great deal of intensive thought.

As a matter of fact, several managers had been making spasmodic experiments in railroad transportation. In 1865, Gilbert Spalding had taken the Spalding and Rogers show out by railroad for an entire season, but had given it up because it offered too many complications—the basic difficulty being the fact that, because railroad gauges were different all over the country, every change in gauge meant a shift from the cars of one railroad to those of another. After a manager packed everything into and onto one set of cars and started forth, after only a few miles he might have to repack all the paraphernalia, animals, and human beings into cars that fitted the width of the rails that went on from there. Such disturbances could happen as often as three or four times in a single night. The process was almost worse than struggling through the mud on the roads.

Circus Takes to the Rails

In the late 1860's, after a uniform rail gauge was established, one set of cars could be used all across the country, and it was feasible for circuses to own their own rolling stock. Even now, however, numerous problems still made circus transportation by rail a tricky business. Only certain properties could be packed into freight cars. Such things as the animal cages, band wagons, and calliope had to be carried on flatcars. The usual method of stowing the wagons and cages was crosswise on the flat, with three or four wagons side by side. Getting them into position was a job for

225

a chess expert, and, in order to fit, none of them could be more than eight or nine feet long. Moreover, a big circus could be carried much more efficiently in longer wagons, but if longer ones were built, lifting the wagons from the ground to pack them lengthwise, and letting them down again, presented a major hazard.

Coup came to the conclusion that the first thing to do was to work out a system whereby the wagons could be easily pulled on and off, without danger of toppling over and spilling poles, seats, and perhaps a lion or two onto the ground. Some gadget at each corner, to which a rope could be attached, would help solve that problem. He devised hook-rope rings for the corners.

Anybody could see that it would also be much easier to load and unload wagons if all of them could be run off the end of a string of cars. For getting them up to the proper level and down again, Coup created the steel "plank" or run. To smooth the process of getting them over the annoying and dangerous gaps between cars, he invented the fishplate, which can be attached between one car and the next, to make a strong, level surface. Snubbers helped slow up the pace of a wagon going down the plank.

Coup's system of "end loading," with snubbers and hook ropes, steel runs and fishplates, is still used today by every circus that travels by rail.

When it came to advertising, Barnum's partner was as ingenious and perhaps even more radical than Barnum himself had been. Coup sent out a whole corps of advance men, increased the size of lithographs, first from one sheet to three, and then to ten, and startled the populace with the blatant notes of the original jukebox, called the Devil's Whistle. For greater visibility in the tent, he replaced the customary kerosene lamps by gasoline lighting.

For 1872, the show set forth by railroad, with sixty or seventy freight cars, six passenger cars, and three engines. Nothing like it had ever been seen. It could go as far as a hundred miles in a night, arriving each day in a sizable town in time to give a parade and three exhibitions. Audiences in these towns included thousands from outlying districts, who often arrived in the night and camped out. Financial rewards were fantastic.

Fire!

At the end of the year, however, disaster struck again. After a tour through the South, the show went back to the Hippotheatron on 14th Street, New York, which had been leased for winter performances, and remodeled at great expense to seat 2,800 persons. The circus opened

November 18th. On the day before Christmas, fire destroyed the Hippo-theatron building, all the equipment, and every animal except two elephants and a camel. The loss was $300,000, with only $90,000 insurance.

Such a catastrophe might well have crushed a man much younger than Barnum, but he rebounded with his usual resilience, and cabled his agents in Europe to spend up to a half million replacing the attractions. In April, the enlarged and expanded "World's Fair" went out on the road with twice as large a tent and two rings.

At the end of the 1873 season, Barnum himself went to Europe where he visited the celebrated European circuses and zoological gardens, looking over the field for novelties, engaging performers and buying animals. From George Sanger he bought the plant for producing the *Congress of Monarchs,* which had been presented with great success in Agricultural Hall, London. According to the contract, the plant included "13 gorgeous carved and gilt emblazoned chariots, and appropriate harness for 62 horses; 1,136 elegant and appropriate suits of armor, court dresses, etc., to faithfully represent all the Monarchs and Courts in the world." When the American got back to New York, the *Congress* was already being shown with the menagerie and other ring attractions, in the Roman Hippodrome that had been built in 1852 by Seth B. Howes and Henri Franconi.

In 1874, on land between Fourth and Madison Avenue, from 26th to 27th streets, Barnum built his own P. T. Barnum's Hippodrome, which was to be replaced later by Madison Square Garden. The structure was 200 by 426 feet over all, with a hippodrome track 30 feet wide and a fifth of a mile long.

Coup's health seems to have suffered as a result of the work he put in on that building, and he took a European vacation. When he returned, he found that Barnum had leased some equipment and the name "Barnum's World's Fair" to John V. ("Pogey") O'Brien. O'Brien had a very bad reputation, and on general principles Coup disapproved of what looked like splitting the show, maintaining that competitors would take advantage of the fact that there were two companies with the same name. Time shortly proved him to be right. The immediate result was that Coup withdrew from the partnership.

After he and Barnum separated, Coup took another partner, Charles Reiche, a German wild animal dealer, who later was to go into business with Hyatt Frost. Coup and Reiche built the New York Aquarium, a huge building at 35th Street and Broadway, spent tremendous sums procuring aquatic creatures, and began to do very well indeed. After a time, however, they too disagreed. Their conflict was about Sunday openings. Coup, the gambler, suggested that they toss a penny, the winner to take the Aquarium and two acres of ground on Coney Island with the storage and supply aquarium (all worth at least a half million), and the loser to take four giraffes and five small elephants that happened to be standing nearby. Coup flipped the coin. Though he was on the side of Biblical pronouncement, he lost.

His record thereafter is of a brief struggle uphill and a quick coast down. Coup organized the "Equescurriculum" with Indian and other equestrian acts, and before the season was over acquired the ten-car John H. Murray show. For two seasons, W. C. Coup's United Monster Shows, combined with Farad's Great Parisian Hippodrome, carrying vast amounts of canvas, made a great splash in the entertainment field. Then came continuous bad weather, and a terrible train wreck north of Cairo, Illinois, resulting in complicated financial difficulties, lawsuits, and other entanglements. W. C. Coup refused the financial assistance offered him, and his circus was sold at auction. After that he started a "dog and pony" show, later founded a small museum, and at last retired again to his Wisconsin farm. He died in 1895 in Jacksonville, Florida.

On November 28, 1875, Barnum had offered all his show property at auction. "This," he wrote, "included my Hippodrome and also my 'World's Fair,' consisting of museum, menagerie, and circus property. My object was to get rid of all surplus stock, and henceforth to have but one travelling show. . . . To this end, my agent bid in all such property as I could use. . . . My travelling show consisted of museum, menagerie and circus of immense proportions. . . . My assistant managers were my son-in-law, Mr. Hurd, and Messrs. Smith Brothers, June and Bailey, late proprietors of the European Menagerie and Circus, which I purchased entire and added to my other attractions."

Coup had sold his interest at the time of the great auction. Things were in a sorry state and, as can be seen from the names, Barnum had now called in the Flatfoots. Those experts straightened matters out and carried on for four or five years with great profit to all concerned. During that time, they presented a mammoth Centennial Show. Barnum, then mayor of Bridgeport, between traveling a good deal and writing several books of fiction, found time to add new attractions. He exhibited a Greek who was tattooed from head to foot, and, during the 1879–1880 season, a "Mlle. Zazel, the Human Cannonball."

Apparatus for a similar act, it will be remembered, was invented by William Farini, a funambulist. His mechanism consisted of a plate in the floor of a stage, which was projected vertically when strong springs underneath were released, thrusting the performer some 30 feet into the air, to reach a rope or the bar of a trapeze, which he seized in flight. A young man dressed in woman's clothes, calling himself Lulu, "The Queen of the Trapezists," first appeared in this act in 1873 in Niblo's Garden, and two years later in the Howes and Cushing Circus. The next modification was seen in the Court Theatre in New York in 1879, when George Loyal, known as the "Human Projectile," was actually propelled by a cannon to the top of the auditorium and caught by Ella Zuila, "The Ethereal Queen," who hung from a trapeze by her feet.

The Human Cannon Ball

When Barnum offered the first human cannon-ball act, in the same year, the "Mlle. Zazel" was Ella Richter, an English actress, who was projected horizontally for 60 feet and landed in a net. She was so popular that during the next few years numerous other performers assumed the Zazel name.

Barnum's advertising blossomed. After 1877 an advance car went out two weeks ahead of the show, now called "The New and Only Greatest Show on Earth," carrying the press agents and a paste brigade of twenty men, with tons of immense colored bills, programs, electrotypes, and almost all the other paraphernalia of the press agent of our own time.

Barnum now owned nearly a hundred cars, and what he characterized as acres of tents and pavilions. Every aspect of the circus was growing bigger and better. One of the Smiths had died, and the other men were old. The Flatfoots retired from the scene.

Meantime, another great American manager had been working his way up to the spotlight, and was trying to edge Barnum into the wings.

22

Culver Service

A One-Man Show

O F ALL memorable characters in the American Circus, none is more fabulous than Adam Forepaugh. Legends grew around him as Spanish moss hangs on a live oak.

Forepaugh was a lone wolf who treated the circus a little as if it were a plump and juicy calf created especially for his benefit. He could not work with a partner, and trusted no one. Yet he was a superlative manager. For many years, the organization he built up was second to none, although it was so much a product of his own personality that it could not survive his death. Like Barnum, he had already built a career and made a fortune before he became a circus owner. Unlike Barnum, however, Forepaugh's first occupation had nothing to do with show business, and his second occupation took him in by a more circuitous route. Primarily, Adam Forepaugh was a businessman of the nineteenth-century rags-to-riches tradition.

The Legendary Forepaugh

Forepaugh, who, because he had a son, Adam Junior, was often spoken of as Old Adam (though he was to die just before he was fifty-nine), was born in Philadelphia in 1831. The menagerie was always an obsession with him, and there must have been many a poor pun and rebus on his name. Unfortunately for the punsters, his name was really Vorback, and he changed it probably at the time he went into show business.

Adam Vorback's father was a poor workingman, and the youngster had to leave school early. His first job was as a butcher's boy, for which he got $4 a month and his keep. At sixteen he left home, worked his way to Cincinnati, and there again went into a butcher's shop. With a frugality that was to endure to the end of his life, in eighteen months he saved up enough money from his small salary to go into business for himself—as a butcher. He went back to Philadelphia.

Now, however, he began also to deal in horses, and to run stage lines, and it was the horses that eventually carried him into the circus. Dealing in horses was a peculiarly lucrative business at just that time. Forepaugh is said to have sold as many as 10,000 a year, for all sorts of purposes; and after the Civil War broke out there was naturally an additional demand for them. By trading in horseflesh, Adam Forepaugh not only made money but became an expert judge of horses. Those who watched him year after year said that he never made a mistake in a horse, and could pick the best with an unerring eye.

The notorious Pogey O'Brien had bought a stud of horses from Fore-

231

paugh, for a small, long since forgotten show called the Tom King Excelsior Circus. After several years, when O'Brien was unable to pay his debt, Forepaugh took a half interest in the circus. At twenty-three, he was in the circus business. When he died, in 1890, he had run a circus for thirty-six years, and never once got into financial difficulties.

Forepaugh and O'Brien bought the E. and J. Mabie Circus and Menagerie, and put it on the road as the Dan Rice Circus and Menagerie, with Dan as the featured performer. But the collaboration was not too compatible, and after a year or two Forepaugh and O'Brien split up. From then on, Adam stayed on his own.

He first opened an indoor circus, which he called the Quadrapantheon, and the following season started out with a wagon tenting show. The Adam Forepaugh Menagerie and Circus was such an immediate and unqualified success that he promptly enlarged it and, when he went out in the spring of 1867, carried a bigger tent than had ever covered a circus in this country—a two-ring tent made up of a 120-foot round top and two 40-foot middle pieces, with three center poles. Five years later he introduced a separate tent for the menagerie. Before that time, the animals had been exhibited under the big top itself, and were lined up along the side walls at the right of the entrance. Under the new arrangement, Forepaugh used the three-pole big top, with two rings and no stages, for ring acts alone.

In 1867, when Adam Forepaugh went out with his circus, he had twenty-two cages of animals, plus an adult elephant named Romeo and a baby elephant. "Professor" Langworthy worked in the lions' den. Everybody except rival showmen said that this was the biggest and best-equipped circus-menagerie on the road, and the Forepaugh show held that reputation for several years. The first great competition came when Barnum entered the business in 1871; and later Howes' Great London gave Forepaugh a lively run for his money.

Never one to ignore progress, Adam Forepaugh went onto rails in his own cars four years after Coup first tried out his inventions. By 1879, the man from Philadelphia had sixty cars full of fascinating attractions. He sent his agents out to Siam, India, and the East Indies for additional and better ones. Representatives of other big circuses were also scouring the East, but Forepaugh managed to keep up a menagerie that amazed the American public.

Adam Forepaugh was always a conversation piece for anyone who

Carroll Seghers: Black Star

saw him in operation. He had a strong German accent, and one of his pronunciations that especially delighted listeners was "west pocket" for "vest pocket," because into his left waistcoat pocket he crammed all receipts from sales of what were known as privileges (mostly the side lines now handled as concessions), and from other small transactions. Sometimes that receptacle would contain as much as several hundred dollars. The cash in the "west" pocket was spending money. The take from the circus itself was put into a bank in Philadelphia. Nobody could fool Old Adam about either account, for he kept track of what was happening in all parts of the lot every day until the ticket office opened, and after that was at the front door as long as money was coming in.

Forepaugh was a stalwart man who attributed his robust health to the fact that he didn't smoke, didn't drink, and usually got to bed by ten o'clock. His appearance is best known nowadays by a picture of him in his later years, showing Gladstonian side whiskers, bushy eyebrows, and a very assured expression. He was never ill, could work inordinately long hours, and required the same regimen from those in his employ. With underlings he was cold, formal, and brusque. In the circus world his niggardliness was legendary. All but top performers were hired for as little as they could be persuaded to take, and found it almost impossible to get a raise. On the other hand, nothing was ever too good or too expensive for the menagerie, and no expense was spared for the big acts.

In the early days, the Forepaugh lot offered a customary amount of "grift," furnished by shell-game players and other hangers on, and connived at by the circus itself, but in later years, the only dubious practice was opening the ticket office an hour early to those who were willing to pay a bonus for seats. Adam Forepaugh's ethics may have been somewhat ambivalent, and he was exceedingly annoyed by any attempt at a "shakedown"—a very usual procedure then, and not entirely unheard of now. He insisted on what he thought were his rights, and managed to get them. On the other hand, he had a strong streak of sentimental generosity. Cripples were always admitted free to his circus, and many a youngster hanging around the edge of the tent felt himself pushed inside, while a gruff, Teutonic voice told him to "Get in dere!"

Rivalry between one show and another, which was always strong, and sometimes bitter, reached a high intensity with Forepaugh. In his hands the unique circus type of advertising known as the "rat bill" flourished brilliantly, with an uninhibited name calling that seems astonishing to our libel-conscious age.

234

Rat Bills

Rat bills are among the rarest of the old advertising papers. Ordinarily heralds were printed in advance, in bulk, whereas these attacks on rival companies were printed locally, for local consumption, and posted in the dark of the night. One bill, put out by Adam Forepaugh in 1881 to attack the Barnum Show, is typical. Under the heading, "A BUBBLE PRICKED! SOLD AGAIN!" Old Adam pointed out that Barnum was promising "100 Golden Chariots, Glittering Dens and Open Lairs, HUNDREDS of Ladies and Gentlemen in Military and Civilian Costumes, A SCORE OF ELEPHANTS," and that every statement was a "GROSS EXAGGERATION! WITHOUT A SINGLE WORD OF TRUTH!" Below was what purported to be a correct inventory of Barnum's New York parade of March 26, 1881, giving 14 elephants instead of the promised 20, 23 cages instead of 100, only 25 mounted ladies and gentlemen in uniform, with a total of 177 horses. "NOTE THE DISCREPANCY! Between the PROMISED and what was REALLY GIVEN! In the OLD RELIABLE GREAT FORE-PAUGH SHOW, due to exhibit soon in Washington and Baltimore, the GREAT FREE STREET PA-RADE" (it goes without saying) will "SURPASS the above in EV-

ERY PARTICULAR. The attendance of a discriminating and truth loving public is respectfully solicited for the . . . LARGEST SHOW IN THE WORLD! Which, moreover . . . EXPOSES Fraud! Falsehood! and Downright Deceit!"

Although rat-bill terminology was attributed to Charles H. Day, representing Adam Forepaugh, this form of advertising probably originated with the owner. At one time or another, most of the famous press agents of the day worked for him, but it is doubtful that they could have gone to such extremes without his authorization.

One of the great contests between Forepaugh and Barnum was fought over the Sacred White Elephant, with Forepaugh coming out slightly ahead. Barnum had sent his agents Davis and Gaylor to Burma to bring back elephants. They decided that it would be a *tour de force* to go home with a real sacred white elephant from the court of an Eastern potentate. After prolonged machinations, for $75,000 they finally persuaded King Thebaw's prime minister to part with a sacred animal called Toung Taloung. The conspirators rented a steamer at Rangoon, with a crew of Mohammedans to whom no elephant was sacred, painted the animal red and blue, covered him with elaborate trappings, and sailed hastily and secretly. Toung Taloung reached New York in March, 1884. Barnum must have been disappointed. As anyone can see who goes to the Cristiani circus nowadays, the white elephant is not white at all, but mottled with pink in a fashion that in no wise increases its attractiveness.

This was Adam Forepaugh's opportunity to call attention to the difference between what Barnum promised and what he gave, and between the quality of the circuses run respectively by P. T. Barnum and Adam Forepaugh. It was no time at all before visitors to the Forepaugh circus saw a real, honest-to-goodness white elephant. Adam's keepers had slipped an elephant out of his herd and given it a coat of whitewash. Moreover, no blotches ever appeared on it. When the paint began to wear off, the keepers just renewed it. Most of the public preferred the nice clean white elephant to the mottled pinkish one.

Old Adam Versus Barnum

Competition between Forepaugh and Barnum became so violent that any sort of dodge was considered fair play, until eventually common sense called a halt, and the two titans made an agreement to route their shows into noncompeting fields, alternating from year to year on the eastern and western routes. Even that armed truce did not restrain Old Adam

236

from playing a trick about Madison Square Garden. The Barnum show had always opened there, but Forepaugh got ahead of his rival by obtaining a lease on the building for dates that traditionally belonged to Barnum. Forepaugh and Barnum compromised. In 1887, they opened in the Garden together, with a program that was one of the greatest of all time. The performance was so successful that they repeated the joint opening the following year under canvas in Philadelphia.

It is easy to misunderstand the character of this collaboration. The combined openings did not mean any real fusing of the two shows, and they never traveled together. Pooling resources simply made for a more spectacular beginning of the season.

Year after year, Adam Forepaugh had built up his circus, ordered new wagons, bought new animals, acquired more remarkable performers, taken in more money. The only season during which he had a loss was that of 1876, when he first went onto rails and Centennial entertainments cut in on everyone's business. At the end of 1889, the great showman was at the apex of success. In January he caught cold. On January 22nd, he was dead. Behind him he left a reputation for being one of the three or four greatest circus operators of all time.

Shortly after Old Adam's death, James E. Cooper bought the Adam Forepaugh show, and took it out during the following season. To keep the great name prominent, Forepaugh's son, Adam Junior, was hired at a high salary to work the elephant and horse acts. Then, in a personal venture, Addie tried to cash in on the great name, and failed. Someone put up capital for a small one-ring circus, which he called the "Only Adam Forepaugh Show." It closed in 1894. Before 1895, the tents of the true Forepaugh circus had been folded forever.

It seems a little sad that the name should have been used from 1896 for nearly fifteen years by Barnum and Bailey, to make the Forepaugh-Sells Circus, in which no Forepaugh ever had a finger. The epic of the OLD RELIABLE GREAT FOREPAUGH SHOW is virtually unique in the history of the American circus. The circus died almost as its creator died—a quick, clean death, cut down in the height of its vigor.

The most aggressive competition to which it had ever been subjected was developed less by Barnum himself perhaps than by Barnum's greatest partner.

237

23

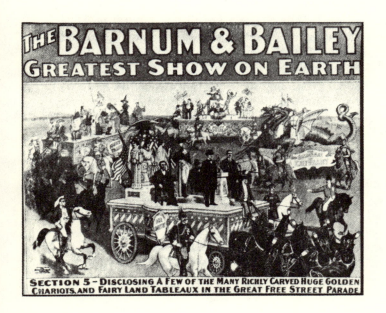

SECTION 5 – DISCLOSING A FEW OF THE MANY RICHLY CARVED HUGE GOLDEN CHARIOTS, AND FAIRY LAND TABLEAUX IN THE GREAT FREE STREET PARADE

The Greatest Manager

of them All

UST who was the non-Barnum half of Barnum & Bailey? The answer is known to almost nobody except circus men and devoted fans. Pose the question to one of them and he will tell you that it was James Anthony Bailey, the most phenomenal manager who ever lived. From Hachaliah on, Baileys have kept cropping up in the history of the circus. The greatest of them all was James Anthony. It is ironic that, despite his achievements, he should have been so overshadowed by his spectacular partner.

J. A. Bailey's name was not really Bailey at all. His life is another story straight out of Horatio Alger. One day in 1859, Fred H. Bailey (Hachaliah's nephew) and Ben Stevens, advance agents for the Robinson and Lake wagon show, drove into Pontiac, Michigan, to "bill" the circus. At the livery stable, they were waited on by a bright and lively lad of twelve named Jim McGinness. The boy's father and mother had died before he was seven years old, and he disliked the people who took him in. Therefore, with a courage and initiative that were to characterize him to his dying day, the boy ran away and went to work for a farmer, at $3.50 a month. When he grew tired of that, he moved on to Pontiac, where he got a job as a sort of bellhop in a hotel. His duties included helping out in the stable, which he did with enthusiasm. Fred Bailey was so delighted with the boy that he decided to adopt him. Consequently, when he was thirteen, Jim McGinness became legally James Anthony Bailey.

Quite unlike Barnum, and scores of other far from bashful figures in the ring entertainment world, James A. Bailey wrote no autobiography. In addition, he was a man who shrank from the spotlight. We know him chiefly through what others have written or told, and almost all of that is laudatory.

Fred Bailey took James Anthony out with him during the season. The boy worked in the winter as bill poster and in other odd jobs. There is a story that in 1863, while he was ticket seller and usher in a Nashville theatre, a man named Green, who was a sutler for the Union Army, offered the young man a bribe to find him a seat. Bailey gave him a seat, and refused the bribe. Green was so much impressed that he made Bailey his clerk.

After the war, Bailey went back to the circus and, in 1866, when he was still only eighteen years old, became assistant agent and bill poster for Lake's Hippo-Olympiad, at $50 a month. Two years later, he was general agent, at $200 a month. In 1870, after Lake had been murdered at the front entrance to his own tent, Bailey became half owner of a "concert" that went out with the Hemmings, Cooper and Whitby show, and the next year (it was then merely Hemmings and Cooper) was hired as general agent at $100 a week—the largest amount anyone had ever received up to that time for such a job.

His next step was a tie-up with George Middleton, to control all concessions with the show. Shortly after that, he bought out Hemmings' interest, and thus, at twenty-six, became proprietor of the Cooper and Bailey Circus and Sanger's Royal British Menagerie.

By the mid 1870's travel by rail was already beginning to be recognized as the best means of transportation for a circus. Many of the old wagon shows had disintegrated, or were about to do so. Writing at that time, Thomas Frost, that careful English observer, recorded the fact that the season of 1868–1869 had been a peculiarly difficult one in America, with almost constant rain. During the preceding winter, many of the shows had bought new tents and equipment—most of which were ruined by rain and mud. Attendance, of course, was poor. It was doubtful, the Briton said, if more than six out of twenty-eight circuses made a profit.

Among those that did were Bailey's (Cooper and Bailey's, of course), Stone and Murray's, the European (by which he meant Seth B. Howes', which was to disappear as such, two years later), and two or three menageries.

In 1876, when J. A. Bailey was twenty-nine years old, he took his circus out to the Far East. By then, long-range transportation problems had become considerably less difficult. It was feasible for a big train of circus cars to cross the United States on rails, and of course circuses had been traveling on ships for nearly forty years.

They had begun to go south by water at least as early as 1837, when Joseph D. Palmer is known to have been in Cuba, initiating more than a century of insatiable demand for the circus, south of the border and in the islands.

When the young Bailey set out, then, he was not opening a completely new path; but he made dramatic history by the extent of his voyage. First he put the Cooper and Bailey show onto rails and took it to San Francisco. There he played to such immense business (as much as $6,000 a day) that he decided to cross the Pacific. He chartered a steamer and set out for Australia, with an excellent ring company and a big menagerie that included a hippopotamus, a rhinoceros, a giraffe, and several elephants.

They played Australia, went on to Tasmania, and started off for the Dutch East Indies. According to a story credited to Willson Disher, historian of the British Circus, the voyage was not uneventful. Just after the circus left Tasmania in the *City of Sydney,* it ran into a storm so violent that the animal cages on the deck broke loose from their moorings. Under Bailey's direction, every member of the company and all the seamen struggled valiantly with the cages, while mountainous waves broke over the deck.

Loose in a Hurricane!

In the first moments of excitement, the rope around the bears' cage broke, and the cage with the lions slid down onto them. All the boxes overturned, and several washed overboard, occupants and all. Above the screams and roars of pain and terror from the animals, the shouts of the men, and the wild shrieking of the storm, a terrific splash was heard as the rhinoceros went into the sea. Cage after cage followed. Nearly half the menagerie was lost, and the giraffe lay dead with a broken neck. When the ship reached Sydney, so the story goes, the giraffe was skinned and stuffed, and a mechanism inserted. In a darkened cage, the head on the long neck nodded gently, and no one was permitted to go near enough to discover the truth.

After buying more animals, Bailey transferred the show to the steamer *Atjah,* returned to Australia and then went on to New Zealand, playing the chief cities and towns. When the company sailed from Auckland for South America in the *Golden Dawn,* the travelers encountered nineteen days more of inclement weather. At the climax of the storm, Chief, the finest elephant, was flung down on deck and killed. The rhinoceros broke loose and charged an elephant. All the animals in the hold, as well as those on deck, began to bellow and scream. Keepers finally fastened chains around the legs of the rhino so that he could be dragged away, and after a while the other animals were brought under control. Years afterward, members of the troupe recalled that in such emergencies Bailey kept calm control of the situation, with everyone relying on his knowledge, judgment, and energy.

The ship finally reached Callao, Peru, and the company gave shows there and then went down the west coast of South America and around the Horn, carrying entertainment to delighted audiences in Chile, Argentina, and Brazil. They arrived in New York on December 10, 1878, after having traveled 76,000 miles.

Bailey was then thirty-one years old. He was a slight man of medium height, who never weighed more than 130 pounds. After he became inter-

241

nationally famous, the world knew his face through pictures on show bills, in which he wore a trim beard and a mustache, his crisp, classic features in striking contrast to the soft, round face of Barnum. Bailey is remembered as being kind and charitable, seldom dismissing an employee except for outright dishonesty. There is a legend, however, that someone once addressed him as McGinness, and did not stay around to do it twice. Whereas other managers were called "Boss" or "John" or (at most formal) "Mr. John," James A. Bailey was always addressed respectfully as "Mr. Bailey." It is as Mr. Bailey that the circus knows him today.

Barnum & Bailey

Soon after his return to the United States, he bought Howes' Great London show, and for the 1879–1880 season made a merger to form Cooper and Bailey's Great London. James Anthony Bailey's star had now risen so high that it threatened to eclipse the light of Barnum himself. On the theory that has always obtained in the circus, "If you can't fight 'em, join 'em," the two men got together late in 1880 or early in 1881, to form the Barnum and Great London Circus, with Barnum, Bailey, and Hutchinson as proprietors. Bailey took over virtually the entire management, and very soon Hutchinson dropped out.

Expenses of the show, according to Barnum's own figures, were $4,500 a day. In the interests of economy, the partners built winter quarters in Bridgeport, bringing even more life into a town that for a generation had profited from the impetus of Barnum's genius.

To celebrate the new partnership a parade of major proportions was held in the streets of New York on Saturday night, March 26, 1881, two days before the season's opening at Barnum's Hippodrome. Seats along its route sold for as much as $10 apiece. In the procession there were 338 horses, 20 elephants, 14 camels and 370 men and women. At Barnum & Bailey's expense, almost a hundred editors of the leading papers between Washington and Boston traveled to New York in drawing-room cars to see the torchlight parade and attend the opening performance Monday night. They were lodged in the best hotels, and went back home Tuesday to write glowing, not to say fulsome, accounts of the wonders they had seen. "A very costly piece of advertising," Barnum remarked, "which yet yielded us a magnificent return."

There were three rings for the performance, with equestrian acts in the two outer ones, and ground acts in the center. "The only drawback to the performance," the New York *Herald* commented a few days later,

The death of Jumbo

"was that the spectator was compelled to receive more than his money's worth; in other words, that while his head was turned in one direction he felt he was losing something good in another."

First came the pageant; then curiosities like Tom Thumb, the Chinese Giant, the Bearded Lady, a pair of giraffes broken to harness, and the baby elephant, Bridgeport, which had been born in February to Queen, a circus elephant. There were extraordinary feats on horseback, juggling, wire walking, trapeze flying, a Japanese perch act, and a military drill by twenty elephants. The program concluded with a spectacular exhibition of vaulting.

During the traveling season, tents were enlarged again and again by adding middle pieces, to accommodate the crowds that often went long distances to see the circus. As many as 20,000 persons were crammed into the big top, for two shows a day, and, at that, thousands were turned away. Barnum & Bailey had produced in 1881 the first American three-ring tent, that triplification of activity under canvas toward which the American circus had been building from the beginning, and beyond which it has

243

never gone. Since the 1880's, any American circus with fewer than three rings has seemed like a one-horse show.

Credit for inventing that system of presentation is almost universally given to Barnum; yet it is one invention for which he probably is not responsible. Certainly he was not the first man to put his performers into *two* rings simultaneously. When Barnum doubled rings in 1873, Forepaugh already had been before him, in 1867. As for the three-ring setup, Lord George Sanger says that he himself showed in three rings and two platforms at once in 1860, on the Hoe at Plymouth, but that the scheme was so unwieldy he discontinued it after one season. With wry amusement, Sanger writes that Barnum carried a three-ring circus to Olympia in London as a novelty twenty-seven years after he himself had thought it up.

Barnum's three-ring tent of 1881 required four center poles. The gigantic covering was to keep on stretching lengthwise until 1919, when Ringling Brothers and Barnum & Bailey put in eight poles. The Ringling tent has now shrunk again to four.

In 1882, Barnum & Bailey initiated a project that was to add a word to the language. They bought Jumbo from the London Zoo, and brought him to this country.

Jumbo was the largest elephant the civilized world has ever seen, and undoubtedly the greatest circus attraction of all time. According to official figures from measurements taken in London, he was 10 feet 10 inches tall, weighed 8 tons, and had a trunk 27 and a half inches in circumference. He had broken off his tusks when he was young. The mighty animal had been three and a half feet tall when he was captured in 1861 in Abyssinia, taken to Paris, shown there for three years at the Jardin des Plantes, and then transferred to London, where he grew to be enormous. Ordinarily Jumbo was very gentle, and was a great favorite with the children. But the zoo authorities began to be afraid he would go bad when the "musth" season came on him.

When Barnum, who had known about Jumbo for years, realized that the time might be ripe for a dramatic *coup,* he cabled his agent, Joel Warner, authorizing him to try to purchase the mammoth animal for $10,-000. The offer was accepted, and a bank draft for 2,000 pounds was dispatched to London.

Immediately a tremendous storm of protest broke out there, and angry communications were addressed to Barnum, urging him to cancel the sale. Phineas Taylor Barnum, even in his seventies not the man to neglect such a heaven-sent opportunity for international publicity, threw onto the fire every kind of fuel he could pick up or concoct. He even fostered sentimental sorrow that poor Jumbo was being torn away from his "wife," Alice. There was actually a suit to test the validity of the sale, but it was upheld, and consequently Barnum began to make arrangements to bring his prize home. That astute gentleman is supposed then to have dickered for the gate receipts taken in from the thousands of persons who went to say farewell to "the pride of the British heart and admiration of every nationality," and thereby to have made a packet.

Then, when Jumbo saw the huge iron-bound cage in which he was to travel, he himself (apparently without prodding) added to the commotion. He began to trumpet, lay down on the ground, and refused to budge. When the agent cabled the owner: "Jumbo has laid down in the street and won't get up. What shall we do?" Barnum cabled back: "Let him lie there a week if he wants to. It is the best advertisement in the world." Finally, after Jumbo had gradually been accustomed to the sight of the cage, he was persuaded to enter—just in time to catch the boat. There are cynics who suggest that the showman engineered the whole incident.

Jumbo was shown first at Barnum's Hippodrome in 1882, and for more than three years served as a drawing card surpassing even Barnum's expectations. The animal traveled in an especially designed "palace" car, and was promoted in every other possible fashion. One of the things that endeared him to the American heart was his making a great friend of a baby elephant, Tom Thumb, named after the midget, who had just died.

On September 15, 1885, two of the Barnum & Bailey circus cars were derailed in St. Thomas, Ontario, Canada. Jumbo and the small elephant were standing on the track when a train rushed upon them. Tom Thumb rolled down the bank. Jumbo was caught between the line of circus cars and the oncoming train. Tom Thumb got off with a broken leg. The great Jumbo was killed. In an attempt to replace him, Barnum & Bailey bought Jumbo's "widow," Alice, and she was shown for a time along with the skeleton and stuffed hide of the departed. Later, Jumbo's preserved carcass was given to Tufts College, of which Barnum was a trustee, and the skeleton went to the Museum of Natural History.

No one knows what happened to disrupt the Barnum & Bailey partnership in 1885, but at any rate (possibly because of ill health) Bailey withdrew.

Late in November in 1887 at ten o'clock at night, Barnum had his fifth great fire. Winter quarters in Bridgeport burned to the ground.

Flames could be seen for miles, and everything was consumed—tents, poles, seats, harness, immense quantities of other properties, and the entire menagerie except thirty of the thirty-four elephants, and one lion.

Nimrod Escapes

The lion, whose name was Nimrod, was led out by his keeper, and was going along quietly when a bystander shot at him. Immediately, the terrified beast broke loose, outstripped his pursuers, and fled into a barn some distance away. The farmer's wife, hearing frantic bellowing, rushed out to find what she thought was an enormous yellow dog eating her cow and calf. She cried "Shoo," and belabored the animal with a broom. The lion growled menacingly. Whereupon the woman ran out crying "A bear! A bear!" Before the circus men could get there, one of her neighbors had shot Nimrod.

Jumbo's "widow" perished in the fire. One elephant, Gracie, rushed into Long Island Sound, where she swam around until picked up in the morning, exhausted. Toung Taloung, the sacred white elephant from Burma, was rescued, but, Barnum said, "determinedly committed suicide," by rushing back into the flames. Those outside could see the frantic beast for a moment, thrashing his trunk about, before he gave one loud cry and disappeared.

Loss from the fire was $250,000; insurance, $31,000. Barnum was an old man, with little more than two years to live. All the same, eleven days after the fire he ordered a whole new menagerie, demanding that it be better than ever. At that time he figured that 82,464,000 patrons had already seen productions he had offered.

Less than a month after the fire, Bailey was back, on terms of full partnership which gave him complete authority. Barnum & Bailey's "Greatest Show on Earth" was born. Bailey issued a statement that marked a milestone in the progress of the circus. Setting forth the terms of incontrovertible honesty and fair dealing under which the circus would be operated henceforth, he announced:

It will be honestly advertised.

The whole of it will be exhibited in every place, large or small, wherever it is advertised to appear, and in no place will a single feature or act be omitted.

The magnificent free street pageant will never be anywhere curtailed by the omission of a single attraction.

Its menagerie and museum tent will never be taken down at night, until

246

after the conclusion of both the circus and the hippodrome performances.

The afternoon and evening performances will invariably be equally complete, perfect, and satisfactory, and, under no circumstances, will the evening performance be, in the slightest degree, abbreviated, cut or neglected; but each and every act thereof will be presented according to the printed programme.

The convenience and pleasure of its patrons will be especially considered.

Its employees will be required to deal fairly and courteously with all, and to answer all proper questions intelligently and politely.

No peddling will be permitted under its tents.

No camp-followers, street fakirs, gamblers or disreputable or intoxicated persons will be tolerated on its grounds.

I shall always be present to investigate any complaints and to strictly enforce the above regulations, and all others that may be necessary to protect both the public and our own good name.

Bailey's pronouncement must have startled any number of persons both on the circus and outside, who were all too accustomed to dishonesty and trickery of every description, even from companies that should have been above reproach.

In 1888–1889 the partners took the show to Olympia in London. There they staged the stupendous spectacle *Nero, or the Destruction of Rome,* which was featured in this country the next year. There were nearly 2,000 in the cast and ballet.

Through the years, the purpose of circus spectacles had changed. From equestrian dramas like *Mazeppa,* designed to show off the riders, the trend veered toward pageants designed primarily to impress audiences with the limitless wealth and marvels at a manager's disposal. They rapidly became attempts at checkmate as each entrepreneur tried to outdo the other. If Forepaugh showed 500 persons on horses, elephants and camels, Barnum naturally had to bring up 1,000; and then of course Forepaugh had to come along with 1,500.

At its simplest, the spectacle was merely a parade around the hippodrome track; at its most elaborate, it became a tremendous pageant and pantomime. The hippodrome track itself increased in size and importance. A print of the Astley amphitheatre that burned in 1841 shows a track between ring and seats, but a narrow one. Quite naturally, more and more of the spectacle action came to take place on that track and, when the circus was in a tent rather than an amphitheatre with its theatre stage, the encircling area became even more important and therefore had to be wider. American heralds for the Barnum & Bailey production of *Nero, or the Destruction of Rome* speak of a 40-foot-wide track, along with three rings and two huge elevated stages. One side of the tent was given over to that spectacle, and the audience sat on the ends and opposite side.

The partners advertise in their herald that "100 Massive Magnificent Golden Chariots" will appear, containing all species of performing and wild beasts. The performance will include all kinds of thrilling races— "Wild Beast, Chariot, Bareback, Equestrian, Classic, Athletic and Gladiatorial contests and combats of the Famed Coliseum and Circus Maximus, and the Olympian Games of Ancient Greece, combined with the most Exciting and Popular Turf Attractions of the present day." Also to be seen are "WEIRD BEAUTIFUL AND SUPERNATURAL ILLUSIONS AND MONSTER DOUBLE MENAGERIES OF TRAINED AND WILD ANIMALS." There will be "STUPENDOUS OPEN MENAGERIES IN THE FREE PARADE," and performances will begin at 2 and 8 P.M.

Like the street parade, the spectacle was becoming so cumbersome and expensive that it was time to call a halt. *Nero* marked the turning point. Bailey may have been responsible for the decision that enough was enough, for while the circus was opening in Madison Square Garden in April, 1891, Barnum died, aged almost eighty-one. Bailey was left as sole proprietor. It is said that he kept 51 per cent of the stock of the mighty company, and gave 85,000 shares to his employees.

The partnership had lasted less than a decade, but without doubt it carried the circus to a peak that has never been surpassed, even by Bailey himself. From the beginning, the collaboration had been a highly successful fusing of complementary elements: Barnum's flair for the spectacular moderated by Bailey's practical efficiency; Bailey's orderly plans and supervision electrified by the *élan* of Barnum's strategems and pageantry. Even when Barnum was gone, the brilliance and verve remained.

The days of the great mergers were at hand. Bailey's first broad step after Barnum's death was to acquire the Adam Forepaugh show from James E. Cooper. He put Joseph T. McCaddon, his wife's brother, in as manager, but the show was not very successful under McCaddon's direction, and Bailey took it off the road at the close of 1894. The greater part of the equipment was used in the Buffalo Bill Wild West, which he controlled with Nate Salsbury as partner.

In 1897, James Anthony Bailey took Barnum and Bailey's Greatest Show on Earth to Europe. Before he left, he arranged to have the Sells

Brothers add the Forepaugh title to their own, and with it to hold the American fort while he was gone. Thus came the Great Forepaugh-Sells Show.

The Greatest Show on Earth opened in December, 1897, in London, and ran until April, 1898, with unprecedented success. Then it traveled around England, on to Germany, and across Europe, getting back to New York on November 6, 1902. The European sojourn was J. A. Bailey's great moment. Twelve years after Phineas Taylor Barnum had passed to his ancestors, that vivid showman's quiet, modest, and almost anonymous partner had created what is still considered the most stupendous and magnificent circus enterprise ever executed.

By the time he returned, those upstarts the Ringling Brothers were offering very serious competition, and soon the story of the great American circus becomes their story. Only four years were left to Bailey. On April 11, 1906, he died of an infection from an insect bite acquired while he was inspecting the menagerie. His estate was estimated at eight million dollars. Barnum himself had left only about half as much.

In a day of tremendous tents, superlative performers, hordes of exotic animals, and parades of incomparable magnificence, the circus of Barnum and Bailey was the greatest of all.

24

The inimitable Felix Adler

Lawrence D. Thornton: Frederic Lewis

The Glittering

Pageant

ITHIN a decade after William Cameron Coup had first made railroad travel practicable, almost every good-sized circus was using the rails. That change in transportation gave an incalculable impetus to the parade. For length, variety, elegance, and colorful elaboration, the glittering pageants of the years between 1880 and 1890 have never been equaled.

Long flatcars, owned by the companies themselves, with Coup's fishplates between them, and his steel runs and snubbing posts ready for loading, made it possible to transport huge amounts of equipment. Wagons and cages could be of almost any size, and were better protected from weather and wear than in the days of wagon trains. It was easier to take care of the animals, and life was somewhat more comfortable for the performers.

The only pieces of equipment that could not be managed on railroad cars were the big telescopes and other abnormally tall tableau wagons. In any event, as overhead telephone and other wires increased in cities and towns, those wagons were becoming a liability. There never were very many of the beautiful, towering structures, but now not one of them remains, and their elegancies linger only in pictures that are usually exaggerated and distorted.

Railroad travel meant also that the whole company and all the equipment went directly to the lot, instead of dividing to let the equipment go ahead to the lot, and the display elements stop at the edge of town to clean up and get into line, and then go through the parade before the personnel even saw the place where the performances were to be given. One result of the change was that parades began somewhat later in the morning.

The circus organization was becoming a sort of glorified supermarket, as shows that already were large bought other shows, to create behemoths that were even more unwieldy. All the expensive imported wagons of Howes' Great London, for example, became the property of the Barnum and Great London when Cooper and Bailey's Great London combined with Barnum's.

A Great Night Parade

Cooper and Bailey's circus had experimented some time before with torchlight parades, and decided that they were a stimulating advertising medium. Consequently, when James A. Bailey found himself in command of his own show and Barnum's, he decided to give a humdinger of a night

251

parade to open the 1881 season. That was the time the newspapermen stayed three days at circus expense. According to one New York newspaper:

The street parade Saturday night was the grandest pageant ever witnessed in our streets, and fully met the expectations of the thousands of spectators throughout the entire route. The whole equipment and display was magnificent, without a single weak feature to mar the general effect. The golden chariots, triumphal and tableau cars were more numerous, more ponderous, more elaborate and gorgeous in finish than any other establishment has brought here; the cages of wild animals were more numerous than usual, many of them were also open, and their trainers rode through the streets in the cages of lions, tigers, leopards, hyenas and monster serpents. There were cars drawn by teams of elephants, camels, dromedaries, zebras, elk, deer and ponies. And there appeared in the grand cavalcade three hundred and thirty-eight horses, twenty elephants, fourteen camels, jet-black dromedaries, a large number of ponies, zebras, trained oxen, etc., also three hundred and seventy men and women. The cavalry of all nations was represented in the various uniforms worn, mounted upon superb chargers, and the costumes throughout were brilliant and beautiful. Music was furnished by four brass bands (one composed of genuine Indians), a calliope, a fine chime of bells, a steam organ, a squad of Scotch bag-pipers, and a company of genuine plantation negro jubilee singers.

The entire route was illuminated by electric or calcium lights. Windows that overlooked it sold for as high as $10.

This, incidentally, was the parade Forepaugh derided in the rat bill "A Bubble Pricked. Sold Again!" but apparently the public thought it was getting something pretty remarkable. Messrs. Barnum and Bailey themselves probably never imagined that it would not hold a tallow candle to the one they were to produce a few years later.

Adam Forepaugh also did himself proud in 1881, as he promised in that same rat bill. Taking a leaf from Barnum's museum book, he put on a $10,000 contest for the most beautiful lady in America, the winner to play the lead in his gigantic spectacle *Lalla Rookh's Departure from Delhi*. The prize fell to Louise Montague, most noted actress of the day, and the theme gave the showman an opportunity to pull every exotic stop, with a great many men and women in Oriental costume, riding on camels and horses, as well as in howdahs on his elephants.

In the parade preceding the spectacle, besides the Lalla Rookh section, color and sound were carried through American streets by 14 ele-

252

phants, 40 big elaborate tableau wagons, a band chariot drawn by 12 black horses, and a calliope. The band wagon was the famous big so-called "Five Graces," one of the few still in existence, which was built for Forepaugh in 1878 by the Sebastian Wagon Works.

Of course, not all parade wagons were enormous, even in the early 1880's. Smaller shows, which had to conserve space at all odds, found it cheaper to continue with short wagons pulled by two horses each, which were packed full and loaded crosswise on the railroad cars. As the sweating men hauled and shoved, lifted and lowered, the cry of "Raise her back!" rang out along the tracks. And that, so they say, is the origin of the word "razorback," designating the circus man who loads and unloads.

Cross cages were then part of the equipment of such ample, but still only moderately pretentious, shows as those of W. W. Cole, Frank A. Robbins, S. H. Barrett, and Batcheller and Doris. After 1900 they were found in only the very small circuses.

Wagons on Parade

By the 1880's, American firms had come of age in the making of parade wagons. In many cases, they now had in their employ highly skilled artisans who previously satisfied their craftsmen's instincts by turning out such creations as cigar-store Indians, figureheads for ships, and religious images. Now they could let themselves go in the fields of mythology, legend, allegory, fairy tale, and Mother Goose.

There were two basic types of what was known as the tableau car—one with flat painting on the sides, and the other with low or high relief carving, often interspersed with mirrors. Originally such decoration had been used to glorify the baggage wagons and the cages. Now, in the true tableau, the car itself became an increasingly elegant float, devised as a stage setting for some still life or living picture on top, or to make a tableau complete in itself. In the most elaborate variation, the contours of the entire car had an articulate irregularity.

Two of the outstanding parade wagons that already had thrilled the country were Van Amburgh's Great Golden Chariot band wagon, used to advertise his show in the '60's, and the tableau St. George and the Dragon, which Forepaugh had had made in the late '70's. The former was a shell-shaped structure, intricately curved at both top and bottom, which rose high at one end to support a kind of canopy that covered the rearmost row of players. The Forepaugh car was a pure tableau in itself. On a curved body were full-sized human and animal figures, adroitly arranged and surrounded by carved ornamentation. Emerging from the top was St. George on a white horse, in close combat with a scaly, winged dragon. It would be difficult to estimate the amount of gold leaf required for either one of these confections.

The oldest of the companies that figuratively and literally got onto the American band wagon were Fielding Brothers (later Fielding and Sebastian, and then Sebastian Wagon Company), of New York; Fulton and Walker, and Caster, both of Philadelphia; and Coan and Ten Brocke of Chicago. More recent were the Moehler Brothers of Baraboo, Wisconsin, the Ohlsen (later the Bode) Wagon Company of Cincinnati, Sullivan and Eagle of Peru, Indiana, and the Beggs Wagon Company of Kansas City. Many of them were near great circus centers.

All kinds of artisans and artists were required—body makers (who perhaps had learned their trade on stage coaches), wheelwrights, and workers in metal and leather, as well as designers, carvers, and painters. These men worked with hard maple, seasoned oak and hickory, carefully concocted paints, gold leaf, the finest mirrors. Still, despite the care and expense that went into making them, only a few of these wagons remain. When its practical usefulness was over, many a beautiful and irreplaceable parade wagon was allowed to stand around in sun and rain, heat and cold, at almost any winter quarters. Over the years, color and gold leaf have worn off. Mirrors have clouded. Even the hardest of woods have disintegrated. Vandals have walked off with bits of carving. Families have used the boxlike cars for living quarters. In many instances, the lovely old creations have been chopped up and burned.

Even a wheel was a masterpiece. For the earlier wagons, wheels were made with simple spokes, or with fan-shaped pieces of wood fastened on the outside of the spokes. As great weight demanded increased strength, webs were added between the radial elements. Spokes up to two inches in diameter were turned from second-growth hickory; thicker ones, from white oak. Yellow poplar made the webs, which were inserted in grooves. Rims were built in sections, and put together with bolts. Hubs were often of steel; boxes on the axles, of bronze. The webbed surface, gay with colors—usually red, orange, and yellow—was known as a "sunburst." Spokes varied in number from 12 to 20, but almost all of the wheels still in existence have 16.

In a day when money had many times its present buying power, just one wheel could cost as much as $150, and on a whole wagon a company often spent many thousands. Such a wagon was built to endure, by men who could not imagine a time without the circus parade. Neither could the public. If the public had been given a choice as to which would go— the circus performance or the parade—many and many a person would have voted to keep the parade.

Back there in the 1880's, when the parade was becoming a seemingly indispensable part of the circus offering, almost everybody tried to get a super-elegant band wagon, even if he had few other display cars. The chariot with the band had a special place in the pageant. On it rode the regular concert players. If, as happened with increasing frequency, one band was not enough, then clowns, side-show workers, ushers, ticket takers and anyone else who could blow or pound a half-acceptable noise rode on other wagons of a less elegant nature.

The most elaborate, most ornate, most costly, second-largest, and most noted of all the great band-bearing cars was the "Two Hemispheres," made in 1902 by Sebastian for Barnum and Bailey. It cost $40,000, and was hauled by a forty-horse team.

For the big hitches, dappled-grey percherons were the favorites, though blacks, Belgian chestnuts, creams, whites, sorrels, pintos, bays, and roans also made handsome turnouts. Many of the well-known drivers are still remembered, and one or two of them are still alive. Back as early as 1848, J. W. Paul had driven the Apollonicon for Spalding and Rogers. Jake Posey and Jim Thomas were to drive forty horses for Barnum and Bailey on the great, five-year European tour.

Even before 1880, every company had to own a steam calliope. The world had grown accustomed to listening for the harsh but exciting blasts that meant, "This is the end of the parade. If you want any more circus, you'll have to come to the performance." As the length of the parade grew, other types of mechanical contrivances were useful for scattering music through places in the line reached by neither band nor calliope. So came

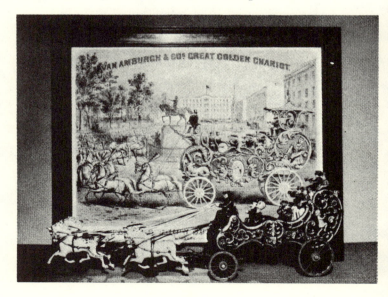

such inventions as the Moscow Chimes, the Orchestmelochor, and the Oriental Music car.

For the Barnum and Bailey parade of 1889, which "Mr. Barnum, as usual, ecstatically viewed . . . from a balcony at the Metropolitan Hotel," music came from twelve places in the line. There were four military bands, a fife and drum corps, four musical chariots of "Campbellican" tubes, an Aeolian organ, the bell chimes car, a group of jubilee singers, and the calliope.

Now, ever since the menagerie had become indissolubly a part of the circus, cages too had to be carried through the streets in every parade. Their size, construction, and decoration became for circus managers a matter for serious consideration and frequent change.

By the ninth decade of the nineteenth century, no longer satisfied with small, tame, or too familiar animals, people wanted to see ferocious jungle beasts and other curiosities, from far ends of the earth. That demand necessitated stronger cages, often with special features for the protection of the animals—and of those who watched them pass or went close to peer between the bars.

Snake dens received special treatment. An especially handsome one, drawn by six horses in Forepaugh parades of the '80's, was of plate glass, with a great deal of gold and silver decoration. A den for the rhinoceros had to be strong enough to restrain that temperamental beast if he went on a rampage. Hippopotami, seals, and polar bears needed tanks, which were accordingly built into the bottoms of their dens. Giraffes, antelopes, and gazelles required tender treatment. In the '80's they progressed through the streets with one side of the cage open. Sliding panels were built in the other sides, to give ventilation without drafts. Today, the giraffe travels in a padded cage.

Gay velvet banners floated from the corners of all these moving dens. Bunting-draped work wagons often went along to fill out the constantly greater length expected by an avid public. At its longest, the circus parade covered three miles from the leading band to the calliope. A pageant might take as much as five hours to go out from Madison Square Garden and return. Among the longest parades of all time were those given by Barnum and Bailey and Forepaugh in 1887 and 1888—one in New York, the other in Philadelphia.

Mother Goose Tableaux

By that time, Barnum and Bailey had the group of legendary and fairy-tale tableaux known as the Mother Goose series, designed especially

256

for children but equally popular with adults. Those tiny floats were integrated with life-sized figures. There were at least seven of the charming little cars—Cinderella, Jack the Giant Killer, Aladdin, Robinson Crusoe, Sinbad the Sailor, Red Riding Hood, and the Old Woman Who Lived in a Shoe. In some instances the bodies themselves were irregularly shaped, and they were always drawn by ponies or by some fantastic, decorative animals such as white mules or zebras. Gold leaf and carved three-dimensional figures made all these tiny cars as expensive as the big tableaux. Nevertheless, a few years later Sells Brothers acquired a similar series.

Though there were still to be many stupendous parades by many circuses, with attractions like the Wild West forming increasingly elaborate sections, or even moving as independent units, there were few innovations after 1890.

While Bailey was in Europe, he paraded as often as possible. After he came back, he bought much new equipment. But the incomparable pageant was on its way out, disappearing gradually, with intermittent spurts of renewed energy. By the early 1920's the big circuses had found street parades impracticable. As the number of motor cars increased, and urban centers grew more crowded, to move through the traffic of any city became more and more difficult. Performers resented the tiresome trek along the streets, especially if they were about to take part in two shows, in which they often risked their lives, in stunts made infinitely more dangerous by fatigue. When a train was late, preparations were delayed, and possibly the parade itself was late getting under way. In addition, license fees grew more and more exorbitant.

Regretfully, the managers decided that the wonderful, the glamorous, the gorgeous, the stupendous, the colossal parade would have to go.

Nowadays, there is the glittering pageant inside the tent—not at all the same thing, especially in its psychological impact. Circuses recognize the nostalgic yearning, and recently a number of American companies have "made parade," in centers where the traffic problems were not too difficult. In 1955, thousands packed the line of march to see colorful processions by Beatty, King Brothers, and Jacob and Sullivan, and joyous youngsters have followed the calliope all the way to the lot.

For most of us, however, little is left of the circus parade except the bright memory. Nowadays when some small circus attempts to revive the street pageant, one feature is indispensable, as it still is in even the smallest tent. That is, of course, the elephants.

25

The Modern
Mastodon

INDIAN or African, male or female, large or small, smoothly taupe or mottled albino, any kind of elephant does something to the human heart. More than the crowded gaiety of the big top, the nostalgic odor of tanbark, the thrill of suicidal danger, the blare of the music, the color and sparkle of the costumes, the beguiling foolishness of the clown —more than any or all of them—the elephants!

Even in the face of long-continued familiarity, elephants still fascinate all human beings, and especially Americans. Perhaps it is because this monster, so fantastically shaped, waving its trunk, swaying perpetually on stumplike legs, peering cynically from alert small eyes, is an anachronistic hangover from the Pleistocene Age, a not-too-much-changed version of the mastodon, and approximately its equal in size. Perhaps the fascination comes from wonder that such a powerful and potentially devastating beast should stand apparently tamed, submitting to restraint, ready to work at command, eating peanuts out of a child's hand.

Everybody delights in watching these seemingly unwieldy hulks in the ring, going through maneuvers requiring the most delicate balance and control—standing on tiny pedestals, rearing onto their hind legs, dancing, forming pyramids. Our trainers are very clever, yet who of us today has seen an elephant walk a tightrope? The Romans watched one walk on a rope in the Circus Maximus; the British saw one thus performing at Astley's, in 1846; and a few years later Americans gazed openmouthed at Dan Rice's Lalla Rookh doing the same trick. To walk a rope is no harder for an elephant than for a man, it is said. The difficulty lies in making the elephant get up onto the rope in the first place. Elephants have played musical instruments, sat at table, juggled, drunk out of bottles, brandished lighted torches, carried almost everything imaginable, including other animals, on their backs, with their trunks, and even in their mouths. Yet none of that is really any stranger than the fact that an elephant will haul a wagon, push over a building, drive stakes, pull on ropes, lift poles, or even go into the formation known as "trunk to tail," when told to do so by a puny human being whom he could eliminate with one blow of his foot or sweep of his trunk.

There are a number of popular misconceptions about the elephant: that he never forgets; that he lives to a much greater age than man; that he is a tame and harmless creature. There is no proof that his memory is extraordinary, though it is true that he will wait for years to avenge himself for some mistreatment. Eighty is a good old age for an elephant. Far from being tame and harmless, he is and always will be potentially dangerous.

This great animal-mountain is a temperamental beast, given to whims and caprices, largely unpredictable even to those who know him best. There is often something between an elephant and his keeper that far surpasses understanding and companionship, yet the most humane keeper, devoted utterly to an animal that appears to be equally devoted to him, may suddenly be attacked without the slightest apparent reason.

In some instances, such sudden violence can be laid to the oncoming of the "musth" or "must" season. Contrary to general belief, must has nothing whatever to do with sex, except that females are not subject to it. Usually once a year, a gland secretes an evil-smelling fluid that runs from a vent in either side of the bull's head. No one knows its purpose, but its advent is a warning that the elephant is dangerous for the time being. Even in the Far East, animals that are working, and have been doing so for years, are chained up during the must season. At that time, as there has been ample proof, one of them will sometimes kill his most trusted friend.

Circus men long ago recognized the dangers inherent in must. That is why all circus elephants today are females, though they are still known as "bulls" ("pigs" to the British). The very few males in the United States are in zoos, where they can be more adequately restrained if they begin to get difficult. Even a usually docile female can, and every now and then does, turn on a trainer, or on some innocent or rash bystander, and in a twinkling bring death and horror into a peaceful scene.

Back in the days when great tuskers were supposed to be the most satisfactory acquisitions for a menagerie, some of them behaved so badly that to this day their names are remembered with shudders. There were Hannibal, Tippoo-Sahib, Columbus, Bolivar, Mogul, Siam, Pizarro, Romeo, Virginius—all bad bulls. Hannibal and Tippoo-Sahib were the earliest, and Hannibal was among the worst.

Hannibal: Killer-Elephant

According to Hyatt Frost, Van Amburgh's advance agent and publicity man, Hannibal was one of the largest elephants ever seen in the United States or anywhere else, when Van Amburgh brought him to this country in 1824. The great tusker is supposed to have killed seven persons, and in a Van Amburgh courier Frost wrote of him as crafty and dangerous, with "an almost unparalleled reputation for viciousness." In those days, it was considered good advertising to play up any jungle beast as dangerous beyond words, and public acceptance was thought to be in direct proportion to the shudders of fear that went through the audience. The publicity man made the most of it. Hannibal was valued at $20,000.

Under the heading of "Curious Tricks of Old Hannibal," Frost tells of an incident that had happened "on the fourth day of November last" (that would be in the late 1850's), "in Williamsburgh," where Van Amburgh's menagerie was showing. While a lad was unloading sawdust from a wagon in the exhibition tent, Hannibal had "one of his fits of fury." He struck at a horse and hit a boy in the neck. The powerful trunk lashed out at the horse again, and the horse ran. Then Hannibal destroyed the wagon, "flinging the wheels about like toys," and proceeded to turn over cages and smash everything within reach. After he finally had been roped, he broke away again, dragging with him a big building stone. At last, the men put on a heavy chain in such a way that they could throw him. Thereupon, as Frost remarks with the utmost casualness, they stabbed the animal repeatedly with pitchforks. After Hannibal had had all he could take, he gave up.

Yet Hannibal had his loyalties. In 1825, in the menagerie in New York, Frost says, two tigers escaped and killed a llama. Joseph Martin, Hannibal's keeper, tried to interfere, and one of the tigers sprang at him. A lion held the tiger while Hannibal lifted Martin into the air and kept him there until help came. There was also a later time in Vermont when Hannibal's keeper at the time fell unconscious from his horse. The elephant picked up the man and held him out of harm's way, on his tusks. Such stories as these have been authenticated by numerous witnesses.

The Zoological Institute and other concerns then leased animals for a season or two to the highest bidders. Animals also changed hands among the showmen themselves. In 1830, Raymond and Waring were featuring Hannibal and Columbus, who did not care much for each other at any time. On December 31st, the two bulls got into a terrific battle on the road outside North Algiers, Louisiana, and were separated with great difficulty. Hannibal was taken on ahead, and Columbus was put into the rear wagon train. As they were entering the town, Columbus suddenly turned on his keeper, killed him and his horse, and then went charging down the line. First he smashed a cage with a llama. Then he met a Negro slave driving some mules. The Negro ran and hid behind a fence. Columbus killed the mules, went after the slave, pulled him out from behind the fence, and crushed him to death. Then the infuriated bull ran through the town, killing a dozen horses, cows, and mules as he went. He was finally stopped by three bullets, which entered just below his eye and left a wound that never healed.

Another tusker, Bolivar, was so dangerous that James E. Cooper finally gave him to the zoo in Philadelphia. Tippoo-Sahib he gave to the New York Zoo.

A Dangerous Profession

Some of the best elephant men have been killed by the animals they literally lived with—for elephant tending is a full-time job. A few have had charmed lives, and lived on, despite long association with mankillers. In the years since the United States saw its first really well-known elephant, scores of keepers have been crushed to death, impaled on tusks, thrown against walls, destroyed in other ways that happened to be convenient for some maddened beast, or killed inadvertently when an animal panicked.

There are those who believe that George and Sam Lockhart were the greatest of all the nineteenth-century elephant trainers. George was killed in 1905 at the station in a small English village by one of four elephants he had named Salt, Pepper, Sauce, and Mustard. A locomotive whistle scared the animal, and she crushed Lockhart against the train.

The Townsend Brothers of Brewster, New York, first topnotch trainers in this country, worked with dangerous tuskers for many years and died in their beds. Orrin Townsend, who was born in 1810, worked thirty-eight years for June, Titus and Angevine, Raymond and Waring, and other early capitalists, handling Hannibal, Bolivar, Tippoo-Sahib, and most of the big bulls of equally sinister reputation. Townsend was called in many times when no one else could manage some great beast on the rampage.

Then there was Stuart Craven (born in 1834, died in 1890), considered absolutely the greatest elephant trainer and keeper this country ever saw. He was a tall, broad, powerful man, who was famous for his courage, patience, and sympathetic understanding of the mighty animals. For some years, he worked for Forepaugh as keeper of Romeo, but quit because he could not get along with Old Adam. Not so long afterward, Romeo killed his new keeper, one William Williams, known as Canada Bill. Romeo was chained securely, but kept giving trouble. In April, 1868, Forepaugh called for Craven, who made his way to Hatboro, outside

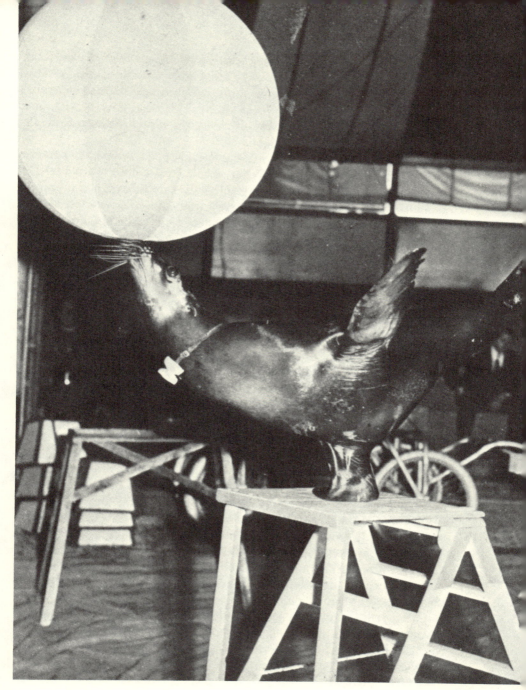

Lionel Green: Frederic Lewis

Philadelphia, where Romeo was being kept. When the bull saw men approaching, armed with chains and other paraphernalia, he flew into a rage. After Craven managed to throw a loop around the elephant's hind leg, and fastened the rope to a triple fall block, Romeo lunged at the man and nearly caught him with his trunk. It took several men from Saturday to Monday to subdue the animal.

Romeo, who weighed 10,300 pounds, had already killed two keepers, and was felt to be so dangerous that he was sold to Van Amburgh. His name was changed to Canada. While the Van Amburgh show was in Connersville, Indiana, the next year, Canada, true to his original name, broke loose in the barn and went to visit his friend Lalla Rookh, who not only could walk a tightrope but was a very attractive female. The keeper tried to lead the bull back to his own stall, and barely escaped with his life. Romeo finally died a natural death in 1872.

When any elephant grew too dangerous, or had killed too many persons even for a sensation-avid public, the owner had several choices. He could shoot the offender; he could give him to a zoo; or he could sell him to another circus where he would appear under another name. The last was one of the commonest procedures—and of course the most dangerous. Only an elephant man who knew this particular animal or had heard about the change could realize that here, standing calm and apparently benign, was a potential death machine. Moreover, names like Bolivar, Queen, Charlie, and Jenny were repeated dozens of times, and it required an expert to tell the individual animals apart.

Keepers and trainers know that elephants have not only strange mass neuroses but idiosyncracies as individual as those that affect human beings. An elephant can swim without any difficulty, but once one gets into the water he is seized by some sort of fixation and almost never will come out again of his own volition. In 1860, Victoria stayed in the water so long that she got pneumonia and died. Albert, who was paired with Victoria, thereupon starved himself almost to death. During the terrible flood in Peru, Indiana, in 1913, Hagenbeck and Wallace turned loose twelve elephants, in the hope that they would swim to high land. Eight of them kept going around and around until they drowned.

The majority of the biggest, most dangerous elephants in captivity have been African; but nowadays almost nothing but Asiatic elephants can be found in our circuses. In general, the African species is bigger. The shape of its back is different, and there are various other distinguishing characteristics. Between the two species, there seems to be no great difference in docility, or the ease with which they can be trained.

264

Elephants are herbivorous animals, and the normal quota of hay for a full-grown animal is 150 pounds a day. Some of them are as choosy as a spoiled two-year-old child; others will eat anything in sight—broom straw, cigar butts, cigarettes, even metal. One member of the Ringling Brothers' herd died in agony after having swallowed a big chain that had been used for tying him to the stakes. Almost any elephant likes whiskey.

Besides the albinos, of which there have been several in American circuses since Barnum introduced Toung-Taloung, occasional other elephantine freaks of nature appear. Major, who played in an act called the "Barber Shop Elephants" on the John Robinson Circus, was an adult who never grew to be more than three feet tall. Tusko, a very dangerous Asiatic bull who was famous all over the United States a few years ago and ended his life in the Seattle Zoo, stood 10 feet 2 inches tall, and weighed 7 tons. Jumbo, greatest of all, was 10 feet 10 inches, weighing 8 tons.

No adult elephant, large or small, ever delights the public so much as an elephant child. In 1955, Ringling Brothers and Barnum & Bailey imported 27 babies of varying sizes, to take their places along with 27 adults. The herd created a sensation in New York on March 27th, when the babies, linked three abreast to their adopted aunties, padded seven miles from the Harlem River to Madison Square Garden.

Elephants rarely breed in captivity. Offspring are rare, and seldom live very long. According to elephant men, who are known to be prejudiced, the elephant is one of the very few animals who show affection for their young. Mother and infant will stand for hours with their trunks intertwined.

That great bulk, which looks so phlegmatic, is in fact a mass of nerves and emotion. The animal gives obvious proof that he experiences affection, love, fear, jealousy, resentment, tenderness, stubbornness, and rage. The sudden noise of a firecracker has thrown many an elephant into temporary insanity. Using that incredibly adaptable trunk, with equal ease the great beast can pick up a pin or kill a man. An elephant sleeps very little, usually just an hour or two at a time, and sometimes, like a naughty child, uses the hours when mankind is sleeping to perpetrate deliberate mischief. Ultra-keen senses of smell and hearing help to make up for poor eyesight.

Back in horse and buggy days, a great many persons discovered that elephants do not like horses—and vice versa. There is no longer any need for someone to call out, "Hold your horses! Here come the elephants!" But at winter quarters in Sarasota, mahouts still have to stand on the alert, bull hooks ready, when these natural enemies come too close to one another.

The way in which mahouts can control these prehistoric monsters is mysterious enough. They seem to do it by a combination of affection, stern authority, eternal vigilance, the threat and occasional use of physical punishment, and a kind of prescience that gives warning of what is going on in the animal's mind. Almost always the keeper walks beside the front left leg. If he suspects a wandering eye or revolt in the making, he seizes that left leg with the bull hook. If a man is quick enough, even an elephant that has started to run can be stopped.

Back in the days when Captain Crowninshield's anonymous exhibit was going the rounds, or Old Bet was electrifying the countryside, one elephant at a time was exciting enough. It was 1838 before as many as two were shown together. At that time, James Raymond's menagerie acquired one big and three small elephants, which were driven tandem on the band wagon—the big one at the rear and the small ones side by side out in front. A few years later, Mabie Brothers set up the same hitch.

Barnum pioneered (in 1852) by getting ten elephants for the New

York Museum, and leasing them to Howes to tour in the summer. Nevertheless, few shows here or in Europe had more than one until after the Civil War. Cooke made a tremendous hit when he took his elephants to Dejean's in Paris for the 1854–1855 season. In the 1870's, Barnum, Forepaugh, and Cooper-Bailey showed five apiece. By 1881, the combined Barnum and Cooper-Bailey show owned twenty, including five Africans and the first baby born in captivity, and for several years the herd stayed at approximately that number. The Ringlings started with two in 1886. In the same period, Forepaugh sent out twenty-five to tour the country, and kept eight more at his winter quarters, or leased them. When the great rivals joined forces to open the 1887 season in Madison Square Garden, Barnum and Forepaugh showed forty each. The numbers continued to grow. In 1931, John Ringling had nearly 100 of the 300 in the United States—undoubtedly the largest herd ever owned by a circus. Today there are 54, including the new babies. According to a census made in 1952, all except six of the 264 elephants then in the United States were female. The males lived in zoos and amusement parks, or were owned by dealers. Out of the 258 females, 124 were in circuses, 92 in zoos, 28 traveled as individual acts, five were in carnivals, and the rest were held by wild animal dealers.

One of the nightmares of any circus is a stampede. It almost always results in loss of human life, and is likely to be very expensive. Even one elephant running amok can occasion damages costing thousands of dollars, and obviously the potentialities are infinitely worse when several of the colossal beasts get out of control at once.

Among the best-remembered crises in circus history was that of 1926, when the Sells-Floto elephants stampeded three times in one week. The circus was in British Columbia, at a fairly high altitude, and the altitude alone made the elephants nervous.

Elephant Stampede!

The first stampede was at Alberta. When the show was unloading in the railroad yards, fourteen huge bodies suddenly raced out through the town and took refuge in the woods. They were coaxed back, and no harm was done, though the boss elephant man had a few bad minutes when he was chased into a cemetery and had to hide among the tombstones. A couple of days later, the same bunch rampaged around in Calgary, but there, too, workmen did not have too much difficulty in catching them. Real trouble came when the show reached Cranbrook. The altitude is

267

higher, and the forest was afire not far away. A small dog, barking at the heels of one of the elephants, sent seven of them off into panicky flight toward the woods, where they scattered. In the first few moments five persons had been hurt.

An old Indian woman spotted three of the animals, and cajoled them with apples until they could be caught. Another one was surrounded, but three of the mighty brutes were still loose in a vast tract of wilderness. Days went by. Townspeople, Indian trackers, and circus men ran themselves ragged. Special trackers were brought in. Trained elephant men were sent from headquarters, but their plane crashed in Colorado. By the time one of the men arrived by train, another elephant had been caught. Two were still out, and engineers on the Canadian Pacific were warned to keep an eye out for elephants on the track. Two professional big game hunters were imported. When an Indian got near enough to one of the truants to try to lasso her, she charged him, and he had to run for his life. The beast took off a lot of her own hide by sliding down a 60-foot bank, was in a sad condition when she finally gave in, and died of pneumonia shortly afterward.

Dashing between one lake and another, following tips that often turned out to be imaginary, the hunters eventually located the last elephant, Charlie-Ed, who had been having a fine vacation but was ready to submit to his keeper. In the meantime, the train had gone on ahead. Charlie-Ed had to be put into a baggage car and shipped by special handling.

In lost business, for the hiring of Indian hunters and trackers, shipping charges, hospital bills, and in lost or damaged circus property, the Canadian stampedes had cost Sells-Floto $60,000.

Now that airplanes are as ubiquitous as birds, it is more difficult for even one stampeding bull to stay at large for very long. In the summer of 1939, Elsie, an elephant in the Russell Brothers Circus, was loose for three days in the Virginia mountains. She fled in panic when she saw a trailer turn over in a ditch, killing one man and another elephant, and injuring four men. After 200 circus folk, police and courageous country people had tracked Elsie for thirty-six hours, a plane spotted her not far from the scene of the disaster. As a very daring measure, two of her elephant friends were sent into the woods after her. Evidently they talked her around, because very soon after that she came back with them, as placid and unconcerned as if she had just been out for a stroll.

Airplanes, trucks, trackers, trainers, and police to the contrary, in

September, 1955, a six-year-old, 2,300-pound Indian elephant named Vickie managed to lose herself only a few miles from the center of Charlotte, North Carolina, and to evade her pursuers for eleven long delirious days and nights.

Vickie was one of the prize exhibits at the Airport Zoo amusement park. One Sunday, when she was startled by a small calf, she took off into the nearby brush, which was so hung with honeysuckle that it must have looked and felt very like a jungle. There she lurked, eating food put out as bait but ignoring other elephants staked out to attract her, and refusing to let her keeper get near, even when he held out her favorite food, bananas. Once when the keeper tried to seize her with an elephant hook, she swept him out of the way with her trunk, and at another time charged three men. No one was severely hurt. After a while, Vickie crossed the main highway, and spent five days in a swampy jungle on the other side, then recrossed and holed up again in the brush.

Authorities called for Lewis Reed, nearly eighty-year-old head trainer for Ringling. When Reed arrived by plane, he tried innumerable ruses, but to no avail. At last, nearly two weeks after Vickie had decamped, Reed picked up her trail and followed it until he was too worn out to proceed. A volunteer posse headed by police continued the chase until Vickie herself had to give up in shaking exhaustion. She was surrounded in an open field, but defiantly faced the human beings. At last, still unbowed and still protesting, with ropes looped around her neck and feet, and ropes making a net over her weary body, she was led off to her stall.

Elephants have done their usually amiable bit toward creating the tremendous enterprise that is the Ringling Brothers and Barnum & Bailey Greatest Show on Earth, from the day when the Ringling Brothers bought their first two elephants for their Carnival of Fun. That was in the 1880's.

26

Harold M. Lambert: Frederic Lewis

The Upstarts
from Baraboo

AS FAR as anyone knows, before 1882 no Ringling was ever connected with a circus. Yet the seven Ringling Brothers were undoubtedly the most efficient and successful group of circus executives who ever lived. The circus was not in their blood, but it was in their minds from the time they were boys—a deep enthusiasm, a compulsion that would not let them rest until they had accomplished their aims and fulfilled their desires.

If there had been only one boy in the family to be infected so thoroughly with the bug, he would probably have run away and joined the first circus that showed up. When all the brothers caught the infection, there was no cure except for them to have their own circus. Starting from scratch, by their own initiative and endeavor they built up what was to be the biggest and most powerful of all circus enterprises. Now, in the middle of the twentieth century, still a family affair, it has been in existence for nearly seventy-five years, and the end is not in sight.

August Rüngeling, a German harness maker, came to this country when he was twenty-one, lived for a while in Milwaukee, changed his name to the more easily pronounceable "Ringling," married Salome Juliar, a girl of Alsatian descent, worked briefly in Chicago, and went on to Baraboo, Wisconsin. During the next few years, he moved frequently, from one nearby Iowa or Wisconsin town to another, looking for work that would permit him to support his growing family in comfort. Ringling *père* did not like to work for others. With an independent spirit that was to characterize his sons, he set up his own harness shop again and again, and just as often had to go back to working for wages. Life was often a matter of bare existence.

Seven Ringling Brothers

Between 1854 and 1868, the Ringlings had seven sons, Albert, August, Otto, Alfred, Charles, John, and Henry. Ida, the daughter who was to be the mother of John Ringling North and Henry Ringling North, was born in 1874.

The story of the boys' first sight of a circus has been told many times. Albert, known always as Al, was sixteen when Dan Rice's Great Paris Pavilion came floating into the Mississippi River town of McGregor, Iowa, where the Ringlings were living. John, the youngest then, was four. Al was indelibly impressed, and doubtless helped to keep the enthusiasm of the younger ones at boiling point.

Al taught himself to ride bareback, to do some simple acrobatics, to

271

juggle, to walk a tightrope. Eventually he became so expert on the rope that he could attract a crowd to the store where he worked by walking across the street on a tightrope stretched between the tops of the buildings. He went on the road for a season with a ventriloquist, playing in vacant stores, hotel dining rooms, and anywhere they could set up their pitch.

Meantime, the younger boys had been trying to learn various acrobatic stunts, and had amused the town by giving performances for which they charged as much as a nickel. Al was married and John was sixteen when the brothers decided they were ready to go on the road for themselves. Then and always, each one of them did those special things for which his temperament fitted him, though in the early days they spread themselves rather thin. As a family, all the Ringlings have been many-talented.

Alf and Charles liked to create music for the show, and their compositions were heard in such spectacles as *Joan of Arc, Cleopatra,* and *Solomon and the Queen of Sheba.* Today, their nephew John Ringling North composes music for current performances. Charles collected rare violins, and even after he had retired would appear, unheralded and largely unrecognized, at least once a season in the big top, to pour forth carefully rehearsed notes from his gold-plated baritone horn. Al built a theatre in Baraboo. In his later years, John Ringling played the great pipe organ in his Sarasota mansion. Charles's son, Robert, became a singer and toured the country with the San Carlo Opera Company; his daughter, Hester Ringling Sanford, is an amateur actress. Hester's son Charles Lancaster is a singer; her son Stuart Lancaster directs his own professional theater.

Back in 1882, the show was called the Ringling Brothers Classic and Comic Concert Company, an amateurish little variety affair, in which the five brothers in the company sang, danced, told jokes, played various musical instruments, and put on a few acrobatic tricks and a bit of juggling.

For the first year, one or two outsiders assisted, but in the autumn of 1883, when their show was called the Grand Carnival of Fun, they ran it entirely themselves. Alf had written the sketches. John, who had a proclivity for dialect, gave "dudish delineations, songs and sayings," presented "Five Minutes in Ireland," with songs, dances and jokes, and his own parody version of "Over the Garden Wall." Later on in the program he became the Emperor of Dutch Comedians, in wooden shoes, in which he danced and gave "Hibdy-Dibdy Fazes." He also took the part of a

Dutchman in a piece called "Room 35, or Trouble in a Hotel," and that of Pat Mullen, a Bad Man, in "Ki-Ke-Kan-Kum." They all made music. Before the next season, Mrs. Al became part of the company. She had always made their costumes, and eventually she not only became a very expert bareback rider but took over the snake-charming act.

It was Yankee Robinson, old and broke, who lent the Ringling boys his name, went out with them as announcer for the better part of a season (dying before they had completed the tour), and gave them their real initiation into circus management and presentation. Up to that time, they had traveled as a "gilly" show, almost entirely in rented wagons. Now they bought two old horses for $50, got a couple of new wagons, and made a tent, cutting the poles and stakes in the woods. They already had a brightly painted wagon which had been fixed up for them by their uncle, Henry Moeller, who from that beginning became one of the most important circus wagon builders in the country. After the 1884 season, the Ringling brothers were seasoned circus men.

From the first, they insisted that their show be clean, honest, and decent. Grift was not tolerated on the Ringling lot. There was no short-changing. No "Monday man" stole clothes off local clotheslines. Employees had to live up to standards the owners set, and in turn were treated fairly. A performer might feel dissatisfied with his salary, but he never had to be afraid he would be cheated in his pay envelope. There is no doubt that the Ringlings were largely responsible for a broad change-over in public attitude toward the circus as an organization, and its employees as a class.

For a good many years, every dollar any of the brothers could squeeze out, beyond those needed for the most moderate personal expenses, went into a common purse. They all had a true dedication to the job at hand, and an ambitious foresightedness that kept them always trying to save enough to amplify the program, and add to the performers, stock, and equipment. The growth was phenomenal. By 1888 they were able to buy two elephants. At the end of 1889, they went on the railroad.

Gradually, each brother found his niche. Gus and Henry eventually went in with the others. By 1890, not one of the seven was taking part as a performer. They were too busy with management. Al became equestrian director, and was always able to achieve spectacular effects by making use of whatever came to hand. Otto, known as King Otto, managed the finances, and spent a good part of his life in the ticket wagon. Alf T. ran the side show at first, and thereafter gave all his time to his earlier enthusiasm—the writing of advertising, press releases, and other promotion. Charles took charge of advertising. John, who had a phenomenal memory, as advance man attended to routing and making arrangements with the railroads. After Gus joined the others, he went ahead in the No. 1 advance car, and Henry worked for his brothers as superintendent and doorman. The circus was never the whole of life for him or for Gus, as it was to the original five, but no Ringling could altogether escape the infection.

Charles had married Edith Conway, daughter of a clergyman in Baraboo, and she promptly made herself a part of the circus world, as Mrs. Al had done. Mrs. Charles helped with costumes, traveled with the show, and in the early days often took tickets. When she was in her sixties, she was manager of the circus for a while, and in 1947 was made vice-president.

There is no better way to understand the extraordinary growth of the Ringling show and its changing nature during the first decade of its life, than to refer to the route book covering that period. In the old days, a route book was a sort of diary, into which every significant fact or figure about the season's peregrinations was recorded, and the Ringlings kept a very detailed book up to about 1900. Thereafter, only the most basic facts about the over-all schedule were recorded officially. The Ringlings were systematic, and began to keep the record the very first year, 1882, when they went out with the Concert Company.

Carnival of Fun

At that time, they opened November 27 at Mazomanie, Wisconsin, and closed at Oregon, in the same state, February 3, 1883. The Ringling Bros. Grand Carnival of Fun opened the next year August 20, and closed April 11, 1884, enlarging the territory.

During the next few years, the title changed several times under Alf's artistic pen. For the summer of 1884, it was Yankee Robinson and Ringling Bros. Great Double Shows, Circus and Caravan, and for the winter, the Carnival of Fun again. The next spring it became Ringling Bros. Great Double Shows, Circus, Caravan and Trained Animal Exposition, and Ringling Bros. Stupendous Consolidation of Seven Monster Shows. In 1889, for a few dollars, they rented the Van Amburgh name, to become Ringling Bros. and Van Amburgh's United Monster Circus, Museum, Menagerie, Roman Hippodrome and Universal World's Exposition. With

274

slight variations, that title endured until Alf thought up World's Greatest Shows, which needed no amplification.

A note appended to the route record for 1891 confides: "At Bolivar, Mo., on September 26th, a very fierce battle was fought between the show and the people of the town and vicinity. Many of the local bad men were badly injured. The show got out after a very exciting experience, without suffering any injury." Such fights, known as "clems," were of course frequent, and often had more serious results.

The 1892 season showed the stupendous rate at which the enterprise was growing. From April 30 to October 29 the Ringlings traveled in a dozen states, with 28 cars plus three advertising cars ahead. The arena was under a 170-foot round top, the menagerie under an 80-foot round top. The circus carried also a 75-foot round top for the side show, a 60-foot round-top dressing tent, a 35-foot round-top wardrobe tent, five horse tents, and two cook tents. The menagerie consisted of six elephants, six camels, one hippo, three lions, three baby lions, two tigers, three leopards, three pumas, two spotted hyenas, one zebra, two zebus (Brahma cattle), one Besea antelope, one American antelope (which died), one tapir, one water buffalo, two elk, two deer, one grizzly, one cage of birds, two cages of monkeys, two llamas, two ibexes (one died), and four kangaroos. Twenty-one executives and a Pinkerton detective went along, and there were 47 performers, of numerous nationalities, plus 16 side-show people, and 18 musicians—none of them Ringlings.

In 1892, the Barnum show is noted as "opposition" at certain cities in Kansas, Nebraska, and Wisconsin, showing that the Ringlings were already really in the big time. The less important opposition at several stands was supplied by the Wallace and John Robinson shows.

Those upstarts from Baraboo were becoming increasingly dangerous to James Anthony Bailey. Bailey made the error of thinking that the Forepaugh-Sells combination he had established before he left for his great European tour in 1897 could hold the field firmly against the inroads of the increasingly powerful Ringling show. By the time he returned in 1902, he had a battle on his hands. His big competitors, with their 83-car show, had moved into a good deal of his territory.

Bailey's answer was to enlarge his own circus until it became so unwieldy he had to skip several stands because it was too cumbersome to be moved quickly. Responding at once to the handwriting on the canvas, he reduced the entourage to 84 cars, making the two giants of approximately equal size. But some sort of compromise was necessary. The two companies agreed to stay out of each other's way. As an additional guarantee of brotherhood, Bailey sold the Ringling Brothers the half interest in Forepaugh-Sells, and in 1905 gave its management to them completely.

It is naturally impossible to predict what the outcome of the armed truce would have been if Bailey had not died suddenly in March of 1906. Even before his funeral, the Ringlings were trying to acquire the Barnum & Bailey properties. Some say that John Ringling was responsible for the ultimate transaction; others, that Otto's hand was in it. At any rate, after Barnum & Bailey had been managed for something more than a year by its stockholders, on October 22, 1907, James A. Bailey's magnificent legacy was sold to the Ringling Brothers. The behemoth—the Big One, Big Bertha—had been born.

After the 1907 season, the Ringlings closed the Forepaugh-Sells show, did away with its old winter quarters in Columbus, and moved everything to Baraboo. A couple of months later, August Ringling died. He left his share of the business to Henry, who now became an equal partner with the others. When Al died in 1916, the remaining brothers acquired his interest from his widow. When Henry died two years later, they also purchased his share.

Circus problems were so magnified during the first World War that it was decided to combine the two great shows, which had been traveling separately in their own territories under their own names. So the Ringling Brothers and Barnum & Bailey Combined Shows was created—the largest circus that ever moved across any country. It then had 92 cars, and by 1922 had reached its maximum size, with 100 cars.

When Alf T. died in 1919, his share went to his son, Richard, who never exercised any authority in management. Charles stayed with the circus constantly, and John was in and out, with numerous other affairs demanding his attention. When Charles, too, died suddenly in 1926, his interest stayed with his family, but of the brothers only John was left.

Partly because he was the last of the brothers, with almost all of the power and authority that once had been divided among them, and partly because his outside activities kept him more in the public eye, John Ringling has often been called the Circus King. To all who worked for and with him, he was known as "Mr. John." For ten years he was to carry on virtually alone, and for another several years to pursue a career that became increasingly dramatic.

He had already distinguished himself by procuring a number of ex-

276

Side show barker

traordinary attractions for the show, such as the only big Asiatic one-horned rhinoceros ever in a circus, the first two of several gorillas that through judicious promotion were to make a great hit with the public, another white elephant, and Goliath, a big sea elephant. John Ringling toured Europe every year, searching out and hiring top-notch performers.

The old winter quarters in Baraboo had been used by Ringling Brothers for the last time in the winter of 1917–1918, and at the end of that season Bridgeport became home base for the combined shows. After the 1927 tour, the winter home was changed to Sarasota, Florida, where John had built new quarters and a palatial winter home for himself. By that time, his show was without peer. In all circus history, so great a property had never been under the control of one man.

Each of the Ringling Brothers had had his own important place in the control of the mighty project. As they fell away one by one, John Ringling gathered up the reins they dropped, and easily held all the lines in his immensely capable hands. He had always had a remarkable aptitude for dealing with transportation problems, and in his head were the smallest details of scores of railroad schedules. Those who knew him recall that, on any road the Ringling circus ever traveled, he could take out his watch at midnight and tell those around him just where they were, or were supposed to be.

277

John Ringling

John Ringling was one of the great showmen of all time, a worthy follower of Astley, Barnum, Forepaugh, and Bailey. As the years went by, he became for the public the embodiment of circus, an international figure recognized immediately by thousands when he appeared in any city here or in Europe. But he never played up to the popular conception of either a great circus entrepreneur or a man worth fifty million. In a day when every man wore a tiepin, he wore no jewelry except a magnificent star-sapphire ring. When he walked on the street, a casual tan topcoat hung across his left arm. He carried a cane, hooked over his forearm.

Though he bought dollar cigars, ten boxes at a time, he never smoked them, but gnawed at one constantly, discarding it as its mass became too soggy and replacing it with another. That cigar-chewing habit was, apparently, due to an exceedingly high-strung and nervous temperament.

John Ringling loved good living and good company. He imported Pilsener beer from Pilsen. Not far from the kitchen door of his Sarasota home, he built a terrapin crawl in the sea wall on the bay, and there kept live sea turtles that could be whisked into the pot to make his favorite turtle soup. When the Old Waldorf was dismantled, he bought the hotel's wine cellar, which in 1920 was one of the best in the United States.

Far into the night, lights could be seen burning in the luxurious Sarasota house, for on the road Ringling was accustomed to eating his main meal of the day after the show was put to bed, and the schedule was continued wherever he was, even when the circus was in winter quarters.

The great mansion, which he called "Ca'd' Zan," meaning "John's house" as a Venetian boatman would say it, created a hospitable background for entertaining all sorts of people, from all over the globe and all walks of life, but chiefly from the entertainment world. In its great hall, where he had placed his Aeolian pipe organ, he hung water-color portraits of himself and his wife, painted by Savely Sorine, a society portrait painter of the 1920's. When those portraits were unveiled, the Ringlings threw a big party, attended by such figures as Tex Rickard, Will Rogers, and Flo Ziegfeld. It was then that Will Rogers perpetrated a wisecrack that John Ringling later repeated with great gusto.

The portrait shows Ringling standing beneath a palm tree, sapphire ring on a finger, tan topcoat over one arm, and the other hand in his trousers pocket.

"How do you like it?" he asked Will Rogers.

"Wa-a-all, I'll tell you," Rogers drawled. "There's just one thing the matter. You've got your hand in your own pocket, instead of in the other fellow's."

Before the last of his brothers died, John Ringling had begun to collect paintings by the old masters, and by 1927 had such a magnificent collection that he built a museum for it, on his Sarasota estate. When he died in 1936, he willed the house and the museum to the State of Florida, as a memorial to himself and his much-loved wife, Mable. The collection, consisting in large part of baroque paintings—dramatic and occasionally flamboyant canvases such as appealed to a man like John Ringling—is now one of the glories of Florida. He founded an art school. His Venetian palace home has also become a museum. And in 1948, two years after the state had taken over the munificent gift, a third institution, called the Museum of the American Circus, was built on the grounds, to house materials about the circus.

One of the projects to which Ringling had given his attention, with Tex Rickard in 1926, was the rebuilding of Madison Square Garden. The circus opened there each spring, as it had done since the time of Barnum, and Ringling came to feel that the Garden was peculiarly his own. In consequence, he was shocked as well as annoyed when, in 1929, he discovered that his dates had been given to a tremendous aggregation of smaller units known as the American Circus Corporation. John Ringling was not the man to take such a blow without protest. He bought the corporation, lock, stock and multiple barrel, concluding the deal on September 6, 1929. He now had title to almost all the circus property in the United States. Even in normal times, and even for a man reputed to be worth fifty million, such a gesture would have been a dangerous one. Ringling had almost unlimited assets, but comparatively little cash. He borrowed a huge amount. And then came the depression.

The next years for John Ringling were of increasing financial difficulties, ill health, and unhappiness. Mable Ringling died in 1929. His second marriage was a failure. He had a stroke. Lawsuits and other involvements bedeviled him. He fought desperately to hold together his circus empire. He owed so much of the money he had borrowed to buy the American Circus Corporation that in 1933 the banks put in Samuel W. Gumpertz (another important man in the entertainment world) to control Ringling Brothers and Barnum & Bailey. For his remaining few years, John Ringling was forced to submit to the bitter humiliation of bowing to another man's authority. When he died in 1936, he left a legal situation that was not straightened out for ten years.

An earlier will had bequeathed a large block of property to his nephews, John and Henry North, and made them, with their mother, executors of his estate. When he decided to disinherit the nephews, he expressed the new intention in a codicil but inadvertently retained in the original document a clause naming them as executors. The result was a decade of litigation.

At length the contest was adjudicated. The property with the great house and the museum went to the state. The circus remained in family hands. And thus it continues today. After numerous changes, in 1938 the presidency settled on the shoulders of John North, who inherited the family resourcefulness and proclivity for dramatic presentation, and proved it immediately by initiating numerous changes. Today, after almost twenty years, in a hundred ways the great circus bears the imprint of his personality.

Ringling Brothers and Barnum & Bailey

In 1944, Ringling Brothers and Barnum & Bailey was an institution of such magnitude, substance, and economic potentialities that, phoenix-like, it was able to rise above the most disastrous fire that ever occurred in all circus history. The scene was Hartford, Connecticut.

The United States was at war, and entertainment enterprises were making the best of old materials and inadequate substitutes. It was impossible to obtain the usual kind of hemp, which has been known to withstand flames while canvas has fallen in charred shreds. Though the canvas was not fireproofed, there are those who blame the rope for the fact that, when fire struck on the afternoon of July 6, 1944, a flaming forest of canvas and poles fell almost immediately onto the thousands who had peacefully and delightedly been watching a performance.

Five of the Wallendas were aloft setting their bicycles on the high wire, and May Kovar was in the arena with her four panthers, when the horrifying cry of "Fire!" was heard. Flames started where the bleachers join the reserved seats, approximately 100 feet from the door. The Wallendas slid down ropes and ladders, and threw themselves into the rescue work. The animal trainer drove her jungle cats into the chute and crawled through after them. Merle Evans started to play the "Star Spangled Banner," broke into the "Disaster March," and continued to play until fire reached the bandstand and the calliope was aflame.

Hearing the notes of warning, performers outside rushed into the blazing tent. Wounded service men who were guests of the circus were helped to escape under the side wall. Workers made a chute of canvas by which children in top seats could slide to the ground. Innumerable adults and children performed miracles of rescue. Others died where they fought wildly and blindly to find a way out, or were so badly burned that they succumbed later in the hospital. One dead child was never identified, and on every July 6 Hartford fire and police officials lay flowers on the grave of little Miss 1565.

In the Hartford circus fire, at least 450 men, women and children were injured. One hundred and eighty-five of them died. Not only was the big top completely destroyed; the show lost a great deal of other property, was forced to cancel engagements for twenty-eight days, and finished the season without top canvas. In 1951, it concluded payment of almost exactly four million dollars—entirely out of profits.

Ringling Brothers and Barnum & Bailey met that frightful disaster, recovered, and went ahead with such effectiveness that, when any American nowadays says "circus," he almost inevitably means the multimillion-dollar attraction created by the Ringling Brothers and carried to its most spectacular amplitude by the brother whose name was John.

27

Underwood and Underwood

The disastrous Bridgeport fire

The Stupendous Merger

U P THROUGH the early 1900's, scores, perhaps hundreds, of circuses were touring the United States—more than ever before or since. By 1929, almost all of them had been dissolved and funneled into one channel, along which they flowed until eventually they became one with the mighty river that is Ringling Brothers and Barnum & Bailey.

Were it possible (as it is not) to follow in detail the history of even the large American circuses, during the last half of the nineteenth century, the result would fill a library. Moreover, it would be so involved that, to the average person, it would read like the genealogical chart of the Smith family.

As late as the '90's, despite the perfection of railroad transportation, innumerable small shows still went about the country on wagon wheels. Some were such one-horse affairs that, owning almost no equipment, they carried no rolling stock, and their performers were forced to travel in hired rigs. The spirit of such a gilly outfit was not much different from that of the old mountebank troupes. They relied chiefly upon the acrobats, tightrope walkers, jugglers, "magicians," and clowns, plus whatever equestrian elaboration could be devised from the material at hand, though the show might carry a cage or two of animals, possibly offer a couple of blackface minstrels, and sometimes put on a Wild West exhibition. Such a circus was an amalgam of odd bits and pieces, stuck together by hard work, ingenuity, and determination, and sent forth hopefully into the byways to take advantage of the apparently insatiable desire for circus entertainment.

The first show the Ringling Brothers got together was that sort of thing, and virtually the only difference between theirs and many others scattered over the country was that the Ringlings kept on expanding, whereas most of the others soon faded quietly out of existence.

Between the time most big American circuses went onto rails, and that when the majority were engulfed in one gigantic maw, there were by conservative estimate at least fifty good-sized ones out in the field. That is to say, fifty can be identified, though that figure does not begin to suggest the complexity of the picture.

Some of those names still carry on. In most instances, trucks have by now been substituted for railroad cars, and the comparatively small concerns usually try to stay out of the path of the titans, whereas the big ones refrain from moving in on the small fry. The days of cutthroat competition, of underhanded methods in routing, roadside advertising, and stealing performers, seem to have vanished. At least, if obstructive methods are still used, they are more subtle. The game is now a cleaner, tidier one, played with the approval of the Better Business Bureau and the blessing of the Chamber of Commerce.

In the old days, attempts to thwart a rival did not always stop short of murder, and the riffraff that attached itself to certain shows made the circus as unpopular in many communities as the gypsies have always been in England. Many a person fell foul of the crooked games of chance, the pickpockets and short-change artists who flourished around the lot. Law-abiding proprietors were sometimes hard pressed to convince the public that their own methods were decent.

Very few owners of that time seem to have had the slightest compunction about forcing rivals to the wall and then cashing in on the resultant involvement or bankruptcy. When a show was sufficiently hard pressed, a man with money and power could snap up its equipment for a song, or buy into the company and force the original owner out. Rivals bought in, dropped out, combined titles, thought up names, discarded them, raked them out again, concealed the line of heritage, and generally muddied the issue. Scores of struggling hopefuls disappeared without a trace.

The result of all these factors was confusion thrice confused. Even a successful show might change management under the same name, elaborate or contract its title, form a hyphenated combination, lose its own identity in merging with another company, or impose its own name to obliterate the other's. Worse than that (as far as identification is concerned), names were leased, lent, or even stolen. Lord George Sanger never came to this country; but in 1874 he sold to Howes the American right to use the "Great London" title. Moreover, from 1911 to 1915, the American Circus Corporation sent out a small show called "Sanger Brothers," just as in 1908 it had used "Howes Great London," and still earlier had taken the Van Amburgh name. As for both executives and performers—they went out of one tent and into another so fast you couldn't see them for sawdust.

It is almost impossible sometimes to follow the confused course of even the most straightforward circus transactions. Take, for example, a show that started as Hemmings and Cooper, and try to trace its pattern and the careers of the men involved in it. Richard Hemmings and James Ebenezer Cooper were both Englishmen, remarkable managers, and men of fine character.

Hemmings, born in 1834, was apprenticed at six to an uncle who

284

was an acrobat, rider and tightrope walker. When the uncle died of cholera in 1849 (in the same epidemic that carried off George Sanger's father), Hemmings was apprenticed again, to William Batty, then at Astley's. The young man appeared at Franconi's and in other continental circuses, doing all manner of acts, including riding tricks. After losing his horses and wardrobe in a fire in 1853, he went on a tour of England, and two years later arrived in New York. After that he worked on his own or with small circuses, went to Cuba, appeared in an equestrian act at Rufus Welch's in Philadelphia, made a tour of the West, and thereafter until 1860 continued to slip in and out of one group or another. Then just before the Civil War, he and Dan Gardner, a well-known clown, organized Gardner, Hemmings and Madigan's Circus. Two years after that, Madigan's name was dropped, and that John O'Brien known as Pogey became partner. In 1863, James E. Cooper bought O'Brien's interest; so the circus became Gardner, Hemmings and Cooper.

The men leased animals from Van Amburgh, and were so gratifyingly successful that they were able to hire Dan Rice in 1866, at $1,000 a week. Gardner sold out, and Harry Whitby, a performer and horse trainer, bought in. The show became Hemmings, Cooper and Whitby. Later that same year, Whitby was shot in Rayville, Louisiana, and then it was Hemmings and Cooper. Finally, in 1873, Hemmings married, retired and sold his interest to James A. Bailey, and the name became Cooper and Bailey —or, to give its mouth-filling, official title, Cooper, Bailey and Company's Great Australian Combination, and Famous International Allied Shows.

In the meantime, James E. Cooper, who was two years younger than Hemmings and had been brought to this country as an infant in arms, had been "driving stage," at first outside Philadelphia, and then in Washington. By 1863, when he had made a good deal of money, he bought O'Brien's interest in the partnership. Cooper is remembered as being the first person to set up a cookhouse, blacksmith shop and horse tents on the lot.

After Hemmings retired, and Cooper's name stood alone with that of Bailey, the two men bought Howes' Great London and Sanger's Royal British Menagerie, which they merged with Cooper and Bailey. On its first trip out, in 1879, one of the great attractions of the now tremendous circus was a baby elephant that had been born at their winter quarters— the first one born in captivity.

After the owners merged two years later with Barnum and his partners, the show was called Cooper, Bailey and Hutchinson. Thereupon,

Cooper sold his interest for a very large sum and returned to business in Philadelphia. However, not content to stay out of show business, in 1886 he joined W. W. Cole to buy out Bailey's interest, and thus became partner of Barnum and Hutchinson. That setup did not last long either, for Bailey was back the next year.

It was this same Cooper who bought the Forepaugh show after Old Adam died in 1890. He acquired a total of sixty-one cars and four advance cars, put in $100,000 for outfitting, and took the circus on a phenomenally successful tour to the Pacific in 1890–1891.

Countless other circuses were developing and disintegrating in equally complicated fashion, and countless circus men went through the same sort of evolutions.

Although by the 1870's everyone had become accustomed to a menagerie tent, with jungle beasts as part of the show, it was still possible for a circus to exist, thrive and even be famous without a menagerie. Such a circus was Stone and Murray's. Quality instead of mere quantity was the standard, and their audiences could be certain of seeing the best possible kind of program, and of finding everything around the lot spic and span and brightly painted.

Perhaps in part because the program emphasis was entirely on the ring acts, Stone and Murray's was extremely popular with the performers themselves. Murray, especially, knew numerous foreign artists, and many of them came to join him. Each of the partners had been in show business since adolescence, and both of them had previously been part of other combinations.

Denison W. Stone, born in Burlington, Vermont, in 1824, was one of the many ring-struck boys who ran away to join the circus. At fourteen he walked twenty-five miles to Brattleboro to join Ira Cole's Zoological Institute, for which Seth B. Howes was equestrian director. The show carried six cages of animals, and the chief arena attraction was trick riding by Seth's nephew, Elbert. After one season, Stone went over to a circus run by Nathan A. Howes, Elbert's father. There he became a clown in *Mother Goose*, which, it will be recalled, had been started in London by Grimaldi about forty years before, and had proved so popular that it came across the ocean. As a full-fledged clown, Stone later worked for Van Amburgh, Orton's Badger Circus, and others.

Then came the chance that he had been waiting for. He became part owner of a circus, now called Stone and Madigan's, in which his partner was the same Madigan who later tied up with Gardner and Hemmings. Just before the Civil War, Frank Rosston, known as a great ringmaster, bought into the Stone-Madigan partnership, and the show became Stone, Rosston and Company. When John H. Murray came along, and it changed to Stone, Rosston and Murray, the circus went actually into the Civil War lines, and entertained thousands of soldiers, going in 1865 as far as Atlanta, and to everyone's surprise drawing big crowds from the impoverished South. There was a wartime law against equestrian entertainment in the circus, but Stone, Rosston and Murray ignored it, and in Vermont alone, in twenty cities, cleared $30,000. Rosston then got out, and there remained just Stone and Murray.

A decade later, Stone too withdrew, and became equestrian director on Howes' Great London—at that time a 52-car show giving effective competition to the mighty Barnum enterprise. Such enormous organizations did not appeal to Stone, so he decided to revive the one-ring circus, with star performers. A tour with the resultant Den Stone's New York Circus and Central Park Menagerie was successful in the East but unsuccessful in the West. After that disappointment Stone went to Europe to present Indian troupes, and soon retired.

John Hayes Murray, the partner whose name is better remembered today than that of Stone, was born in New York City in 1829, and started out early as a blackface minstrel, appearing at Barnum's Museum, and traveling with Jane and Company's Circus. Taking advantage of a magnificent physique, he learned a number of acrobatic tricks and feats of strength, and appeared in 1848 in Seth B. Howes' Circus as one of the Roman Brothers, acrobats and strong men. After several years, the "brothers" went on a tour to California and South America, where they presented their acts in many theatres, and sometimes even between acts at the opera.

Murray now began to find better opportunity for his gifts. In England for three years with Howes and Cushing, he not only continued in the brother act but directed the entertainment and exhibited an "educated" horse, Black Eagle. When on May 14, 1858, he acted all those roles in a command performance for Queen Victoria at the Royal Alhambra Palace in Leicester Square, he so caught the popular fancy that the *London Illustrated News* devoted much of its full-page report of the event to him and his horse. For another five years, the brother act delighted audiences at such circuses as the Renz in Berlin and Price's in Madrid.

Gargantua

When Murray came back to the United States in 1864, he became a partner in the Stone and Rosston circus, which, when Rosston left, became simply Stone and Murray.

Because of his own wide acquaintance in England, Murray was able to persuade several members of the famous Cooke family to come over to present, among other novelties, their famous jumping jockey act, in which a person jumps onto the back of a horse going at full speed—a stunt that with elaborations has become a specialty in our own day with the Cristiani brothers and the Loyal sisters. Several other British artists were in the Stone and Murray troupe, and Whimsical Walker was one of the clowns. J. H. Paul, later to be the first man to drive a 40-horse hitch, was superintendent of the baggage stock.

Management eventually filled Murray's whole time, and after Stone withdrew he became sole owner and carried on alone for three years. Misfortune struck in 1878 when, on a trip to the West Indies, all of his horses but one were lost in a storm. He sold his equipment—including fifteen railroad cars—to Coup and Barnum, and another fine circus passed into history.

A most distinguished lineage lay behind William Washington Cole, who was little known to the public, but made an indelible impression on the showmen of his day. His grandfather was Thomas Taplin Cooke. When Cooke's Royal Circus Company visited America in 1836, his daughter Mary accompanied him. She married William H. Cole, an English contortionist, and stayed behind when, after two disastrous fires, the circus returned to England. Their son William was born in 1847. She herself was an *haute école* rider and wire walker, and after her husband died she initiated young William very early into the profession.

The Aloof Mr. Cole

W. W. Cole himself entered circus business when he was eighteen, getting practical experience in every phase, from side show spieler to advance agent. A year later, he owned a part of Cole and Orton, which started out with fifty horses, one cage of performing lions, and an elephant. After the show was enlarged by buying ten more cages of animals from Pogey O'Brien, it became W. W. Cole's New York and New Orleans Circus and Menagerie, with headquarters in Louisiana—never one of the biggest circuses, but for its size the greatest money-maker in history. Before he died in 1915, its creator was worth ten million.

Cole was a cautious, retiring man, disliking personal publicity as much as J. A. Bailey did, and so aloof in his manner that he was dubbed Chilly Billy. However, he was a remarkable organizer and manager. One of his first projects was to take his show to California and back in 1873 by rail—the first circus to depend entirely on the railroad for a trip of that length. No combined circus and menagerie had ever been seen in the Far West, and Cole was received with such avidity that business was turned away during the whole three-week stay in San Francisco.

His show was also the first to invade the Puget Sound territory, using boats wherever railroad gaps existed. After several trips to the Pacific Coast, in 1880 the circus went out to Australia and New Zealand, returned to California, and went back East across country by a zigzag that included Nova Scotia, before returning to its headquarters, which was then in Utica, New York.

Repeated success made it possible for Cole to replace his 25 small cars by a new 42-unit train of 50- and 60-foot railway cars with all the latest gadgets. New wagons were built to fit the cars, with a few nine-footers retained so that they could be loaded crosswise, along with nineteen short menagerie cages. Big dens for the rhinoceros, hippopotamus, and lions, parade chariots and six-horse baggage wagons were put on lengthwise. The show carried 150 horses and five elephants, including Sampson, the biggest one then in America. The tent was a 170-foot round top with four 40-foot middle pieces, and the menagerie tent was 70 by 200 feet.

It was William Washington Cole who joined with Cooper in 1886 to buy Bailey's one-third interest when the latter went into temporary retirement from his partnership with Barnum. At that time, Cole sold his own show at auction. When Bailey decided to return to Barnum, Cole sold the interest back to Bailey, and himself retired to his real estate investments. Like others of his kind, however, he found it difficult to stay off the lot, and in 1898 made another brief excursion into circus business by buying a one-fourth interest in Forepaugh-Sells plus the same share of Buffalo Bill, and managing both shows while Bailey was absent on his famous European tour. After Bailey's death, Cole's participation in circus enterprises became merely nominal, and he retired permanently. At just that time a Cole Brothers show sprang up, but apparently it had nothing to do with William Washington Cole.

Nobody keeps cropping up more frequently or in more places between 1861 and 1890 than the strange figure called Pogey O'Brien. Not a soul had or has a good word to say for him, and it is no wonder Coup was disgusted when Barnum let O'Brien use his name for a circus. The ubiquitous Pogey was a fat, asthmatic, flamboyant man, who could scarcely write his name. He was known far and wide for his shady tricks and chicanery. Appalling grift flourished wherever he was, and his shows were always "wide open," permeated by gamblers, thugs and thieves, including a notorious gang called the Irish Brigade, who hung around the lot and took care of any victim having the temerity to protest. Furthermore, O'Brien picked up show names, made them up, rented them, and dropped them again, so fast that anyone trying to trace his career is soon lost in a mass of verbiage.

O'Brien had originally pulled himself up by his bootstraps to a point where he had enough money to buy horses and operate coach lines. In 1861, he invaded circus business through the back door, by renting horses to Gardner and Hemmings. The following year he bought an interest in their show, and became assistant manager. That lasted for another year, and then O'Brien sold his interest to J. E. Cooper, and organized his own company.

His next venture was with Adam Forepaugh as partner, but naturally the two men could not get along. Thereafter, for some years, O'Brien's success was spectacular, and in less than a decade he had accumulated an incredible amount of circus property. In the year 1871, he owned or had a controlling interest in four shows, with totals of 103 wagons, 455 persons, 85 animal cages, 7 elephants and 590 horses. In another five years, however, he had made himself so thoroughly disliked and mistrusted that nobody wanted to have anything to do with him. He died broke at fifty-three, in 1889.

Perhaps no career gives quite so clear an indication of the glut of circuses with fantastic and now completely forgotten names, as does that of Pogey O'Brien. Among the shows in which he was involved were: O'Brien's Caravan, Monster Menagerie and National Kingdom; Sheldenburger's European Menagerie and Grecian Circus; J. E. Warner and Company's Great Pacific Menagerie and Circus; John O'Brien's Great World's Fair; A. B. Rothschild and Company's Royal Victoria Circus and Menagerie; Campbell's Great Circus; and Lowande's Brazilian Circus. Most of those names were just other ways of saying "O'Brien."

Robbins was one of the famous circus names in the last quarter of the nineteenth century, and has been revived recently. There were two Robbinses, not related.

Two Robbinses

Burr Robbins (1837–1908) had had a varied career before 1871, when he bought the defunct John Stowe Circus and gave it his own name. Two years later he took over the European Circus from the Flatfoots, added equipment, and set forth under the impressive title of Burr Robbins' Moral Museum, Circus and Menagerie. It was quite an affair, which went by rail, with a large staff of executives and performers, a musical car, three tableaux, and a band wagon drawn by ten cream-colored horses. Not quite a decade later, Robbins bought the Myers and Shorb U.S. Circus, in which Den Stone was then clown and equestrian director. Though that show did very well, it was discontinued after six years. Thereafter Burr Robbins backed other circuses, showing such financial acumen that when he died he left an estate of $2,000,000.

The second Robbins, Frank A. (1854–1920), started at fifteen with Hemmings, Whitby and Cooper as a "candy butcher" and, after nine years on that show and elsewhere peddling for other people, bought for himself the privileges of the Hamilton Circus.

That buying of "privileges" was frequently a quick road to easy money. Controlling the side show and the sale of such side lines as popcorn and peanuts, lemonade (over which no lemon ever cast its shadow), programs, the "concert" at the end of the show, and sometimes the tickets, meant that a great deal of cash could find its way into the pockets of even an honest entrepreneur. For the unscrupulous concessionnaire, naturally, the returns were much greater. Many a slippery customer paid a proprietor large sums for the privilege of mulcting the public on the lot by all manner of sharp practices.

F. A. Robbins may have been above such things, but he soon managed to make enough on the privileges of the Hamilton to launch a five-wagon show of his own, which had all the attractions, including a ceiling walker and a snake charmer. Going back to the European formula, he not only ran a tenting show in the summer but started performances in the winter of 1887 at the American Institute Building, New York, using two rings and a stage. Although that, too, was successful, he borrowed beyond his credit, and after eleven years had to give it up. Despite further vicissitudes, he made another try in 1905, and until 1915 sent out the Frank A. Robbins Circus and Menagerie. At the end of his life, Robbins promoted carnivals, vaudeville, and other allied types of entertainment, until he died as the result of a 20-foot fall through a skylight.

Wes Foree: Black Star

Though the European tradition of family circuses has never been so strong here, in addition to Ringling Brothers there have been a number of American family enterprises. Among the longest-lived and most consistently successful was the John Robinson, which (though its founder was born in Little Falls, New York) usurped the Southern territory, and made that whole section of the country its own, under the slogan "Southern Men, Southern Horses, Southern Enterprises, Against the World."

John Robinson, whose Scottish father had come to this country with the British army during our Revolution, was born in 1802, and at sixteen became a trick rider with the small Rockwell's Circus, at $5 a week. One of his most spectacular stunts was to ride around the ring, as Astley had done, with only one foot on the horse. Progressing from Rockwell's through a succession of circuses, he found himself with a small company in Eastern Tennessee when the employees mutinied and took over. The mutineers offered Robinson (who had a magnificent physique) a bargain interest in the show, if he would fight their battles and put affairs into running order again. That tiny show was turned by John Robinson into a huge money-maker, which he eventually passed on to his sons and grandsons. The John Robinson Circus was always characterized by remarkable riding, with some of the best of it done by James Robinson, who had been born Fitzgerald but had taken the name as Gravelet had taken Blondin. For years, the great Stickney, who had been at Astley's with Ducrow, was equestrian director; and Bill Lake was clown.

293

Sells Brothers

Throughout the country, except for Ringling, the most familiar family name in American circus history is probably Sells, and from 1871 to 1905 "Sells Brothers" was actually run by the family. The circus was created by four brothers—Ephraim (known as Old Man Eph), William Allen (called Ad), Lewis, and Peter—all born between 1834 and 1845, and all to die between 1898 and 1904. The Sells brothers began their careers in Ohio, in fields that bore peculiarly little relation to the circus. Eph owned a truck garden. Lewis and Ad were auctioneers. Peter clerked for them. Ad wanted to try circusing, and started out with a small indoor hippodrome show. By 1871, the others had so caught the contagion that they chipped in to buy some cast-off circus property, which included a few animal cages. The following spring, Lewis and Ad started off, sending Peter ahead as advance agent. For that expedition, Peter's ingenuity evolved as a title the "Paul Silverburg Mammoth Quadruple Alliance, Museum, Caravan, and Circus, A. and L. Sells, proprietors." Headquarters was in Columbus.

The show consisted of 19 wagons, 13 cages, one tableau car, 130 horses, an elephant named Julius Caesar, and a few camels and dromedaries. Even for those days, Lewis and Ad made their money stretch a very long way. Business was bad, with muddy roads and a great deal of rain, and Eph had to help out with what cash he could scrape together. Then, when the outlook was uncertain, Eph really plunged—mortgaged the truck garden for $3,000 and joined his brothers, acting as treasurer. His contribution bought horses and more equipment. It also turned the tide.

With unimaginable rapidity, the company became gigantic and affluent. In 1878, after the brothers had bought the Montgomery Queen Railroad Circus at auction, they started out from Columbus with thirty-two cars, as Sells Brothers' Great European Seven Elephant Railroad Show. The "seven elephant" part was a slap at Barnum and Coup, and at Bailey, who owned only six elephants apiece.

With James Anderson as partner, the brothers soon started a second show, the Anderson and Company Great World's Menagerie and Circus, using Topeka as headquarters. After one season, Anderson dropped out and the name was changed to the New Pacific Circus and Menagerie, with Lewis Sells in charge. Ad went into hotel business, and in 1882 Sheldon

294

Barrett, who had married a Sells girl, was made general agent, and the show became S. H. Barrett's Circus and Menagerie.

Thus the Sells Brothers owned two circuses, both of which traveled by railroad and were of high quality. The most modern equipment was used on the No. 1 show, which in 1885 had 68 advance men, and carried 389 other employees, 253 horses and mules, 45 (60-foot) cars, 10 elephants, 10 camels, 51 cages of animals, and 4 tents. In that same year, the No. 2 circus sent out a show of almost identical size. After 1887 the two parts were combined, to make Sells Brothers and Barrett's Colossal United Shows, keeping the best property from both, and getting rid of the remainder.

Primarily, the Sells circus traveled in the West, calling itself the "corn and wheat belt show." The owners spoke of themselves as agriculturists, and routed carefully according to crop conditions. They made an excellent team. Eph was hard-boiled and, it was said, somewhat stingy, watching the gate. Peter was polished, immensely liked by everyone, and very clever at promotion.

The first break in the continuous upward sweep came late in 1891, when they went out to Australia. An epidemic of glanders destroyed many of the horses, and the show lost a great deal of money. In 1890 the Sells interests combined with Bailey's Forepaugh title, and thereafter the circus name was a hyphenated one. For several years it traveled with sixty cars, maintaining the high quality expected from a Sells circus, but the Ringling competition was becoming increasingly devastating.

Eph died. Barrett died. Peter died. Only Lewis was left, and in 1905 he sold out at auction to J. A. Bailey, who promptly transferred a half interest to Ringling Brothers, and put Al Ringling in charge. For two years the show traveled as usual, but did not go out in either 1908 or 1909. In 1910, Ringling closed the Sells Brothers headquarters in Columbus and, though he put the show onto the road again, 1911 was its last season. The title still belongs to Ringling.

Eventually the Sells name was joined to Floto, to make another hyphenated combination, but the marriage was somewhat irregular. Ad Sells had an adopted son named Willie, an excellent equestrian and tumbler, who wanted to be an executive. By devious means, a circus was acquired from one Charles Andress, and sent out as the William Sells. The story goes that, taking advantage of a flaw in the title, Willie tricked his employees out of their pay, then took advantage of J. N. Renfrow, who supplied cash but soon found himself holding an almost empty bag, and finally treated one Hummel in similar fashion. Because the family name was being used contrary to agreement, Willie's uncles leapt into the fray and sued Ad and Willie. A long, bitter family row ensued, with suits and countersuits which never were settled.

Willie finally met his match in Messrs. Tammen and Bonfils of Denver, who had taken on some circus property for debt, caught the circus bug, and arranged for Otto Floto, a friend, to run the show for them. Willie Sells persuaded them to take him in, and the circus became the Sells-Floto. Everything was rosy for one season, until Willie abandoned a number of acts in Mexico City. Tammen discharged him and, as part of the bargain under which he agreed not to prosecute, required that Willie sign over to him the right to use the Sells name in perpetuity. Thus the great name of Sells passed entirely out of the family. Tammen moved the winter quarters to California, and ran the circus from there until 1921, when it was bought by the American Circus Corporation.

Another important circus, the Al G. Barnes, in the tradition established by Hachaliah Bailey and Isaac Van Amburgh, was unique at the time in offering only wild animals.

Like Adam Forepaugh, Al G. Barnes was a lone wolf who built up his own show, ran it for years without help or interference, and then stepped out of the picture. Barnes was not his real name. He was a Canadian, born Alfred Stonehouse, who as a young man made a reputation for training horses and ponies. While he was working for the Sig. Sautelle Circus and other organizations, he changed his name, and by 1910 had acquired his own show, which he built up slowly to a 30-car project. Public interest in wild animals continued unabated, and thousands thronged to see the fine specimens and remarkable trained acts that Barnes presented. He took the Western territory for his special routing, for several years wintered in California near Los Angeles, and developed what was probably the best of all animal circuses. When John Ringling bought the American Circus Corporation in 1929, the Barnes circus had already been swallowed up by that combine. Though the name went on, Barnes himself went out of business.

Hagenbeck-Wallace

Hagenbeck-Wallace, one of the most familiar couplings of names in American circus annals, did not come into existence until 1906 and was operated by both its originators for not much more than a year. At the end of that brief period, it was run for a time by Wallace alone, in 1913 passed into the hands of six new owners, in 1918 became the property of the men who three years later constituted the American Circus Corporation, and through that organization passed to the Ringlings.

The collaboration was the idea of Carl Hagenbeck of Hamburg, who had invaded the American field with exhibitions at the 1893 Chicago World's Fair, and at St. Louis in 1905. With his son Lorenz, he came to this country, organized a large company of high quality, played one season, and then (no one knows why) placed his show on the market. After B. E. Wallace, John Talbot, and Jerry Mugivan had had a turn at running the erstwhile Hagenbeck project, it was taken over by Wallace alone.

Benjamin E. Wallace, another able, hard-working, rags-to-riches American, had had a long circus career before he ever saw Carl Hagenbeck. He was born in Pennsylvania in 1848 and, after serving in the Civil War, became a hostler in a livery stable in Indiana, then branched out on his own as a horse dealer. He soon had accumulated enough money to invest in a small circus. Having outwitted a group of shysters who tried to do him in, Wallace organized a good-sized wagon show in partnership with James Anderson and Al G. Field, both of whom had been a part of the Sells Brothers organization. Their show went on the road in 1884 under the imposing title: "Wallace and Company's Great Menagerie, International Circus, Museum, Alliance of Novelties, and Mardi-Gras Street Carnival." The actuality was fairly impressive, too, including not only the usual and some unusual ring acts, clowns, side show and concert, but also a special attraction of fifteen Comanche braves and three squaws, and a feature for the street parade that reminds one of Astley's platform-on-horseback.

Grift flourished in the Wallace circus to an unconscionable degree, and there was even a special car that carried roulette wheels and other games through which the sucker could be induced to part with his money. Public opinion so resented these conditions that, between 1892 and 1894, the circus was known as Cook and Whitby. When Wallace began to use his own name again, the grifters were on the way out, and eventually were eliminated.

Two terrible wrecks wrought havoc with Wallace shows. The first one in Durand, Michigan, on August 7, 1903, with twenty-two fatalities, caused Benjamin Wallace to decide to quit the business. Instead, when shortly afterwards Hagenbeck proposed the animal show merger,

Wallace went into it. In 1918, five years after he finally did pull out, one of the most appalling catastrophes in circus history hit the Hagenbeck-Wallace show near Gary, Indiana. Eighty-five persons were killed, and 150 injured. That disaster made the new owners decide to sell out, and the entire equipment, including 49 cars, was acquired by the future American Circus Corporation for $36,000—surely the most amazing circus bargain of all time.

After giving up the show, Wallace confined himself to business in Indiana until his death in 1921. He was another one-man showman, quick in decisions, hard in his business dealings, and in some instances apparently not unwilling to conform to the questionable ethics prevalent in his day and profession.

During the 1920's, those circuses that had managed to survive met a new era characterized by business methods with which even many long-established enterprises were unable to cope. The spirit of the new day was embodied in the American Circus Corporation. That corporation, which functioned between 1921 and 1929, was a sort of mammoth file cabinet, filled with circuses that had collapsed or strayed into receivership, or whose owners for any reason had lost their enthusiasm for taking an active part in the circus enterprise. Running a circus was becoming less and less an exciting and rewarding game, and more and more a big business, played according to its own peculiar rules.

Before the day of that corporation, circus business had involved a constant reshuffling of properties, mergers, and withdrawals, but it remained for three men, Jeremiah Mugivan, Bert C. Bowers, and Edward Ballard, to take over the field with devastating pen and document, and to reduce it largely to a game on paper. Titles were juggled as if they were stock market shares. By 1929, when the American Circus Corporation met John Ringling head on, with the exception of the Ringling properties it owned virtually every circus of any importance in the country.

The leading spirit of the combine was Jerry Mugivan, who was born in Indiana in 1873. His career began as a candy butcher on railway trains. After a few years Mugivan joined the Raymond Circus as a ticket seller, and the next year went to a show owned by one Frank Smith, which called itself the Sands and Astley Circus. There Mugivan met Bert Bowers, with whom he was to form a lifelong association.

After passing from one show to another, in 1900 Mugivan joined Sells and Gray as legal adjuster, then went on to the Great Wallace Shows, and to Howes' Great London. In 1904, with Bowers, Mugivan started his own 10-car Great Van Amburgh Shows, which rapidly became Howes' Great London Circus. Then the partners took over the Dode Fiske, which they rechristened Sanger's Greater European. The next acquisition was Dan Robinson's Famous Shows, the title of which was applied to the Sanger, with Mugivan operating it, while Bowers took out the Howes. Such division of management set a pattern they followed for some time.

The next to go into the hopper was the John Robinson, in 1916. Then the Dan Robinson Famous Shows title was discontinued. The Howes circus was taken off the road, and 45 cars went out with the John Robinson. Circus properties were shifted back and forth between one unit and another, and the group kept adding new ones. Hagenbeck-Wallace went in, in 1918, when Mugivan and Bowers formed a corporation with Ballard who owned it, each holding an equal share. In 1921, the American Circus Corporation, as such, came into being.

Soon after taking over the Hagenbeck-Wallace, the corporation acquired the Sells-Floto and the Buffalo Bill Wild West, and the Yankee Robinson title. The Gollmar name, leased in 1922, was dropped after being used for a year. Eventually the two original members of the corporation retired from active management, but kept on purchasing—first the Sparks circus, and then the Al G. Barnes. By 1929, they had reshuffled their holdings to such an extent that five circuses were listed as property of the American Circus Corporation: Sells-Floto, Hagenbeck-Wallace, John Robinson, Sparks, and Barnes. After disposing of all of them to John Ringling, just before the depression hit, the three members of the company retired to enjoy the results of their prowess.

Except for Ringling Brothers and Barnum & Bailey, the only railroad circuses now left in the country were Miller Brothers 101 Ranch Wild West, Robbins Brothers, Christy Brothers, Gentry Brothers, and Cole Brothers. A few family truck shows still churned their way along the roads. The long period of free-running enterprise was virtually finished. Management of the great American circus was being fitted into a mechanized pattern. The brightest glories of that fabulous enterprise were being revealed chiefly through the achievements of individual performers.

Large and small circuses had grown, changed and perhaps disappeared. The parade had developed into a fabulous pageant, and then faded out. Trainers had modified their methods. The clown too was going through a series of metamorphoses.

28

Lawrence D. Thornton: Frederic Lewis

Lew Jacobs

New Faces for the Joey

ARNUM once said that the clown and the elephant are the pegs on which the circus hangs. In the early days, Philip Astley had neither clown nor elephant, but he was not long in inventing a comic who became a clever and ubiquitous feature of the ring entertainment.

Though Joe Grimaldi of the British pantomime established the pattern of the modern Joey, the name Clown must have been used in the circus arena to denote the comic even before the small Grimaldi fell through the trap door and broke his collar bone. As early as 1780, for the benefit of his London company, Philip Astley jotted down a note on a scenario—just such a prompter's scenario as the *Commedia* used to tack up backstage. "The Clown," he wrote, "to interpret and articulate better." Moreover, the name must have come across the ocean very soon afterward, for when Ricketts took his circus on tour in 1795 his comic rider, Mr. Sully, was already known as Clown.

Mr. Merryman

In the great days of the fairs, the jokester who accompanied the mountebanks had been known as Zany, Jack Pudding or Merry Andrew, in obvious descent from jesters of an earlier day. When the buffoon invaded the arena, he was known at first as Mr. Merryman, and in the very early days Philip Astley billed him thus. But all those names were soon old-fashioned.

In an 1829 herald headed "Surry Theatre," Dickie Usher from the Theatre Royal, Drury Lane, is billed in "Clown's Trip to the Moon." In the same year, Usher, who had been presented first by Astley, after a career of "pitching" in the streets, was setting all London agog with his "Stud of Real Cat." After going down the Thames between bridges in a washtub drawn by four geese, Gibble, Gabble, Gobble and Garble, he was conveyed to the theatre in a carriage hitched to Four Thorough-Bred Mousers, who covered the 951 yards in a minute and a quarter.

By that time two basic types of circus comic had begun to develop everywhere—the versatile acrobatic clown, and the talking clown. The riding clown-acrobat of Astley's ring very early began to be supported and even supplanted by a tumbler who performed his tricks on the tanbark itself; and with him came a humorist who achieved his effects not by action but by jokes, songs, grimaces, and ludicrous gestures, as Grimaldi had done in the pantomime.

Change was gradual. As the nineteenth-century style of acrobatic clown developed, though he was a tumbler, vaulter, ropedancer and juggler, he often also continued to be a rider. The speaking comedian, while gaining in popularity, seldom completely forsook his acrobatic capers.

Making a fool of the ringmaster is one deathless type of jesting that can be adapted to any kind of routine, horseback or afoot. When Emmett Kelly guyed the Ringling equestrian director, he was following a pattern that was created at least as long ago as the time of John Esdaile, ringmaster at Astley's for many years, who learned his tricks straight from Grimaldi. A print of 1840 shows Esdaile, known as Widdicomb, making fun of the clown Barry, who is seated on a tiny donkey and doubtless is getting ready to wipe that smug smile from the ringmaster's countenance.

Ringmasters in both hemispheres were made ridiculous in a trick called the "Peter Jenkins Act," which was really a cross between *The Tailor's Ride to Brentford* and *The Peasant's Frolic*. An attendant whispered to the ringmaster, who apologized to the audience. The equestrienne had had an accident, and would not be able to appear. Thereupon, a seedy-looking and very inebriated gentleman would rise from the benches and weave his way into the ring, protesting that the show was a fake. "Maybe *you* can ride!" the director of the ring would remark satirically. In a moment, the man had clambered awkwardly onto a horse; in another, his outer garments had fallen off, and a daring acrobatic rider was revealed, in tights and spangles.

"Whoa, January!"

Another artless favorite in American rings of two or three generations ago was a distant cousin of the Peter Jenkins, known as the January Act. The clown came in, showing off the paces of his mule, and calling out "Whoa, January!" After an interchange with the equestrian director, the clown traded with him—the mule for a horse. The mule then balked uncontrollably, until the clown was bribed to take back the horrid animal, which promptly recovered its manners as the clown drove off.

That **foolishness** was perpetrated of course by a talking clown—a **genus that** first developed when a host of Grimaldi imitators adapted the great Joey's pantomime manner to their own uses. One of the first talking clowns to invent an original manner was the British William F. Wallett, the "Shakespearian Jester," who, it will be remembered, was a competitor, friend and associate of Dan Rice's in this country shortly after mid-century. Wallett had started his career at Astley's in 1831 as a "posturer," and an early herald shows him vaulting through a hoop above the backs

302

of two horses. As the Shakespearian Jester, the lanky comic dressed himself up in peculiar motley, and poured forth a continuous stream of bizarre sallies and long recitations.

English comics were then popular all over the world. Paris liked them especially, as far back as 1785, when Billy Saunders appeared with Astley's company, and captivated them by his accent. "Volé-vo joer avé moâ?" Saunders would ask, and the French would roll in the aisles.

The Whiteface Clown

The whiteface clown acquired a full make-up in Paris in 1825. Grimaldi's white moonface, a throwback to the Pedrolino of the *Commedia*, may have helped inspire the creation of the French Pierrot, by Gaspard Debureau, at the Théâtre des Funambules. However, Grimaldi's influence was felt more directly by way of Clément-Philippe Laurent, one of the earliest modern clowns, whom Astley discovered showing marionettes in Paris, and who introduced the essentials of British pantomime into the French ring.

By mid-nineteenth century, exciting modifications were occurring in circus rings everywhere. Dejean was the leading entrepreneur in France, where the immortal Auriol had already glorified the Pierrot costume; Renz and Wollschläger controlled Germany; Paul Cuzent was in Russia; a host of pioneers vied with each other in the United States. Performers in each arena were trying to outdo their rivals, and the result was a magnificent burst of innovation in every field.

The tumbling clown was now coming into his own. The English Little Wheal could make an entrance with 100 consecutive somersaults. Lavater Lee could leap over 40 horses. Ludovico Viol, an Italian headliner, was a contortionist. These men were artists of very high caliber.

Acrobatic Clown

It should never be forgotten that the acrobatic clown, on a horse or on his own two feet, must be at least as proficient as the serious artist, and often far more skillful. He must be able not only to perform all the tricks but also to make them appear simple and spontaneous; and while risking his neck the clown must always be working for laughs.

Among the most demanding of all circus professions is that of the wire-walking clown, who appears aloft, often in baggy garments, lurching, tottering, appearing to fall, recovering, and always assuming a deliberately burlesque manner, which complicates a feat that is hazardous enough when presented straight. There is a clown in one of the smaller American circuses who tops off a superlatively awkward slip by calling out to the audience, "I'll bet I scared the hell out of you," and who always draws forth a murmur of relieved agreement.

The few comic riders who are left also set themselves that same kind of task, just as Saunders and Fortunelli did in Astley's ring. Among the most versatile of them today are "Poodles" Hanneford, now with Clyde Beatty, and Giustino Loyal, now with Ringling. Hanneford came from Ireland with his family years ago as a young man, and has been vaulting onto, off of, and between horses ever since. Loyal is a more recent arrival, whose emphasis on the comic is less persistent.

Nowadays many a clown has won his chance in the ring merely because he has a funny make-up, and often the farthest he goes, acrobatically, is falling flat when he is slapped.

During the first hundred years, in appearance the ring comedian was a polite fellow, dressed either in cheerful motley reminiscent of Harlequin, or (toward the end of that period) in baggy white trousers like those of Pedrolino. His manners were inherited from the *Commedia*, but more from its later days of comparatively pallid court appearances than from the earlier lusty and outrageous slapstick. When the amphitheatre was young, the clown obtained his laughs chiefly by calling attention to his own awkwardnesses. Later, much of his comedy depended on the sort of devices Grimaldi had used in the pantomime.

The August

In approximately 1870, the low-comedy buffoon reappeared, in a reincarnation of a type that goes back to Greece, and was christened the "august." How the august came into being is still argued. One version (obviously apocryphal) has it that Tom Belling, a young rider in the circus controlled by Ernst Renz, was amusing himself one day by dressing up in the clothes of a stableboy, which were much too big for him. When Belling heard Renz approaching, he fled in terror from the director's notorious temper, and blindly ran into the ring itself, while a performance was in progress. The audience greeted him with roars of mirth, which redoubled when he stammered apologies and tried to get out of the ring. Renz, who had followed him, immediately saw the possibilities of that extemporaneous appearance, and encouraged the young man to elaborate the act. Tom Belling became thereafter the kind of awkward helper still known to modern circus audiences, who tangles himself up in his own feet when he tries to place the props.

Another version is that Renz saw Belling outside the tent, arrayed in the stableboy's clothes, and kicked him into the ring. Still another places the scene in the Renz circus, but insists that the protagonist was a moronic *Lump* named August.

It might be logical to suppose, at any rate, that the august was a German creation, for he could easily have been an outgrowth of a primitive German comic, Hans Wurst, an awkward, talkative creature, whose bumbling humor contrasted strongly with the dead pan of the British and what has been called the "simple boobery" of the French. In actual fact, however, the character of the august seems to have been created by the English Chadwick, and to have been taken over by Belling, who made a great hit with it. Chadwick was especially popular in France, where he used to convulse audiences by turning to the orchestra and calling for what sounded to them like "Miousic!"

The appeal of the great clown is universal, although the form in which he casts his humor may vary with his particular audience. The comic has always appropriated anything he has been able to adapt to his own needs. Yet, though his costume and make-up are supposed to be sacred, even when he is famous and powerful he is not safe from copyists.

In 1855, John and William Price (famous British acrobats and equilibrists, who later built the Circo Price in Madrid) played a flute and a violin while careening around in all sorts of odd postures. The French took such delight in their antics that numerous Gallic comedians tried to copy them, and making music of some kind has been an almost inevitable feature of the French circus ever since.

Billy Hayden, embodiment of the British talking clown, spent much of his time in Paris. Though an excellent tumbler, he was the first comedian since the Shakespearian Jester to achieve his effects chiefly by words. Almost always he was accompanied by a trained pig, just as is Felix Adler today in the Ringling ring. A trained pig also accompanied Medrano, once head of the Parisian circus that still bears his name. That Spaniard, who began as an acrobat and became one of the early experts on the flying trapeze, made his first appearance at the Cirque Fernando in Montmartre, crying "Boum! Boum!" as he ran on stage, thus giving himself an ineradicable nickname.

Between 1860 and 1880, the ring clown was almost always a tumbler, whether he appeared alone or with others in little pantomimes known as knockabouts. Those knockabouts were always crude and, as the popularity of the august increased, often brutal, being built around falling, tripping up, and buffeting.

All sorts of exaggerations of face, costume, manner, and dialogue were adopted in the later nineteenth-century circus ring. There was the grimacing clown, who was to reach his zenith in the French circus with Footit; the musical clown of the Price Brothers; the singing clown, created by Barry and Williams, Americans; the rubber clown; the vanishing clown; and Charles Keith's vagabond clown, ancestor of Emmett Kelly's tramp.

Basically, however, since the 1870's, there have really been only two types of comics—the whiteface and the august. At least thirty-five styles of make-up have been identified in the American arena, and some persons add a third category (the grotesque) to include such deviations as the man who dresses as a woman, the dwarf, or the creature so padded that he can scarcely waddle. All of those grotesques are actually variations of the august.

The whiteface is not unpleasant to look at, has decent manners, and wears an expression put on with red or black paint. The august is he of the big nose, baggy clothes, and huge shoes, usually untidy, sometimes ragged, and often dirty. On occasion he may be impeccably garbed, but in clothes that do not fit him. He is likely to wear a false nose and ears, a fiery wig, or a hat that rises of itself. He carries gadgets that burn or explode, and other ingenious articles that perplex and frustrate him. He is always butt of the joke, and always in the wrong. It is the august who spoils the trick the clown is doing, by appearing at the inopportune time, giving the incorrect cue, tripping over himself, or messing up some vital prop.

There are as many types of august, of course, as there are ingenious comedians. One type, who wanders around alone, diverting the audience while the scene is changing, is known technically as the carpet clown. In his costume, he or any other august often parodies the whiteface, wearing the characteristic baggy trousers, but exaggerating them, perhaps with a balloon inside, which will explode before the performance is over, or substituting a silly hat for the pointed cap of Pierrot.

Traditionally, a clown and an august work together, and there have been several remarkable clown-august duos. The most famous was the French Footit and Chocolat, who for twenty years after their debut in

ıveau Cirque held the French public spellbound. In ad-
ble to tumble, vault, ride and go through other acrobatic
ho wore a typical Pierrot costume, could do amazing
ce. Chocolat, his Negro august, dressed in black breeches
th a hat perched on the side of his head, let himself be
and buffeted, keeping a straight face through it all.
ented all manner of parodies—on a telephone conversa-
rider, a railway trip during which Chocolat was kicked
he carriage. As time went on, and the vogue of the talking
, Footit and Chocolat relied more and more on dialogue.
ıics copied them, and the kind of act they made piquant
ieteriorated into the grossness of the "Dutch" comedians
i burlesque—clown-august acts of greater vulgarity than
ı the circus.
terpoint can be written for more than two, and there have
nous groups of clowns, of which the greatest was also
ratellini. Three brothers, Paul, François, and Albert
of an Italian acrobat and clown, transformed the clown-
great art. For a decade after 1919, the Fratellinis, at the
: Cirque d'Hiver, were the greatest drawing card in all

s were incredible foils for each other. François, an ele-
Pierrot of the classic tradition, surrounded everything he
/. Paul and Albert, his augusts, also had a clown-august
h each other. Paul, the supreme artist, evolved fascinating
types of the respectable *bourgeois*—the poor little man
tunes and very upset by the burlesque absurdities of Al-
a grotesque make-up and affected an air of stupidity.
er, the three were irresistible.
ne of the Fratellinis, the "entree" of clowns had been only
r. After them, it was an essential part of all circus. The
own as an entree is descended directly from the *Commedia*,
and recalls the parade with which mountebanks called attention to themselves at the fairs.

It was the Fratellini who glorified the accessory. Their favorite ad-
juncts were musical instruments—either normal ones, or such monstrosi-
ties as a bass fiddle that strolled around by itself and a clarinet that telescoped. The ingenious brothers made the most of the shock inherent in
abnormal size, and took advantage of the sense of unreality created by

the juxtaposition of normally unrelated objects. Into the ring the Fratel-lini would carry a saw or a safety pin as big as a man, an ineffectually mi-nute umbrella, a terrifyingly enormous spider, huge puppets, grimacing skeletons. And always they made merry with saxophones, drums, cornets, cymbals, concertinas, and other musical instruments or noisemakers.

The Great Grock

Music was also the special tool of Grock, whom many persons con-sider the greatest clown of modern times. Grock's real name was Adrien Wettach, and he was the son of a Swiss clockmaker who had joined a traveling circus. The child, born *en route,* probably in 1883, was brought up in the business, and when he was still tiny learned to ride, juggle, do acrobatic stunts, and walk a rope. He also became something of a con-tortionist. In addition, he was a true musician, especially expert on the piano, which he played with such virtuosity that he was taken on as a musical partner by a clown named Alfredo.

After Adrien parted from Alfredo, he worked with various other part-ners until he met a clown named Brick, whose partner, Brock, had gone into military service. Adrien Wettach thereupon called himself Grock, and as an assisting comic to Brick made his debut with the Swiss National Circus. The collaboration was not epoch-making, but it did give Grock a chance to produce lugubrius howlings on a violin and to make startling noises with various other instruments—a type of foolishness that he devel-oped later into some of his most hilarious episodes. By the time he himself took another partner, some three years later, Grock was already estab-lished as a comic in his own right, and from that time on anyone who worked with him was scarcely more important than a prop.

The great Swiss clown was a master of grimace, and had a voice of tremendous flexibility. Men recall their hysterical laughter when, as children, they heard Grock merely spell his name. For years, two of the expressions he perpetrated in his inimitable voice were public catchwords —"Pourquo-a-a?" (Why-y-y?) and "Sans blague!" (No kidding!) He was a remarkable mime, and could send an audience into helpless laughter merely because he could not decide what to do with his hands, or because the cover of the piano refused to stay up. In the 1930's the great comic was so popular that he sometimes held the ring for as much as an hour. Finally, after years in circuses, Grock went into the music halls.

He was a combination of musical eccentric and talking clown, and in arenas on the other side of the Atlantic many later arrivals have followed

308

his pattern of dialogue. In this country, where nowadays a clown seldom speaks, even when he is at close range, a great deal of the contemporary clown's business has been adapted from tricks thought up by Grock.

Especially after the early 1900's, a sharp difference developed between Continental and American clowns. In both instances, dangerous acrobatic maneuvers were on the way out. But in the vast three-ring tent the grimacing pantomimic took over, whereas in the European circus, with seats set up around a single ring, where a voice could be heard without too much difficulty, the talking clown continued to be a headliner.

A roster of famous American clowns since Joe Pentland and Dan Rice inevitably includes Pete Conklin, Marceline, Slivers Oakley, Poodles Hanneford, and Emmett Kelly, sad butt of the cosmic joke. Slivers Oakley, who once was honored above all his fellows by a five-minute solo in the Garden, was the one-man baseball team remembered by millions. An ingenious group a generation ago used to bring down the tent with the burning house and the clown fire company. The burning house is gone, but we still have the automobile of miraculous capacity, and new entrees are constantly being devised.

All over the world nowadays, in any arena, clowns play three parts. Especially gifted and well-known characters move around alone, improvising when the spirit moves and the occasion permits, as when Kelly seats himself near some giggling female and gazes at her long, dolefully, and speechlessly. Large or small groups of large and small clowns come on in organized entrees. Any number of comics appear and disappear in informal commotions known as shivarees.

The clown has come a long way and changed his motley many times since Porter fell off a horse at Astley's, but his present position is somewhat anomalous. Such amazing things have been happening on trapezes and wires and down in the ring itself that poor old Clown seems to have been passed by. It may be that he is now getting ready for a new incarnation.

His difficulties began in the 1920's and 1930's, when no one could take his eyes for long from the incredibly skillful and dazzling figures that were risking their lives many feet above the tanbark.

29

Culver Service

Lillian Leitzel

The Radiant
Galaxy

NO NAME in the modern circus is so imbued with magic as that of Lillian Leitzel. All circomanes breathe it with something like awe —and with infinite regret. To Fred Bradna, for thirty years equestrian director for the Ringling show, Leitzel was the supreme star of his time. John Ringling said, "She was the greatest performer we ever had." She was circus itself.

Her act was high in the big top, a solitary achievement while the house lights were dimmed, the spotlight picked out the tiny figure, and the drums rolled a crescendo accompaniment of mounting excitement, for the most famous and highest-paid woman circus performer in the world. The feat for which she was best known demanded almost superhuman strength of arm and shoulder, and was made more dramatic by the fact that she was exceedingly small. Her personal life fascinated the public, for her husband also was a supreme artist. And her death, in a moment of flashing horror, sent headlines screaming around the globe.

A Tiny Star

Lillian Leitzel, born in 1891 in Breslau, Germany, was christened Lillian Alize Elianore, and took as surname the Leitzel (which circus folk pronounce "Leetzel")—a diminutive of Alize. While still a youngster, she toured Europe with her family, who were remarkable gymnasts, and in 1910 came to this country with her mother and her mother's sisters, who called themselves the Leamy Ladies, after Edward J. Leamy, manager of the troupe. Long afterward, the great artist acknowledged her affection for that manager by each year putting flowers on his grave.

That kind of gesture was typical. Performers who worked with her say that Leitzel was an endearing person, generous, friendly and outgiving, and though she had an uncontrolled temper her outbursts subsided as quickly as they arose, leaving her penitent and insistent on making amends. In the days when she was the star of the Ringling show, if something went wrong in the dressing tent she might slap her maid sharply as an immediate release for her feelings, and then apologize with the utmost sweetness and give the maid a magnificent present.

Leitzel reached the Ringling circus by way of vaudeville, in which, after she left the Leamy troupe, she and another girl played for several years as Queens of the Air. John Ringling saw them, and hired Leitzel as an aerial gymnast. She traveled with Ringling Brothers and Barnum & Bailey in the summer, and in winter either appeared in Europe or worked

311

in the *Ziegfeld Follies*. In 1928 she married Alfredo Codona, whose position in the Ringling circus was comparable to hers.

Leitzel was only four feet eight inches tall, weighed less than 100 pounds, and wore a 1½ A shoe, yet her muscles, especially those of arms and shoulders, were so strong that in the air she could control her slight body with incomparable grace. Her specialty was the one-arm plange, in which she threw her body over her arm again and again, at least 75 or 100 times during each performance. Her record was 249, and she acquired such ambidexterity that when her right arm became temporarily incapacitated she could use the left one.

Her entire routine was accomplished on three pieces of apparatus—a web (a long rope that hangs from roof to floor), two Roman rings hung side by side on ropes fastened at the top to swivels, and still another rope ending in a loop, to pull her up to a high point above the tanbark, where she created her innumerable repetitions of the plange before being pulled down again. On the rings, she performed a series of very difficult maneuvers, including a handstand during which she "cut" her feet in a series of twinkling little flicks.

First she would go up the web—not climbing as almost everyone else does, but rolling up, making every motion a beautiful one. Then came the handstand on the rings, culminating in a drop over backward, after which she rolled down the web again and seized the loop of the other rope, to be pulled up for the plange. Contrary to general belief, it was not while doing the plange that she fell. Nor did the rope break.

On February 13, 1931, Lillian Leitzel was appearing in a night club in Copenhagen. She had not wanted to, especially as Codona was in Berlin and she disliked being separated from him; but with characteristic generosity she had agreed to accept the engagement to help a struggling young booking agent. Frank McClosky (for several years manager and general manager of the Ringling show), was in Leitzel's entourage, and had charge of the rigging. A couple of weeks before the Copenhagen engagement, he had hung the rings from new swivels, but the arrangement felt awkward to the artist and she insisted that the old ones be put back. Replacing the swivels had been merely a matter of routine, and no one had the faintest suspicion that anything was the matter with the original swivels, though afterward an analysis revealed that the metal in one of them had crystallized. Afterward too, McClosky remembered that, just before she went on, Leitzel had remarked to him that she would much rather be at home reading Edgar Wallace.

312

Tragedy on the Ropes

A few minutes later, while she was doing a handstand on the rings, a swivel broke. The sudden jerk when one half of her support fell away was so unexpected that she lost her grip on the other ring and plunged head-first to the floor. The distance she fell was scarcely more than 20 feet, but it spelled death.

The Copenhagen engagement was the first time Leitzel and Codona had been separated. She was not killed outright, and he rushed from Berlin to her side. The severity of the concussion was not immediately apparent, and she appeared to be improving. Two days after the accident, Codona started by train back to Berlin; before he reached the German capital she was dead.

The world mourned. As the ship carrying her ashes sailed into New York harbor, a plane flew over and scattered flowers on the deck. Codona erected a sculpture memorial, consisting of two more-than-life-sized figures, of a wingèd man sheltering a feminine form in his protective embrace.

The story was not yet finished. Codona continued in his own, even more dangerous performance, and sometime later married again, but a few years afterward shot both himself and his wife.

All circus people—those keenest of critics—say that Alfredo Codona was the greatest flyer of all time. As there were no flying trapeze artists before 1859, their contention is one that can be supported by many eye-witnesses. Codona won the profound admiration of his fellows and the ringing applause of circus audiences, not so much because of any unusual tricks, but because of his grace, beauty, and apparently effortless ease in action. To those who watched him, he seemed almost superhuman—curving, whirling, flashing through the air, pausing for a moment to seize the strong waiting hands, and then hurling himself again into space.

Codona's Triple Somersault

In 1922, Alfredo Codona mastered the triple somersault, which the Italians, with reason, call *salto mortale*. That feat was not unique. Others had done it before him, and others have done it since. Some of them have lived. The first person to accomplish it, according to performers, was probably Ringling's Ernie Clark. Then there were Ernie Lane and Charles Siegrist. The former lasted only a short time, the latter for years; but both broke their necks doing the triple. Codona is said to have figured

that, in the triple somersault, he had to travel sixty-two miles an hour.

Since the time of Léotard, the art of the flying trapeze has developed amazingly in scope and complexity. It involves one or more flyers, or leapers, and a catcher. Alfredo Codona's brother, Lalo, was his catcher. Vera Bruce, whom he married after Leitzel died, was the second flyer. Both beauty and safety depend on perfect timing. The flyer grips the bar, swings forward, lets himself go, turns the somersault or somersaults and, with his arms outstretched, but body doubled up, falls toward the arms of

314

the catcher. Their hands grasp each other's elbows, slide to the wrists, and hold there while the bodies swing together, in perfect synchronization, preparatory to another flight. A fraction of a second can make the difference between the perfect catch and death.

Flying trapeze artists always work with a net, and have done so since the act was young. The wire walkers, the artists on perches and ladders, the other equilibrists working high in the air, the performers on the fixed trapeze (the men or women whose act, like Leitzel's, consists of a routine in lofty rigging), may risk their lives above bare tanbark or concrete, but they at least have some physical object—a wire, rope, or piece of wood— at which they may clutch in case of emergency. During the greater part of the flyer's routine, however, he is alone in the empty air, with no support except his own nerve and his perfect sense of timing. Even the net is a tricky thing at best. Falling into it correctly requires knowledge and practice. Hitting it at a wrong angle can easily break the neck; but it is at least something tangible and concrete, designed to break the worst of the fall. No flyer in his right mind, however expert, would relinquish the slight but essential security represented by that filament below.

The Flying Concellos

A little after Codona's time came the Concellos, Arthur and Antoinette. They worked on the flying trapeze for nearly twenty-five years and never had a serious accident, though many times they both performed the triple somersault, as well as numerous other dazzling feats. Both are familiar with the kind of prolonged, spontaneous applause that is the response to great artistry, and Antoinette has long been called the greatest woman flyer of them all.

Her slim but muscular body will never be forgotten by those who have seen her flashing and swirling above the arena. She is the only woman who ever did the triple somersault in the air, and she was incredibly skillful in the double-and-a-half somersault, which is concluded by the catcher's grabbing the flyer's feet.

Antoinette Concello had no thought of becoming a performer until after her sister joined the circus. Then, in five years Antoinette reached the top. Her career began in 1928 with the Sells-Floto, and by the early 1930's she and her husband, with Everard White as catcher, made the most phenomenal flying team ever seen in a circus. They opened their act with stunts so hazardous and dramatic that nowadays they are used in finales. For more than a decade after 1930, the Concellos went out with

315

the Ringling show in the season, and in the winters alternated between European circuses in amphitheatres and the traveling Shrine Circus in this country. In 1945, out in the West, they realized every performer's dream by having their own little circus; but the dream lost its freshness after a year or two, and then they were back in the big organization. Arthur and Antoinette did not quit flying until the fall of 1953, and Antoinette still keeps her hand in by training aerial ballet for the Ringling show.

It was Arthur Concello who, as general manager of the Greatest Show on Earth, invented a seat wagon that has revolutionized the whole system of setting up the big top, and into the bargain has helped solve the problem of performers' dressing rooms.

In the 1920's and 1930's, the American circus fostered an unusual number of superlative artists in many fields, perhaps because competition was tremendous. To make the big time a performer had to be, and remain, very good indeed. Flyers worked so hard at their art that they even maintained their own winter quarters, in Bloomington, Illinois, where they practiced assiduously under the direction of Edward Ward, a remarkable trainer. There were also exceedingly expert wire artists, and riders whose names belong with those of the great days of Astley and Ducrow.

The wire artists Con Colleano, Bird Millman, and the Wallendas used to thrill audiences all over the world. Colleano and the Wallendas continue to do so.

The Great Colleano

Colleano (pronounced Collyáno) came to this country from his native Australia in 1924. His family owned a small circus there, and he was already a finished artist when he crossed the world to work on a sixty-week contract with the Keith-Orpheum vaudeville circuit. When John Ringling saw Colleano in the London Colosseum, he arranged for him to come to America, and to work out his Keith contract through a number of years. As a result, the great funambulist stayed with the Ringling show for twelve successive seasons, and returned to it again as late as 1954.

Colleano's is the art of the bounding tight wire. In his bull-fighter's costume, with his darkly handsome features, black hair, and graceful body, dancing and posturing along what is really a knife of steel, a single strand about a quarter-inch thick, he is the modern version of the *funambulus* of Rome, the medieval cord dancer. Such an artist goes through his paces close to the audience, and therefore must not only control his medium but also make every move, every gesture, elegant and graceful.

316

Con Colleano, say the other performers, is one of the most expert cord dancers of any day.

The cord is a treacherous ally. It can slip, break, draw taut, loosen just enough to toss the dancer too high in the air and move away from him as he returns. For the past fifty years the "cord" has usually been a wire, which is even more dangerous than hemp if the performer falls across it. To conquer and control the wire requires a serene nervous system, quick automatic reflexes, a strong, well-balanced body, and the ability to keep the eyes fixed on a chosen point no matter what the distraction of sight or sound. It demands also constant practice and vigilance. There are those who say that it requires youth; but Colleano, in his fifties, still leaps, dances and turns somersaults on that thin wire as if he were on the ground. The high point and conclusion of the performance is, as ever, the infinitely dangerous front somersault.

From time immemorial, acrobats have recognized the fact that, except on the ground, the forward somersault is much more difficult and dangerous than the backward. No man can see where his feet are going to land, when they are coming down behind his head, whether he is on a horse, or on a wire.

Colleano has had several accidents, though not in the somersault. In one instance, when the wire snapped, he almost broke his neck. When a limelight blinded him, in New York, he fell and cut a deep gash in his chest. A dramatic feature of his performance is that, though most low-wire artists manipulate a parasol for balance, he merely stretches out his arms.

Bird Millman used a parasol. Her father and mother were wire and trapeze performers, and she herself made her debut riding a pony. From then on for some years, the Millmans worked together—the mother in an "iron jaw" act, Bird with the ponies, and then all three of them in a trapeze and tight-wire feature. The girl was pretty, extremely versatile, and moved beautifully. When she was still very young, she began to be presented as a solo low-wire artist, and soon became one of the headliners on the Ringling show. At only fourteen, Millman made an appearance for royalty in London; and later was commanded to a performance before Kaiser Wilhelm II in Berlin. While she was at the peak of her fame, she married and retired.

For more than a quarter of a century, the Wallendas have presented one of the most famous of all high-wire acts. The high wire is a cable about three-quarters of an inch in diameter. Like Émile Blondin, the Wallendas offer an art that is a matter of balance, pure and far from simple. Long

317

ago, they developed two distinct specialties—one moving across the wire with a bicycle, the other a high pyramid tableau with a chair. Up in the sky, often without a net, the Wallendas for years have given onlookers shivers of apprehension by their daredevil exploits. Nevertheless, as it has done to others through the centuries, the wire has taken its toll of the Wallendas.

In Glasgow one day in 1932, just as the group was crossing in its finale, carrying the chair, one of the landing platforms gave way. The performers began to fall, but managed to seize the wire and hang on—all except the girl at the top, who fell too far out. As she plunged past, the nearest man caught her between his legs, and held her thus until he, like the others, could make his way hand over hand to the end of the wire. She had fainted, but recovered before she reached the ground, and stepped forward with the others (who ignored their painful though minor injuries) and came back with them for the bow. In 1933, in Sweden, fate was not so kind. The back wheel of Willy Wallenda's bicycle slipped off the wire, and he crashed to his death.

As with many another troupe, not all participants in the Wallenda act are now members of the original family. As they join the company, outsiders take the name. Nowadays, the troupe often travels great distances with foreign circuses.

Another star of the 1930's was Kannan Bombayo, a small, slight Hindu who hurled himself into a series of somersaults and other acrobatic maneuvers from a bouncing rope, set with a spring at either end, so that he was propelled high into the air. This procedure is much more dangerous than leaping about on an ordinary slack rope, which, in turn, is usually felt to be more difficult than performing on a tight-stretched cord. Bombayo clung to the old-fashioned hemp, rather than using wire, and was one of the last performers to do so.

The bareback riding of May Wirth, which also was seen in American tents a quarter of a century ago, was so remarkable that her contemporaries in the ring insist that no one will ever equal her. Like Colleano, May Wirth is an Australian. She acquired her training with the Wirth family circus Down Under, and with them came to the Ringling show. She was the only woman ever to do a somersault from one horse to another, and could stand with her face to the horse's tail and do flip-flaps on his back —an almost equally difficult feat. Moreover, she could turn a back somersault with her feet tied up in baskets. Like Bird Millman, she retired to private life while applause was still ringing in her ears.

318

The 1920's and 1930's were the days when Ella Bradna was also at the height of her fame as a rider, graceful and elegant in tableaux recalling Ducrow's *poses plastiques,* while her husband, Fred Bradna, as equestrian director, controlled the program's continuity.

Blown from a Cannon

One of the sensational headliners of that period was Hugo Zacchini's cannon-ball act. Though a similar stunt had been invented in the 1870's, it was Hugo Zacchini who made it famous for the twentieth century, first in Europe and then in this country. Hugo and his family also invented the mechanism by which they and others are still propelled—a cannon having a barrel at least 24 feet long, which shoots the human projectile the length of a huge big top.

The great acts continue, or pass out of the arena as new ones enter. It is difficult to make a true comparison between those of today and yesterday, or yesterday and the day before; but certainly the circus-going public of our own time, accustomed to the miraculous, increasingly demands something new, something different, something spectacular. One man shot out of a cannon becomes commonplace. We must have not only two, but two simultaneously. Since our brokers of the stupendous, the gigantic, the supercolossal sold us the three-ring tent, the true artist in this country has been less and less appreciated. In the enormous arena, where innumerable simultaneous motions and sounds impinge on the senses, creating a confusion of impression, no onlooker can possibly concentrate on watching the intricate beauty of precise motion and timing, even though he may know that great skill is required to produce it. Moreover, because the superlative artist makes the most difficult feats seem effortless, a hasty observer may fail to appreciate the underlying skill. A simple-looking but technically almost impossible feat is likely to be greeted by a belated spatter of applause, whereas a trick that looks spectacular but is really comparatively easy may bring forth wild bursts of enthusiasm.

There are those who say that the true art of the circus has disappeared, in favor of loud noise, flashing lights, and thrills that are often cheap; but certainly that is not true. If the circus goes the way of pantomime and vaudeville, that death will not be the fault of the performers. Circus artists as a class are men and women of profound integrity, who take infinite pride in their work. No matter how disheartening the inadequate appreciation of the audience, almost any artist will continue to give his best, and will try always to make that best incomparable.

30

Rudolph Matties at work

Foldes: Monkmeyer

Great Modern Trainers

FROM the days of the Pharaohs, through the thousands of years, have come reports of miraculous control of animals—especially of the great jungle beasts. Nevertheless, despite brief expositions by such observers as Apollonius of Tyana, no one knows the actual methods the ancients developed for training wild animals, with what weapons they protected themselves, or how many of them were killed by their pupils.

In modern times, the whole world knows when an animal escapes, even for a few moments, or when one turns on his trainer in the cage. Famous trainers write their memoirs, and some even allow the curious to watch them at work. Yet we still actually know almost nothing about how a comparatively puny man can bend a great and treacherous beast to his will.

During the early years of the twentieth century, the Hagenbeck tradition had inspired a whole generation of remarkable men and women trainers. A few of those geniuses still live, and some of them still go into the cage. A handful of their disciples continue to demonstrate variations of the methods and manners that have made international figures of Julius Seeth, Louis Roth, and Mabel Stark.

What makes a great trainer of jungle beasts?

There he is, standing quietly in the cage, moving with alert assurance, speaking firmly but seldom harshly. Often he holds nothing more formidable than a tiny switch. If he has the slightest fear, he never shows it. With caressing voice, he sometimes draws forth startling demonstrations of affection from those supposed natural enemies of man. How does he do it?

He must have indomitable courage, patience, and respect for the animals with which he is working, and an almost intuitive understanding of their individual and group psychology. But most important of all, he must have a deep and inborn conviction that he will be able to control his animals. The person who can make a beast of prey obey does certainly have some unusual force, an inexplicable authority, which the mighty predator immediately recognizes and accepts.

Such a power is given to only a few human beings. Julius Seeth gave dramatic evidence of it when he stepped into the cage of lions in Abyssinia. Henri Martin showed it when he first faced Atir. No one knows its origin, and no one can explain why one potential trainer should want to control only lions, whereas another is obsessed with tigers. But given the power and the obsession, the trainer is eternally dedicated. He may be torn almost to bits, and still insist on going back into the cage. His urge is incurable.

In any group of animals there is one dominating individual; but domination does not necessarily remain fixed. Lions, for example, are very quarrelsome, and the slightest change in routine may precipitate a crisis. If two of them fight over the females, the entire group reacts to the tension. The mildest animal may suddenly rise to take part in the controversy, and the leaders may be threatened, or even overthrown. Therefore the trainer must be on the alert every second to cope immediately with the slightest hint of insubordination. From the lion's point of view, the trainer believes, he himself is, if not exactly another lion, a kind of lion god, whose demand is law—at least for the time being. Let the god beware, however; if the power begins to slip from his grasp, it will go back at once to the dominating animal in the cage, who is almost certain to turn on his master and try to tear him limb from limb. In addition to eternal vigilance, the most effective protection for the trainer is his heaven-given assurance. He must assume without question that he is all-powerful, that these mighty, dangerous beasts will obey him, and that he himself can not be hurt.

The ability to dominate wild animals must be inborn, but it may not always be immediately recognized. Louis Roth, one of the most remarkable trainers of all time, might never have known his own gift if fortuitous circumstances had not revealed it. On the other hand, Mabel Stark knew from the time she was a young girl that nothing on earth could satisfy her soul except training and exhibiting tigers. Julie Rand Allen, a protégée of both Roth's and Mabel Stark's, has always yearned to train jungle beasts, preferably lions. The gift recognizes no nationality and no class. Roth was a Hungarian peasant. Mabel Stark grew up as an unwanted orphan in a little Kentucky town. Julie Allen is a Boston doctor's daughter.

The Phenomenal Roth

Professionals who knew him insist that no trainer could have surpassed Roth. He had a deep affection for all animals, especially lions, among which he worked for a half century, and the manner in which he made them respond was phenomenal.

Roth was born in Hungary in 1889, and came to this country alone when he was twelve years old, to stay in Pennsylvania with a man from his native village. Not long afterward, looking for any kind of work, he got

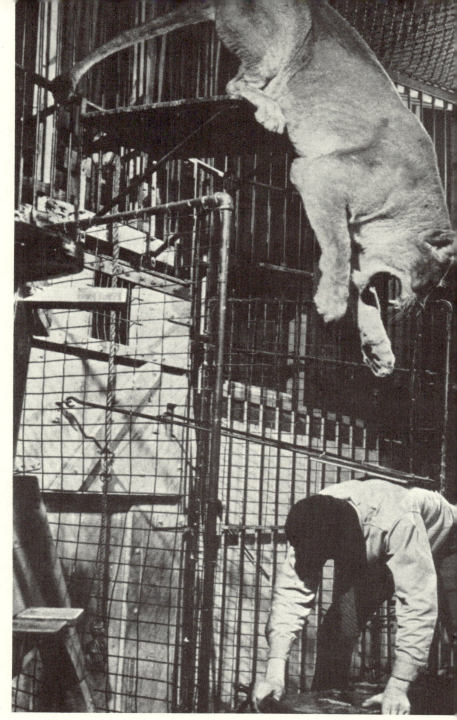

a job as cage boy at $3 a week, on Louis Rohe's Wild Animal Farm on Long Island.

Through a hole he made in the fence at the farm, watching the trainers secretly at work with their animals, he learned all he could absorb about their methods and about the animals themselves. Then, thinking he might be taken back to Pennsylvania because he was still so young, he ran away and went to work at Frank C. Bostock's Wild Animal Show in another part of Long Island.

The English Bostock, who at that time was one of the best known and most successful owners and trainers in the world, let the boy practice training several young lions. At that time, Bostock had four shows on the road, and somewhat later he sent the boy to a unit in Rochester, New York, to "work" a group of tigers Louis himself had trained.

There the young man found proof of his growing conviction that even the jungle killers respond to affection. Sultan, one of the lions in the Rochester show, had been with Rohe's. Louis had taken care of him there when he had a wounded leg, and the lion had become particularly attached to him. One day in the Rochester arena, Sultan attacked another man who was his keeper. Roth fought his way in. Hearing a command in the beloved voice, Sultan dropped his prey. The man was already dead, and it was assumed that the animal was now too dangerous to be approached. When Roth was reluctantly permitted to try to put Sultan through his paces once more, the animal responded perfectly, and never misbehaved again.

The acts Louis Roth trained through the years became spectacular. In Europe, Togare, a Persian blacksmith's son, had taught a menagerie-born lion to wrestle. With the utmost care, Roth trained a lion that had been born in the jungle to do the same trick. He taught three lions to ride a horse simultaneously, a tiger to ride an elephant, a leopard to ride a zebra. He himself rode on a lion. In 1910 he went to the Al G. Barnes Circus as head of the menagerie. At that time the circus was just a little gilly show, but under Roth's direction it grew to such proportions that, when Barnes sold out in the late 1920's, it was considered one of the greatest animal circuses in the world.

Like every important trainer who ever lived, Roth had numerous narrow escapes. Lions broke loose, and he went through the harrowing business of recapturing them—six of them once, in New York City. He bore scars, but was never severely injured, and after risking his life in the arena for a half century he died of cancer.

Tiger Woman

The greatest of all women trainers is undoubtedly Mabel Stark, whose world-wide reputation was acquired chiefly through her work with tigers. The tiny, slender blonde began in her early twenties to train those mighty carnivora. Now in her seventies, she still shows her tigers—at present in Japan, where the act is a continuing sensation.

Although she trained to be a nurse, she had been fascinated by tigers ever since her first circus, at eight years of age. When she finally persuaded the manager of the Al G. Barnes show to take her into the organization, she put away her nurse's cap forever. She was going to be a tiger trainer!

The men thought it a joke. While she bedeviled them persistently, she rode horses (an exercise she loathed), and finally was permitted to work with lions (which she feared more than tigers). Finally Roth, Barnes, and the others grew tired of her pleadings, and she was permitted to try out with three tigers. To everyone's surprise but her own, she came out of the cage alive and unharmed, and gradually progressed from the original three until she trained and controlled an act in which sixteen of the mighty cats obeyed her will—or almost always obeyed her will. At times she has been mauled, bitten and torn. Surely no other living trainer, man or woman, has been so nearly destroyed, on so many occasions; yet she has never lost either her enthusiasm or her affection for her tigers. Even after one has turned on her, she has always raised her voice to protect it from destruction. She is an animal trainer of the great tradition, who insists that to train any wild beast one must first win its confidence, and that kindness and patience are the most important factors. In fact, she insists that a trainer who tries to beat an animal into submission always gets into trouble. The animal hates the trainer, and bides its time.

Working in her own way, she has taught jungle-bred tigers to roll a ball and even to ride a horse. Millions of circus-goers have shuddered while she wrestled with one of her deadly pets. Many have seen her fall under their teeth and claws.

One of her most terrible experiences occurred when she was riding in a parade, cooped up in a cage with four male lions. A horse ran away and fell under the wagon, and immediately three of the terrified lions began to throw themselves against the bars, while the fourth caught her by the leg and tried to drag her into the center of the cage. Beating about her with a stick—her only weapon—she succeeded in backing into the safety cage at the end of the wagon, while onlookers screamed. Another time, while she was in the ring with twelve tigers, there was a blow down. Canvas and center pole fell, tearing the runway tunnel loose. Mabel Stark kept the beasts under control while men desperately fought to get the top up, and afterwards took her bow as if nothing had happened.

The injuries resulting from less fortunate experiences have often carried her close to death. When Zoo, the biggest and meanest tiger in her Ringling act, jumped her one day after she slipped in the cage, he bit completely through her leg, leaving a wound that became infected and cost her weeks of agony. Because one of her wrestling tigers, Rajah, unintentionally hit her too hard on the head with his paws, she developed a brain tumor, which was not recognized and operated on until after she had worked for a year in what she calls "a fog of pain." One day when the temperature was 110° under the big top, Nellie, the ball-rolling tiger, sank her teeth into the trainer's elbow, and ripped her shoulder with poisonous claws. For a week, Mabel fought tetanus and the threat of amputation.

At the Mercy of Tigers

The worst accident of all happened in 1928, when Mabel Stark was exhibiting on the John Robinson Circus, and the show was playing Canada during torrential rains. The ring was slippery, and the animals in a state of terrific tension. Sheik, a tiger she had refused to eliminate though he was said to be a killer, sneaked up on her when she slipped and fell in the mud. In a flash he had ripped her left thigh, almost severing the leg above the knee. Immediately, Zoo closed in to seize a portion of the prey. Despite the fact that Terry Jacobs, the lion trainer, ran to her aid, the tigers slashed and tore at her and at each other. Finally Jacobs succeeded in forcing them into the chute, and attendants were able to take her out. She had a hole in her neck near the jugular vein, a permanent hole in her shoulder, a torn deltoid muscle, an ankle that stiffened for months, and a terribly mangled leg. It took the doctors four hours to sew her together again. Plastic surgery and X-ray and radium treatments later helped to obliterate some of the scars on her face.

Two months after that accident, Mabel Stark was back in the cage, going on as she always had, in response to an obsession stronger than fear of disfigurement or death itself.

Julie Allen, still a beautiful young woman, looks so fragile that it is almost impossible to believe she too could exert her will on predatory jungle beasts. She was Louis Roth's favorite protégée and watched him work by the hour. After his death she showed his lions, but no longer goes into the arena.

Roman Proske, another superb tiger trainer, whose silver-clad figure was long a familiar sight in circus rings both in this country and in Europe, has retired to live in Florida. Damoo Dhotre, who worked for a long time with Alfred Court, has gone back to India. Court, greatest of French trainers, is living in retirement in his villa near Nice, and recently published his memoirs.

Court was born in 1889, son of a well-to-do family in Marseille. As a youngster he was very athletic and became so proficient on the parallel bars that a professional acrobat offered to take him as partner. Young Court accepted, and soon found himself in a Montpellier circus; but because he was still less than fifteen years old he was promptly hauled back home by his outraged family.

As soon as his fifteenth birthday came, he badgered his father into letting him return. After several years at one act and another, he began to concentrate on animals, for what he called his Zoo-Circus, and discovered his life's work. In the next fifteen years, during many of which he exhibited with Ringling, Court's reputation as a trainer of all kinds of groups of animals grew steadily. He exhibited a group of ten lions, one of nine tigers, one of twelve bears, black and white. He also made four mixed units of lions, tigers, pumas, bears, and great Danes, an extremely difficult achievement with adult animals, although some trainers maintain that, with a heterogeneous group, if the animals get out of hand they are as likely to attack each other as to turn together against the trainer.

"They're Loose in the Streets!"

One of the most spectacular and potentially devastating animal escapes in all circus history occurred in May, 1925, when Alfred Court was showing a mixed group as a feature of his Zoo-Circus in Saint-Amand, Flanders.

At the end of the evening performance, which had been seen by nearly 4,000 persons, four lions and seven tigers were sent off together through the tunnel. Because of a cage boy's carelessness, a door at the other end had been left open, and in a matter of seconds the animals were loose in the streets, rushing through the terrified crowd, which scattered frantically in search of cover. After persuading the gendarmes to let the circus men handle the capture, Court and his assistants started a search

327

The circus comes to town

Barlow: Frederic Lewis

that lasted until noon the next day, all over town and into the country, and caused damages for which Court paid almost $10,000.

Some of his tigers cowered under wagons. One of them slid into a house and up the stairs to besiege the nuptial chamber of a newly married couple, forcing them to leave by the window. The lions took to leaping through plate-glass windows, gaining temporary sanctuary in a café, a modiste's, an ironmonger's and a pork butcher's shop, and later running across the countryside. Though Court and his men were mauled and had several narrow escapes from death, by the next morning, using lassos, chairs and pitchforks, and bringing up cages at strategic moments, they had captured all but two of the errant animals. Finally, one of these was outwitted on the staircase of a school, and the other, eventually recognizing her master, permitted herself to be seduced out of hiding from a thicket several miles from town.

Even Court, who undoubtedly accomplished his training through kindness and understanding, in the ring bowed to the same old desire of audiences to watch an exhibition that might at any moment become a struggle to the death. Playing up to the public delight in danger, he combined gentle and affectionate play with spectacular demonstrations of mock ferocity.

Americans especially seem to enjoy such demonstrations, for Clyde Beatty, who is famous for them, draws immense audiences. Shouts, yells, snarls, growls, the snapping of whips, the explosion of firearms, and a carefully exaggerated atmosphere of sound and fury are always a part of Beatty's exhibition, as they were of Van Amburgh's. Because of its popularity, we are likely to see this type of performance more often in the future than we are the Hagenbeck-Roth method. Few young trainers are following in the steps of those giants, either here or in Europe. In our day, the whip, the iron bar, and the pistol with blank cartridges are standard for many a trainer, and the audience still finds ample opportunity to indulge its sadistic instincts.

Exponents of the less violent manner hope that the present reversion to violent exhibition methods is only a brief swing of the pendulum. They are not too optimistic, however, for the great natural sources for wild beasts are rapidly being depleted. In a few years, they say, the only important collections of jungle beasts in captivity may well be those in zoological gardens. The time may be coming when the menagerie will again be separated from the circus, and the only animals exhibited will be those that can be easily bred and will thrive under domesticity.

When and if that time comes, there surely will still be *haute école* to delight thousands as it always has done. To train a horse for that type of exhibition requires its own peculiar understanding and skill.

Among those who excel in such training is the Dutch Captain William Heyer, noted as a magnificent high-school rider, as trainer and exhibitor of such horses as Starless Night and Yo-Yo, and as an authority who for years has prepared other horses and riders for all sorts of circus acts.

Heyer's father owned stables in both Holland and the British Isles. Even as a boy of five, when his father's saddler took him to see Ringling Brothers and Barnum & Bailey at the Hague, William wanted to meet the horses and someday ride in the ring. At ten, he bought his first horse for 100 gulden (then about $35), a twenty-five-year-old black so well trained in *haute école* that the boy learned from the horse.

Later, Heyer trained one horse and then another, and after he had finished his army years was associated for some time with a European circus. In 1927, he was invited to ride in competition in the private manège of the King of Sweden, who gave him a medal. In Sweden he also trained for himself a remarkable horse named Louvain, which he later sold for two other horses and 42,000 francs (about $6,700). In 1936, William Heyer came to the Ringling Circus, and has been in or around it ever since.

The art of persuading horses to dance goes back a very long way—at least to the Greeks; though we do not know exactly what figures the horses of the Greeks went through. After Julius Caesar's men discovered they could control their steeds in a cadenced trot, they taught them various other figures. Nowadays, such riding is divided into two basic types, usually known as *auf der Erde* and *über die Erde.*

In its essence, high-school riding is not a circus act. It was a royal system of horse training, a revival of classic methods taught in the Spanish Riding Academy in Vienna, which came into being in the middle of the sixteenth century. From that center, the art of *haute école* has spread all over the world.

For ultimate perfection in *über die Erde,* the horse should be what the Germans call a *Lipizzaner*—a mixture of Spanish, Italian and Arab blood carefully developed through centuries. For *auf der Erde,* many trainers prefer a thoroughbred, or an American three-gaited saddlehorse.

Über die Erde is peculiarly Viennese, presented with or without a rider, and seldom seen in the circus. Certain aspects of that style developed out of military maneuvers, and the horse springs into figures in which all four feet are off the earth. *Auf der Erde* is a quieter, gentler and more elegant style.

Training a high-school horse sufficiently for exhibition can be done in one year, an hour every day. Perfection takes at least two years. To make a perfect rider, a lifetime is too short. All control of the high-school horse is by the wrists, calves and subtle shifting of the weight of the body. The rider sits apparently immobile in the saddle, while the horse walks, trots, waltzes, side-steps, gallops backward, and pirouettes.

That poor relation, the rosin-back, usually a Percheron, is trained simply by tightening the check rein, fastening a rope to his bridle, and guiding him around and around the ring, until he is willing and able to plod on and on, without breaking rhythm.

Liberty horses—those charming animals that are shown without riders, and usually appear in matched groups—require careful and prolonged training, but are much easier to develop than the high-school horse. Heyer can train a 12-horse liberty act in three months. At first,

330

each animal is taught his place, to walk, trot, canter, kneel, lie down, sit up, or rear, at command. With a gentle "*À moi*" or "*Yes,*" and a carrot as reward, the trainer then teaches the horse the letter S figure called *changer,* the small circle known as *volte,* to balance on his hind legs, and all the other figures. After each horse knows his routine and his cues, the act is put together. Thereafter, any intelligent director can put the horses through their paces.

Trainers of all kinds of beasts have taught audiences to expect fabulous results, and have filled the arenas of Europe and America with dramatic and complex acts. Simultaneously, the public has become accustomed to superlative quality in equipment, costumes, and accessories. Yet, despite all this progress, travel by rail, that once seemingly perfect solution of transportation problems, is almost a thing of the past. As their ancestors did in the beginning, the circuses of the world again are moving along the highways.

The Big Top folded its tents for the last time when Ringling Brothers and Barnum & Bailey announced it would not reopen under canvas. This historic photograph was taken at the last performance in Pittsburgh, July 16, 1956.

Wide World

31

Lawrence D. Thornton: Frederic Lewis

The Loyals

Where Past and
Future Meet

ODAY, in methods of presentation, America and Europe seem almost to have changed places. The largest American circus is becoming increasingly reluctant to travel, whereas many European companies are giving the majority of their performances in tents, far from home base.

Though this change has only recently become apparent, it has been going on for a long time. Even if there had been no American example to follow, tenting might of course have come logically to England and the Continent. Outdoor canvas-protected performances of ring acts, of groups of traveling animals, and of side-show abnormalities were part of European culture long before Astley took them indoors; and the tradition never completely died out. Moreover, in Great Britain especially, certain companies began to show under the round top almost as soon as Aron Turner invented it.

In the British Isles nowadays there are only two permanently based circuses—one in Blackpool, with a thirty-week season, and one in Yarmouth, with fifteen weeks. In both, incidentally, the arenas can be sunk and filled with water in the fashion invented by Thomas Cooke.

Of the great traveling companies, the most important now is the Bertram Mills. Its creator was what the British call a funeral furnisher, whose hobby was driving hackneys and four-in-hand coaches in horse shows, and who found himself at the end of World War I with insufficient outlet for his equestrian enthusiasms. While he was watching a rather poor circus at Olympia in London at Christmas in 1919, Mills bet his host that he himself could put on a better one for the next holiday season. The obvious way to win the bet was to import Ringling Brothers and Barnum & Bailey to fill the engagement, and Mills arranged to do so. Then the agreement fell through because of transportation difficulties, and he was forced to get something together by himself. Mills picked up the best performers he could get from the Continent and from other American circuses, built up a staff with no preconceptions (because its members had no more circus experience than he had), and presented a show that brought down the house. Though many companies were forced out of existence when the economic aftermath of war hit Britain a devastating blow, by drastically trimming his sails Mills kept going until the tide of depression turned. When smoother waters at last appeared, he was riding high.

Other companies came and went. By 1930, Mills led the field, seconded by John Sanger and Sons, and Carmo's (which never recovered

333

after a heavy "snowdown" followed by a disastrous fire that year), and with more than a dozen other good-sized circuses traveling the British Isles—four of them confining themselves to Ireland. Although motor transport had already become the order of the day, in 1933 Mills changed to rails, and each year nowadays travels out of its Berkshire winter quarters in four trains, for a tenting season initiated in 1930. In consecutive years the show tours the South of England, the Midlands, and the North of England and Scotland, and repeats, always leaving an interim at Christmas time for several weeks at Olympia where it was born. Since the death of Bertram Mills himself, in 1938, his sons, Cyril and Bernard, have carried on. Though almost all other British circuses are privately owned, the Mills is a public company, with shares sold on the stock exchange.

Nowadays, in addition to the Bertram Mills, four other large companies tour England—Chipperfield's, Billy Smart's, Sir Robert Fossett's, and the Robert Brothers. Each maintains headquarters in some country district, and arranges for special programs during the winter. At Christmas, Chipperfield and Smart occasionally appear in some provincial amphitheatre, but usually go to London, though they have no buildings of their own. Robert Brothers travels from theatre to theatre, presenting its programs on the stage.

The American oval with three rings has been tried and rejected, and all British circuses now confine themselves to one ring, which on the road is set up in a round tent of larger or smaller dimension, holding sometimes as many as 7,000. Some of the menageries are remarkable, and so big that groups of animals are sent to tour the Continent also. The famous Sanger name is no longer up in big letters, for Lord George's circus faded out with its founder, and Lord John's was sold in 1941. To be sure, John's son, named for his uncle, revived the Lord George in 1942, but the resultant show is comparatively small. In the lower brackets there are now more than a dozen other companies that still maintain English headquarters, and four continue in Ireland.

On the Continent, the system is even more fluid. Of all the fabulous and tradition-steeped arenas of Paris, only two are left—Medrano and Cirque d'Hiver, where programs, changing monthly, are to be seen throughout the year, except in August. Although some sort of suitable permanent building exists in almost every large provincial town of France, circus is to be seen in any of them for only short periods during the year. The longest engagement now scheduled is the six annual weeks in October and November at the Cirque de Rouen.

In all Europe, the longest season in a permanent building is twenty-four weeks at Schumann's in Copenhagen, but across the continent, under tents, large and small circuses constantly carry their glittering wares from town to town, after a style set in approximately 1920 by Alfred Court's Zoo-Circus. France especially is now full of companies showing under tents, which follow the American system of one-day hops, in contrast to the Central Europeans, who change their stands only two or three times a week. Long ago, the French began to copy the American oval, and now the tendency is for the oval to expand, and to contain more than one ring. German companies, on the other hand, have always preferred the round tent, with one ring, extended as circumstances demand—a type that now finds its mightiest exponent in Krone, who goes to Italy for the winter months with a luxurious production. The Krone is now so tremendous that its menagerie contains seventy elephants (sixteen more than Ringling owns).

Ringling Brothers—The Greatest Show on Earth

On this side of the Atlantic, just after 1929 when John Ringling acquired the American Circus Corporation, a good many independent circuses were still left. Today almost all of them have disappeared, and only one goes by railroad. Some of these shows cross and recross the country; others confine themselves to small, familiar areas. None of them attempts to compete with the amplitude of Ringling Brothers, which continues to prove that it is the Greatest Show on Earth. It is biggest in tent acreage, in numbers of performers, in supporting personnel, in animals and equipment. It offers more of the unique artists.

The program seen under its big top is a superb summation of circus history through many centuries. Jugglers, carpet acrobats, contortionists and equilibrists, who once delighted the Pharaoh, his nobles, and the common people of the great cities of the Nile, here demonstrate their cleverness, suppleness, and sense of balance. Ropedancers, who thrilled the populace on the street corners of Rome, draw forth the same shuddering apprehension and delighted applause. The clown, whose ancestor first appeared in the towns of early Greece, bumbles around, looking for an opportunity to be funny. Wild beasts, perhaps no more skillfully trained than those shown in Roman amphitheatres, obey the behests of of their masters, in cage-arenas like those invented by Hagenbeck. Tiny dogs amuse the spectators as they did at Halfpenny Hatch. A wire walker proceeds to the high top of a sloping strand, as that now nameless funambulist did in sixteenth-century Venice, and slides down so fast he reminds one of Cadman, the Wingless Bird-Man, who left a trail of smoke at Southwark Fair in 1733.

In the manner of Jules Léotard, men and women swing and fly and somersault. Acrobats balance on unsupported ladders, on the rolling sphere, on perches, on fixed trapezes. And always, the horses appear in *haute école* figures like those the Greeks devised, and in acts such as Astley invented. Although the spectacle (long since become scarcely more than a walk-around) continues to be a gala introduction for almost every company except Ringling, on the Big One it is offered later on the program, as a kind of dramatic demonstration of the richness, elegance, and variety the circus offers.

Here are still the old, the new, the spectacular, the bizarre, the improbable, the impossible; making the circus, today as yesterday, and—despite any change that may come—as it surely will be tomorrow.

Changes are upon us already, to be sure. Now that television can carry the delights of circus into the most isolated home, entrepreneurs and performers must accept the challenge and take advantage of the opportunities. As the audience becomes increasingly mobile, and the economic scene becomes constantly more complex, the circus itself may somewhat restrict its travels. There are signs even now that it may turn full circle, and go back, at least periodically, to the amphitheatre from which it sprang. But in whatever place or setting, and however adapted to our time, the joys of circus will surely endure, as they have endured already for nearly two hundred years. In its essence, the circus is indestructible.

It will defy dissolution not only because its colorful delights hold irresistible appeal for men and women as well as children, but because the performers themselves can imagine no other kind of life. For them the circus is a perpetual obsession, a way of life, a true and infinitely demanding love to which they give undivided and undying loyalty. Their heritage goes back far beyond Astley, for they are the descendants of caravan and fair, of mountebanks and wandering animal trainers, of artists who appeared on street corners.

There are those nowadays who shake their heads despairingly, insisting that the traditions of the arena are dying. Consummate skill, they say, can be acquired only through early training and long practice, and such training is no longer possible. Artists all over the world are giving the lie to that criticism, by passing their skills on to their children, as their ancestors did for countless generations.

Circus City

This training for the future is especially evident in Sarasota, Florida, where Ringling Brothers and Barnum & Bailey has its winter quarters. Overnight in 1927, John Ringling turned Sarasota into the center of circus activity in this country, by setting up winter quarters on 200 acres, three miles from the center of what was then scarcely more than a little fishing village. Since then, that Florida town has become a thriving community, and the entire area surrounding it has increasingly taken on the color of the circus. Stand at Sarasota's Five Points any day from just before Christmas until almost the end of March, and you may well see the giant, idly looking out far above the heads of the crowd, and a couple of midgets hurrying their tiny steps along Main Street. A dwarf careens by on a motor scooter. Unrecognized except by friends, because he is without make-up, a world-famous clown pauses to look into a window. A great juggler stands talking in a doorway. Officials, trainers, other performers are to be glimpsed in restaurants, in bars, in theatres, or sitting on the terrace of the John Ringling Hotel, which is owned by the circus.

Despite the fact that in season the town may hold thousands of visitors, it is essentially a city of homes, many of which belong to those who are, or have been, of the circus. Out in the back yard of an average-looking house, a girl stands on her head on a wire. Not far away, a family practices on the bars, or a boy on a trampoline. Beyond a fence, a man puts small trained dogs through their paces. Rigging of various kinds looms here and there. A clown suit hangs on a clothesline.

In that city, many circus families prepare for the future. Four of them are typical. All are Italian, though one has its roots in France. Among them they represent such a great number of skills that they alone could easily present a performance of major proportions. Those families are the Loyals, the Zacchinis, the Cristianis and the Canestrellis, all of whom came to this country to work with Ringling. They have intermarried until it is hard to tell where one family begins and another ends, and the children and grandchildren play together, are taught together, and practice together.

The Loyals, who first of all are riders, trace their lineage to Claude Loyal, who established a dynasty in France a century and a quarter ago, and whose innumerable descendants have gone out all over the world. The adult members of the Sarasota branch were born in Italy, where they had their own circus. Nowadays, counting husbands and wives, there are nearly a dozen of them who are at home in the ring. Giustino, with two sisters, produces a headline riding act for Ringling. Four of the Loyal girls are the only members of their sex ever to accomplish the spectacular stunt of vaulting onto a horse simultaneously.

The name Zacchini, of course, first of all means human cannon ball. In 1921, Ildebrando Zacchini and his son Edmondo invented a much more effective mechanism for propelling a human projectile than any of those that had been used when Barnum was presenting the original "Mlle. Zazel." For their first cannon ball, the Zacchinis shot another son, Hugo, who continues with the act to this day. Nowadays even the family daughters defy danger in the same manner. As a group, the skills of the Zacchinis are multiple—riding, trapeze, tumbling, and wire walking. Being mechanically minded, they even make cannons, other circus equipment, and dramatic "rides" for carnivals.

Ottavio Canestrelli and his wife joined an Italian circus traveling out of Italy when they were very young, and with it not only played the Mediterranean area but went across the desert to Baghdad, and on to India, where they stayed for five years. There they met Bombayo, great bounding-rope artist, and with him came to the Ringling show. Under his tutelage their daughter Tosca became the only female performer on the bounding rope. As a family they too can offer enough acts to make a lively program.

The Cristianis, who came to this country in 1934, now have their own circus, a three-ring affair that travels by truck, and employs between 200 and 300 persons, with the family (fourteen in all) forming the backbone. Their circus background goes back to the 1870's when, with the help of King Umberto I himself, one Pilade Cristiani established a show in Italy. Pilade was a trick rider, and many of his descendants have inherited his equestrian ability. His son Ernesto became such an expert tumbler that Medrano gave him a medal for his tumbling. Medrano's son Jérôme gave Ernesto's son Lucio a medal for his bareback riding. Today, five Cristiani brothers are famous for various riding acts, including somersaulting in series from one horse to another, and all vaulting onto a horse at once, as the Loyal girls do.

In all these Sarasota families—typical of circus families all over the world—almost every adult is expert in at least one ring act, and many of them are proficient in several. The majority began as children, just as their own offspring are doing, and the smell of tanbark is irresistible. Even when the sons and daughters marry, move away, and supposedly settle down into more mundane professions, they cannot altogether stay away from the circus. The yearning to be a part of it is a compulsion impossible to overcome, for almost more than any other people of the entertainment world, circus folk require the sense of belonging, the gratification of achievement, the glorification of the limelight, and the recognition of applause.

In Sarasota, there is an additional sense of unity and fellowship. This is home to all those whose lives are of the circus. It is a home, however, that many of them must desert every year. Early each spring, the people of the Florida city prepare for the annual tour.

At Ringling Brothers' winter quarters, a few weeks before the show is to leave, the old big top is set up for practice. Raising it is now a simple procedure. Elephants used to do most of the work, but nowadays they help only with poles and side walls. The bale ring with the top canvas is pulled up by a winch. Manpower too has been replaced to a large extent by motors, and around the lot it is an infrequent treat to hear the old chantey with which the canvasmen used to pull the rope: "Heave it, weave it, shake it, take it, break it, make it, move along," though occasionally one may hear the guying-out gang chanting: "Ah hebie, hebby, hobby, hole, go 'long!"

In the big top, acts requiring wire and rope rigging are practiced by experts and taught to novices, while acts that need only the actual ring are practiced out on the lot in an area measured to the correct size, and known as Madison Square Garden. That area, surrounded by seats, has three permanent rings and two stages, and its long sides are always called 49th Street and 50th Street. On 49th Street the director stands with a microphone, calling or singing his orders, commendation or criticism, or merely emphasizing the rhythm, while the rehearsal organ music swells out over the arena, stops and starts again. Timing is worked out to a split second, and toward the end of rehearsals John Ringling North sits on the band wagon, which has been pulled up alongside, and watches from under an enormous umbrella. On Sundays there are public performances.

As travel time draws near, the pace of all affairs at winter quarters quickens. Performers seize every available moment for practice. New acts shape up. New equipment appears from the shop. Gorgeous and fantastically expensive costumes, accessories and other paraphernalia are finished.

The Caravan Rolls On

At last comes the day when the first section sets forth.

Early in the morning, winter quarters already wears an air of comparative desolation. The old big top is down, and the new one will leave next month with the second section, which will carry equipment needed for tenting after the hippodrome engagements in New York and Boston. Many of the menagerie pens are empty. The private cars have rolled off the spurs. Out in the back lots stand a few old floats. The silvery coaches and the flatcars that are to travel wait on the rails.

Animals have been coaxed into closed boxcars. Trucks have been loaded endwise onto flats—three large trucks and one small one, or four medium-sized ones, to a car. Extra pieces are tucked in here and there, some uncovered, some mysteriously draped in canvas. It is easy to identify the exposed units, for red wagons carry rigging and props for the acts, and green ones the cookhouse and concessions.

Here, and in the section to follow later, will be found the whole great dream world that rises in the morning and is gone in the night.

On the day of departure, throughout winter quarters there is a purposeful air of bustle, a spirit of mingled sadness and excitement, as the travelers take leave of their families. Automobiles and taxis wheel up and stop between the rows of cars. A locomotive shunts back and forth. Performers appear, alone or with families or friends, and climb into the coaches.

The time to take off has almost come. With his altar boys in their white cottas, the Monsignor arrives and passes up and down between the lines of cars, bestowing a blessing on the journey.

The train begins to move.

The acrobats and jugglers, the riders and tumblers, the mountebanks and mimes are off again, about to resume the life of the road, as their ancestors have done for untold hundreds of years.

The caravan is leaving.

The circus again is on its way.

Circus Lingo

ANY ESOTERIC fraternity has its own lingo, and the circus is no exception. Some of the strange words and expressions used by the initiate were inherited from the old peripatetic mountebanks, along with the itching foot, the ready tongue, the sense of unity with others of their kind, the loyalty, courage and fortitude. Some words are thieves' argot or gypsies' Romany. Certain expressions were evolved on the lot, to denote specifically and definitely the equipment, animals, and human beings in and around a circus, its peculiar ways of life, and its high moments of danger or achievement.

The British have many expressions never heard around an American lot, and vice versa.

Lists have been compiled again and again, but perhaps the most complete American one is a glossary made by, and especially for, members of the Circus Fans' Association. It contains several hundred items. Here are some of them:

Ace, A dollar

After Show, Concert

Alfalfa, Paper money

Annie Oakley, Ducket or Ducat, Fake, Paper Skull, Broad, Fluke, Ticket

Back Yard, Space between big top entrance and dressing rooms, where wagons, wardrobes and properties used during performances are kept

Baggage Stock, Heavy draft or work horses

Bale Ring, Heavy steel ring, around center pole, to which open sections of tent are hitched before pulling up

Bally, Ballyhoo or spiel in front of side show

Banners, Side show fronts painted to depict the wonders within; cloth signs used by the advance for advertisements on buildings, etc.

(**Banner-Line,** series of banners in front of side show)

Bible, Magazine, program

Big Top, Big tent used for main show

Bladders, Toy balloons (Can it be that, probably quite unknowing, this is a hangover from the goatskin bladders used in the earliest buffoonery?)

Block Watch, Square pine blocks, 6 × 6 inches, put on ground as footing legs for seat jacks

Bloomer, Poor stand

Blow Down, Heavy storm that levels tents

Blow the Stand, Cancel a town chosen or billed; leave the show

Blues, Cheap seats, general admission, usually around ends of big top

Booster, Capper, Sure Thing Man, Confederate of gamblers

B. R., Roll of currency; bank roll

Broad-Tosser, Three card monte dealer

Bugs, Chameleons

Bull, Elephant

Burn Up, To exploit a route, territory or circus with grift to such an extent it is unprofitable

Butcher, Peddler of lemonade, candy or other refreshments

Cake Cutter, Shortchange artist (**Cut cake,** to shortchange)

Camel Punk, Boy who tends camels

Cattle Guards, Sets of low seats placed in front of blues, for overflow

Chain to Rails, Prevent show from moving, by legal measures

Charley, Wastepaper can on bill car

Cherry Pie, Extra work

Chockers, Men who handle wagon wheel blocks on flatcars

Clem, Fight

Clown Alley, Dressing tent reserved for clowns; corps of clowns

Clown Stop, Brief appearance while props are changed

Come In, Interval between gate opening and grand entry

Come Ons, Suckers, boobs

Concert, Extra show after main performance

Connection, Areaway between menagerie and big top

Convicts, Painted Ponies, Zebras

Cook House, Dining tents

Damper, Front door cash register

Daubs, Noncustomary places for posting outdoor bills

Day and Date, Simultaneous town and day with opposition show

Deemer, Dime

Dog and Pony Show, Derisive term for small circus

"Doors!", Call meaning to let public start in

Donagher, Latrine

Down Yonder, Southern states

Ducat Grabber, Door tender or ticket seller (often spelled "ducket")

Dukie or Duckie, Handout at cook tent for workmen

Equestrian Director, Performance manager, who blows whistle (ringmaster never used in circus parlance)

Extras (or Double-Staking), Extra stakes put in ground in threatening weather

Finish, Concluding number by performer

Fink or Larry, Broken novelty, as torn balloon

First of May, Novice, greenhorn

Fixer, Agent who pays fees or adjusts damages (also squarer or adjuster)

Flag, Signal over cookhouse when meal is served

Flash, Appearance

Flookum, Powder with synthetic flavor and color for soft drinks

Flying Squadron, First section of show

Framing a Show, Planning to start one

Front Door, Main entrance; line up in front of side show

Gaffer, Circus manager

Gaffs on the Joint, Gambling devices are crooked

Garter, Tape held for a performer to leap over

Gawks or Lot Loafers, Townspeople watching loading, etc.

Getaway Day, Last day of engagement

Gilly or Gilly Wagon, Extra wagon or cart, usually small, hired when needed, to carry lighter pieces of equipment around the lot; any unusual method of carrying (formerly, hired wagon for transportation)

Gone Sunday School, Has abolished the grift

Gorge, Scoffins, Food

Grafters, Slickers, Luck Boys, Gamblers trailing show, sometimes along with it, sometimes merely on same route

Grease Joint, Hot dog or hamburger stand

Grind Show, Side show or small show playing continuously

Grouch Bag, Money bag worn inside clothes

Guys, Heavy ropes or cables that guy up center poles

Hammer Gang, Men who drive stakes (Stake driver is machine, never man)

Hard Tickets, General Admission tickets

Haul, Distance from railroad to lot

"Heads UP!", Warning cry, to avoid being hit

Heel Box, Last ticket stand, inside big top

Hefty, Performer who does strong man act

"Hey Rube!", Rallying cry for help in a fight, used in clems between circus people and toughs or irate townspeople

High Seat, Induce people to move up to top row of blues

Hip, Hippopotamus

Hogger, Greedy showman

Home Sweet Home, Last stand of season, when bill posters usually post one stand of paper upside down

Home Run, Trip from Home Sweet Home to winter quarters

Hook Ropes, Ropes with hooks on ends, to be fastened into rings on wagon sides, to help pull, or to hitch on extra teams

Hook-up Teams, Teams used for loading or unloading at trains

Horse, Thousand dollars

Horse Feed, Poor returns from poor business

Horse Opery, Any circus (jocular)

Howdy, Elephant howdah; chair carried by camels

Hump, Camel

Iron, Iron stake for hard lots

Joey, Clown

Joe Hepp and Bill Hepp, Imaginary characters, brothers

Joint, Concession stand

Johnny Tin Plate, Small town marshal or constable

Jonah's Luck, Unusual bad weather or mud

Jump, Distance between places of showing

Jump Stand, Extra stand near front door, to sell tickets in rush

Kicking Sawdust, Following circus or being part of it

Kid Money, Admission for children under age

Kid Show, Side show, freaks

Kiester, Trunk or wardrobe box

Kife, Swindle the suckers

Kinker, Originally acrobat, now almost any performer (once called also "Spangles")

Kush, Kale, Jack, Money

Lacing, Small rope loops by which sections of big tent or its middle pieces are tied together to make one top ("Bust the lacings"—to separate lacings when dismantling)

Layout Man, One of first men on lot, who measures and designates placing of tents

Lead Stock, Ring Stock, Zebras, camels, horses, etc.

Liberty Act, Horse performing without rider

Little People, Midgets or dwarfs

"Light Wagon's On!", "We're ready to go" (Electric light wagon is loaded last)

Long, Pass with reserved seat coupon

Long Side, Side of cookhouse in which workmen eat

Lot, Show's exhibition grounds

Lotlice, Townspeople who hang around lot

Lumber, Loads of seats, poles, etc.

Main Guy, Guy rope that holds up center pole in big top

Make an Opening, Make first spiel in front of a show

Manage, Act with horses and riders (erroneous, though traditional, from *manège*)

March, Street parade

Mitt Joint, Fortune teller's tent

Monday Man, Man once permitted exclusively to steal from village clotheslines

Mud Show, Show traveling by wagon or truck (sometimes "overland trick")

Mug Joint, While-you-wait photographer's tent

Nigger Boards, Boards spread on ground in old days for concert acts, etc.

Notch House, Brothel

Nut, Operating expense for the show

Office, Sign of understanding, as "give him the office" means "tip him off"

Old Man, Owner or director of show

On the Show, Performers and all others ("With" the show is never heard)

Strawing, Seating patrons on ground strewn with straw when all seats are taken

Packed to the Ring Curb, Crowded

Pad Room, Dressing room, so called because pads for riders used to hang there

Paleface, Whiteface, Pierrot type of clown

Paper, Circus posters

Paper Section, Section for those with passes

Pay Off, Pay day

Perch Act, Pole balancer's act

Picture Gallery, Tattooed man

Pipe, A letter

Pitchmen, Salesmen for concessions of various kinds

Pole, Wagon tongue (Tent poles are qualified, as "quarter pole")

Possum-Belly, Compartment under railway car for extra storage

Pretty Boy, Bouncer or strong-arm man

Privileges, Refreshments or other articles sold around show

Punkpusher, Petty boss who supervises work of young town boys

Razorback, Man who loads and unloads railroad cars

Reader, Town, county or state license

Read the Lot, Look for tent stakes, etc. after show is down at night

Red Light, To eject a person from a train, or leave him behind

Red One, Good stand

Ridge Rope, Strong rope or cable stretched length of tent at tops of center poles, like ridgepole on house

Rig, Put up aerial rigging

Ring Barn, Building with regulation-sized circus ring for practice at winter quarters

Ring Banks or Curbs, Wooden curbing in sections, around ring

Riot Panic, Great applause

Risley Act, Three acrobats lying on backs and tossing a fourth from one to the other

Roper, Cowboy

Rosin-Backs, Horses for bareback riders (backs sprinkled with rosin to make surer footing for riders)

Roustabouts or Roughnecks, Common laborers (men on tents usually canvasmen)

Rubber Man, Balloon vendor

Runs, Place where trains are held

Sap, Cane

Second Count, Shortchanger's method

Shanty, Chandelier, Man who attends to lights

Sheet Up, To post bills

Shill, Come-on man who entices suckers; to pass in free; one who is purposely passed by the door

Short, Pass without reserved seat coupon

Short Side, Side of cookhouse tent where performers and staff eat

Slough, Tear down preparatory to moving

Smoke Wagon, Two strong small wheels mounted on axle for carrying heaviest poles and so on

Sniper, Bill poster who sneaks up at night to place his paper

Soft Lot, Wet or spongy ground

344

Spindle Man, One who operates novelty gambling wheel

Spec, Entry, Grand pageant in tent

Spot, Location on lot

Stake and Chain, Wagon used only to transport tent, rigging, stakes, chains, bale rings, halyards, hammers, etc.

Stand, Any town that is played

Star Backs, Reserved or more expensive seats

Staubs, Stakes in ground, to which guys are tied

Stiff, Legal attachment or writ

Stores, Gambling games in old crooked outfit

Strawhouse, Tent so crowded that some spectators must sit on straw in front of seats

Stripes, Tigers

Sucker, Circus-goer

Sweep-Rope, Rope sewed into canvas top, in elliptical shape or following contours of entire tops, for strength

"Tail Up!" or "Trunk to Tail!", Command to elephant to grab next elephant in parade or march

The Advance, Contracting and billing agents who go ahead of show

The March, Parade on streets

The Trick, Entire show

The Wagon, Main ticket or bookkeeping wagon, where accounts are kept

Threesheet, To boast

Thumper, Bass drummer

Toot Up, Attract attention by calliope

Top, Tent

Side Wall, Vertical portion of tent; to creep in under side wall

Tourist, Lazy workman

Towners, Townspeople where show visits

Traps, Trapeze

24 Hour Man, Official who goes on one day ahead to make sure everything is in order

Wait Brothers Show, Ringling Brothers and Barnum & Bailey, because their posters read "Wait for the big show"

Walk-Around, Procession of clowns all around hippodrome track

Walk Away, Money left by persons forgetting change

Wardrobe, All dressing (costumes for performers, elephant blankets for parade, etc.)

Web Sitter, Groundman for aerialist

White Wagon, Main office on circus lot

With It, Loyalty to the show

Work, Stage a performance with animals

Zulu, Negro who participates in spec

In many instances, naturally, British lingo duplicates American—or, possibly, the other way around. But it includes any number of words our circus never uses, with some that have descended directly from the time of Astley. As might be expected, British terms are often closer to French or Italian than ours are. For example:

Artiste, Performer (pronounced "artist")

Balloon, Paper hoop through which rider jumps from horseback

Barney, Fight

Black Tober, Site where there is no grass, as slag or wasteland

Bona or Cushy, Good

Buffer, Dog (**Slanging buffers,** performing dogs)

Bunch, Profits

Charivari, Whirlwind entrance of clowns (cf. "shivaree")

Crocus, Patent medicine man

Cul, Col, Friend

Denarlies, Denari, Money

Dona, Woman

Entree, Extended act by clowns or group of clowns

Graft, Formerly work of any kind

Josser, Gajo, Flatty, Yob, Outsider

Kip, Abed, sleeping

Letty, Bed (**Letties,** lodgings; **scarpering letty,** unpaid bill for lodgings)

Nanty, Nothing, no, not

Nobbings, The take

Omey, Man

Pitching, To go out and set up shop (especially of small shows and acts)

Parlari, Talk

Parni, Water

Pig, Elephant

Ponging, Somersaulting

Prad or Grai, Horse

Pull-Down, Dismantling of circus

Reprise, Single gag of clown or clowns

Ribbons, Silk ribbons over which ballerina jumps from galloping horse

Ridge Pole, Horizontal pole at top of tent, from which much of rigging hangs

Rum Col, Circus proprietor

Run-In, Wide passage from stables, through ring curtains, into ring

Saulti, Penny

Scarper, Run away

Slang, The performance

Tober, Pitch, The lot

Trick Line, Any rope used to pull anything into or out of action

Uncle Friday, Paymaster (Friday is payday)

Like everybody in show business, most circus men and women, on any continent and in any tent, are as superstitious as Fiji Islanders. Almost all of the regular superstitions upset them, and they have their own set of peculiar hoodoos to boot. Some are the result of association with disaster. Some have existed for centuries, no one knows why. Some are personal idiosyncrasies.

Those old camel-back trunks are bad luck. But, whatever the shape, never move a trunk, once the place for it has been spotted. If you kill a monkey, three persons will die. Playing or whistling "Home Sweet Home" will send some aerialist hurtling to his death. If one of the performers counts the audience, someone in the show will die during the performance. If a trouper gets hit with a riding crop, there will be an accident within two weeks. If you stroke an elephant's trunk, and he lifts his trunk into the air, that is a sure sign that someday you will own your own show.

Individuals have their own peculiar phobias, such as spiders or snakes or certain animals. Almost everybody believes in his soul that a Jonah can ruin the show. The old John Robinson show had trouble all one season till they got rid of a side-show spieler who wore a bright-red necktie. There was a plate spinner who wrought havoc with the Barnum outfit. For another company, there was a peg-legged cook. And the hoodoo for Adam Forepaugh, who had been a candy butcher in his youth, was a cross-eyed candy butcher.

346

Bibliography

Franz Ackerl und Arthur-Heinz Lehmann, *Die Edlen Lipizzaner und die Spanische Schule*. Alexander Duncker Verlag Ottfried Kellermann, München, 1952.

P. T. Barnum, *Humbugs of the World*. J. C. Hotten, London, 1866.

P. T. Barnum, *The Life of P. T. Barnum*. (Edited by George S. Bryan.) Alfred Knopf, 1927. Orig. Ed., 1856.

Richard Bernheimer, *Wild Men in the Middle Ages*. Harvard University Press, 1952.

Fred Bradna and Hartzell Spence, *The Big Top*. Simon & Schuster, 1952.

James Henry Breasted, *Ancient Times: A History of the Early World*. Ginn & Co., 1916.

Maria Ward Brown, *Life of Dan Rice*. Published by the author, 1901.

Benjamin J. Bump, *The Story that Never Grows Old*. Privately printed, 1953.

Jacob Burckhardt, *The Civilization of the Renaissance in Italy*. (Trans. from the German by S. G. C. Middlemore.) Phaidon Press, Oxford and London, 1945. Orig. Ed., Switzerland, 1860.

W. C. Coup, *Sawdust and Spangles*. Herbert S. Stone & Co., 1901.

Nicole Decugis et Suzanne Reymond, *Le Décor de Théâtre en France*. Compagnie Française des Arts Graphiques, Paris, 1953.

Alice Curtis Desmond, *Barnum Presents: General Tom Thumb*. The Macmillan Company, 1954.

T. F. G. Dexter, Ph.D., B.A., B.Sc., *The Pagan Origin of Fairs*. New Knowledge Press, Berranporth, Cornwall.

Pierre Louis Duchartre, *The Italian Comedy*. (Trans. by Randolph T. Weaver.) John Day Company, 1929.

J. Dwight Duff, D.Litt., *A Literary History of Rome*. T. Fisher Unwin, London, 1910.

Frank Foster, *Pink Coat, Spangles and Sawdust*. Stanley Paul and Company, Ltd., London.

Gene Fowler and Bess Meredith, *The Mighty Barnum: A Screen Play*. Covici-Friede, 1934.

Harold N. Fowler, Ph.D., *A History of Roman Literature*. The Macmillan Company, 1937.

C. P. Fox, *Circus Parades*. Century House, 1952.

Ludwig Friedländer, *Roman Life and Manners Under the Early Empire*. (Trans. from the German by Leonard A. Magnus from 7th Enlarged and Revised Edition of Sittengeschichte Roms.) 4 Vols. George Routledge and Sons, Ltd., London. Orig. Ed., 1864.

Hyatt Frost, *A Brief Biography of Van Amburgh*. Printed by Samuel Booth, New York. (No date, but was late 1850's.)

Thomas Frost, *Circus Life and Circus Celebrities*. Tinsley Brothers, London, 1875.

E. Norman Gardiner, D.Litt., *Athletics of the Ancient World*. Oxford at the Clarendon Press, 1930.

Isaac J. Greenwood, *The Circus: Its Origin and Growth Prior to 1835*. Dunlap Society, New Series No. 5, New York, 1898.

Carl Hagenbeck, *Beasts and Men*. (Trans. from the German by Hugh S. R. Elliot and A. G. Thacker, A.R.C.S.) Longmans, Green and Co., London, 1910.

Alvin T. Harlow, *The Ringlings*. Julian Messner, Inc., 1951.

H. Hediger, *Wild Animals in Captivity*. (Trans. by G. Sircom.) Butterworth's Scientific Publications, London, 1950.

W. D. Howells, *Mark Twain, Prof. Nathaniel S. Shaler and Others, The Niagara Book*. Doubleday, Page and Company, 1901.

Horst W. Janson, *Apes and Ape Lore*. Warburg Institute, London, 1952.

George Jennison, M.S., F.Z.S., *Animals for Show and Pleasure in Ancient Rome*. Manchester University Press, 1930.

H. Stuart Jones, M.A., *Companion to Roman History*. Oxford at the Clarendon Press, 1912.

J. J. Jusserand, *English Wayfaring Life in the Middle Ages*. (Trans. from the French by Lucy Toulmin Smith.) G. P. Putnam's Sons, 1889.

Emmett Kelly with F. Beverly Kelly, *Clown*. Prentice-Hall, 1954.

Hugues Le Roux, *Les Jeux du Cirque et La Vie Foraine*. Illus. Jules Garnier. E. Plon, Nourrit et Compagnie, Paris, 1888.

George Lewis as told to Byron Fish, *Elephant Tramp*. Little, Brown and Company, 1955.

Gustave Loisel, *Histoire des Ménageries de l'Antiquité à Nos Jours*. 3 Vols. Octave Doin et Fils, Paris, 1912.

Pierre Marill, *Histoire des Trois Clowns*. Societé Anonyme d'Éditions, Paris, 1923.

Earl Chapin May, *The Circus from Rome to Ringling*. Duffield and Green, 1932.

George Middleton as told to and written by his wife, *Circus Memoirs*. Published by the author, 1913.

Henry Morley, *Memoirs of Bartholomew Fair*. Chapman and Hill, London, 1859.

R. G. Moulton, *The Ancient Classical Drama*. Oxford at the Clarendon Press, 1890.

Allardyce Nicoll, *Masks, Mimes and Miracles*. George G. Harrap and Company, London, 1931.

Alois Podhajsky, *Die Spanische Hofreitschule*. Verlag Rudolf Hans Hammer, Wien, 1948.

Nicolai Poliakoff, *Coco the Clown* (by himself). J. M. Dent and Sons, Ltd., London, 1941.

Alfred Ringling, *The Life Story of the Ringling Brothers*. R. R. Donnelley and Sons Company, 1900.

Dave Robeson, *Louis Roth: Forty Years with Jungle Killers*. Caxton Printers, Ltd., 1941.

Gil Robinson, *Old Wagon Show Days*. Brockwell Company, 1925.

Gerhart Rodenwaldt, *Die Kunst der Antike*. Propylaean-Verlag, Berlin, 1927.

Joseph Andrew Rowe, *California's Pioneer Circus*. (Ed. by Albert Dressler.) Printed in San Francisco, 1926.

Maurice Sand, *The History of the Harlequinade*. Martin Speicher, London, 1915.

Ruth Manning Sanders, *The English Circus*. Werner Laurie, Ltd., London, 1952.

"Lord" George Sanger, *Seventy Years a Showman*. (Sec. Ed., after orig. of 1910.) J. M. Dent and Sons., Ltd., London and Toronto, 1926.

Serge, *Histoire du Cirque*. Illustrations, Photographiques et Dessinées de l'Auteur. Librairie Gründ, Paris, 1947.

Lady Eleanor Smith, *British Circus Life*. George G. Harrap and Company, Ltd., 1948.

Mabel Stark as told to Gertrude Orr, *Hold That Tiger*. Caxton Printers, 1938.

John Stow, *The Survey of London*. (Introduction by Henry B. Wheatley.) J. M. Dent and Sons, Ltd., London, 1912. Orig. Ed. 1598.

Henry Thétard, *La Merveilleuse Histoire du Cirque*. 2 Vols. S. Guida, Paris, 1947.

Jules Tournour as told to Isaac F. Marcosson, *The Autobiography of a Clown*. Moffat, Yard and Company, 1910.

Sir Garrard Tyrwhitt-Drake, *The English Circus and Fair Ground*. Methuen and Company, Ltd., London, 1946.

Giorgio Vasari, *Lives of the Most Excellent Architects, Painters and Sculptors*. (Orig. Ed. of 1568, abridged and edited by Betty Burroughs.) Simon and Schuster.

M. R. Werner, *Barnum: A Biography*. Harcourt, Brace and Company, 1923.

A. E. Wilson, *Pantomime Pageant*. Stanley Paul and Company, Ltd., London.

David Worcester, *The Art of Satire*. Harvard University Press, 1940.

White Tops. Magazine of the Circus Fans of America. All copies.

Le Cirque Dans L'Univers. Magazine of the Circus Fans of France. All copies.

Index

353

354